D1110845

Private Sectors in Higher Education

Private Sectors in Higher Education

Structure, Function, and
Change in Eight Countries

Roger L. Geiger

Ann Arbor
The University of Michigan Press

1989   1988   1987   1986   4   3   2   1

Library of Congress Cataloging-in-Publication Data

Geiger, Roger L., 1943–
   Private sectors in higher education.

   Bibliography: p.
   Includes index.
   1. Private universities and colleges—United States.
   2. Public universities and colleges—United States.
   3. Comparative education.   I. Title.
   LB2328.5.G45   1986   378'.04'0973   85-24501
   ISBN 0-472-09368-1 (alk. paper)
   ISBN 0-472-06368-5 (pbk. : alk. paper)

Grateful acknowledgment is made to Oxford University
Press for material from *Private Education: Studies in
Choice and Public Policy,* edited by Daniel Levy. Copyright
© 1986 by Yale University. Reprinted by permission of
Oxford University Press.

For my parents

Acknowledgments

This study originated in curiosity about the nature and extent of private higher education outside of the United States. In a sense this subject emerged from the collective work of the Yale Higher Education Research Group. The founder and director of this group, Burton R. Clark, had written of the distinctiveness of private institutions and the diversity of the American system of higher education. Daniel Levy, having discovered the growing importance of the private sector in Mexican higher education, was then beginning to investigate public/private dynamics throughout Latin America. And I had recently studied an increasingly strained relationship between private universities and the state in Belgium. Moreover, some general developments in higher education indicated that it might be a timely moment to attempt to fill the void in comparative knowledge about private higher education. In the United States concern was growing over the capacity of private colleges and universities to deal with rapidly mounting costs and declining college-age cohorts. In a wider perspective, the Western world had experienced two decades of rapidly growing government involvement in higher education. A general issue seemed to present itself: the continuing viability of private institutions in the face of the growing publicness of higher education systems.

It was with such considerations in mind that this study of private higher education was undertaken. For this purpose comprehensiveness was neither desirable nor feasible. Instead, the strategy of this study was to identify the principal structural types of private higher education, to analyze their chief exemplars, to compare these patterns to the private sector in the United States, and to explore systematically the interactions between government and private institutions. Approaching this subject as a problem in the comparative analysis of educational systems, I began without predilections for or against private control. Thus, the modest endorsement of the potential benefits of private higher education with which this volume concludes represents an *a posteriori* judgment rather than an *a priori* bias.

A study of this scope requires the assistance of many individuals and organizations. For providing a stimulating environment for this work I am heavily indebted to the Yale Institution for Social and Policy Studies and to two of the programs that it has harbored. The Higher Education Research Group, in just seven years of existence, achieved wide recognition for its contributions to the comparative study of higher education systems. As a member of that group I benefited greatly from association with Burton R. Clark, whose understanding of higher education has informed this analysis in a manner too pervasive for footnotes to acknowledge adequately, and who has generously written a foreword to this volume. Daniel Levy proved to be an invaluable colleague as we worked our respective sections of the globe; as did Rune Premfors, who first convinced me to investigate the Stockholm School of Economics, and then made arrangements for my actual fieldwork in Sweden. Upon the termination of the Higher Education Research Group in 1980, I was exceedingly fortunate to be able to conduct the second half of this study, as well as subsequent projects, in the Yale Program on Non-Profit Organizations. Participating in this ongoing effort to elucidate the distinctive features of private not-for-profit institutions deepened my understanding of the nature of private colleges and universities. I particularly value the advice and the acumen of the program director, now chairman, John G. Simon.

This study never could have been accomplished without the assistance of individuals, too numerous to name, in these seven foreign countries who helped me to learn about their respective systems. I would like to express my gratitude to all of them.

Tapping the unusually rich sources on Japanese higher education required considerable assistance. Indispensible helpers and delightful companions were my two Yale assistants, Akiko Hashimoto and Isao Kiso. I would like to thank the Institute for Higher Education and its director, Isao Amagi, for assisting my research trip to Japan, and for confiding me to the capable hands of Michiko Aoki and Fujiko Kawakami while there. Ikuo Amano, Akira Arimoto, and Kazuyuki Kitamura shared not only their knowledge of Japanese universities, but their hospitality as well.

Although the Japanese may have had to go to the greatest lengths in order to facilitate my inquiry, I encountered friendly cooperation in all the localities that I visited. I should take this occasion to apologize once more for the inevitable impositions caused by this peripatetic form of research. For helpfulness beyond the call of academic duty, I would especially like to thank Adriano Arcelo, Hans Daalder, Robert De Moor, Simon Ellis, Ignace Hecquet, Henri Janne, Rune Premfors, Isidro Ramos, and Jef Verhoeven. In addition, Juan Francisco graciously placed the resources of the Philippine-American Education Foundation at my disposal, as did Ladislav Cerych with the Institute of Education.

An author owes particular thanks to those who are willing to read and comment upon his early drafts. Although they bear no responsibility for any inaccuracies in what follows, these individuals can be sure that their efforts have improved this volume: Robert Birnbaum, James Douglas, Robert deMoor, Maurice Kogan, Graeme Moodie, Harold Perkin, and George Weisz. In addition, I received valuable comments from the Higher Education Research Group, particularly, Burton Clark, Dan Levy, and Rune Premfors. Finally, I would like to thank the Exxon Education Foundation for supporting this work.

This volume constitutes one portion of an extended journey into the study of higher education—an undertaking ultimately motivated by a belief in the importance of universities, despite manifold imperfections, and the commitment to rational understanding that they embody. For their assistance and indulgence in getting me started on this path I dedicate this book to my parents.

Foreword

One of the fascinating issues in the support and operation of higher education in the latter part of the twentieth century is the relative merits of public and private control. In the United States, public and private universities and colleges have long existed side by side. In recent decades there has been a decided shift toward the public realm, with predictions swelling in the 1970s and early 1980s that the private sector will inexorably shrink further in size and importance. Yet the private institutions, large and small, university and college, continue to have impressive prestige, retaining a powerful hold on the American imagination. Are the private colleges and universities then largely a romantic survival from an earlier time? Do they duplicate, at greater cost, the efforts of public institutions? Do they have any special functions? Indeed, is the American commitment to private higher education not an international anomaly? Higher education is certainly a public good and therefore the state can and ought to take care of it. A number of other advanced societies, notably Germany, France, and the United Kingdom, seem to find private support unnecessary, even injurious.

What then do we know internationally about the public-private distinction, the interplay between these two realms, and the contribution of each? Very little, it turns out, since the topic has not been subject to serious cross-national comparison. With this volume, Roger Geiger is the first to do so, centering squarely on the size, nature, and contribution of private sectors in the higher education of eight countries. His effort has required a mastery of far-flung, fugitive materials, quantitative and qualitative, supplemented by field trips to institutions in other countries for firsthand observation and discussion with informed observers and key officials. The countries that he selected—Japan, the Philippines, Belgium, the Netherlands, France, Sweden, and the United Kingdom—are thought-provoking exemplars of three different types of private sectors: those that carry the main burdens of expanded higher education; those that have a virtually parallel status to the public institutions; and those that exist on the periphery of dominating public sectors.

Noteworthy is the way that the huge Japanese system, virtually on a par with the American in rates of access and participation, managed its expansion the private way, with significant benefits and costs. Near the other extreme is the development in the United Kingdom in which formerly independent universities gradually came under state control as they received more public financing, to the point where a formalized national system managed in the early 1980s to give a university charter to one new private institution, the University of Buckingham, only after considerable controversy and struggle. And then there is the American case, ambiguous in its many complications. Placed within a cross-national frame, its many different types of private sectors can be seen as fulfilling the many functions one finds in private sectors internationally—and more. Private research universities, with seven or eight ranked among the top ten universities, set the pace in their particular sphere. Private urban universities perform a number of services, including part-time education for adults. The entire domain of liberal arts colleges that includes the best and the worst of four-year programs is a private-sector monopoly. The American system is exceptional in its multitude of private sectors and their wide range of sources of financial and moral support.

Finally, there is the simple fact that the two largest systems of higher education among the advanced democratic nations, those of the United States and Japan, have invested heavily in private sectors alongside their massive and impressive public ones. Diversity in several basic senses characterizes these systems. Whatever their defects, they are undoubtedly robust.

This important study connects to a body of social thought that has developed outside the literature on higher education, appearing principally as a part of political economy. Some economists and political scientists have converged in recent years in the study of the respective contributions of the state and the market. The former is seen as depending mainly on authority and the latter on free exchange for the coordination of human effort and the general ordering of society.[1] Analysts have learned to speak in general terms of "market failure" as a cause of state intervention, and of "state failure" as a source of a return of certain activities to the private sphere and more marketlike interactions. This suggestive mode of thought has been extended by the introduction of the "Third Sector," that realm of voluntary, nonprofit organizations and associations, that is neither driven by the authority of the state nor the exchanges of profit-seeking enterprises, but which exists significantly in all advanced democratic nations, particularly in the United States.[2] The Third Sector can carry out functions that most people are not prepared to leave to the vagaries of the market, fearing its deficiencies in handling a public good. These functions may also be mishandled when subject to the "categorical constraint" of government, that is, the compulsion in government, under law and norms of fairness, to apply regulations across the board and hence to require uniformity and to enforce conformity. We all have some interests not shared by the general population, and a plethora of minority concerns may voluntarily turn to nonprofit and nonstate institutions to reach the ends they collectively desire.

Such large categories of thought need careful specification and reformulation if they are to be applied effectively to such different sectors of society as health, welfare, the arts, elementary and secondary education, and higher education. In each, the market, the state, and the Third Sector will take somewhat different forms, conditioned by different tasks, technologies, and traditions. And so it is in Geiger's careful depiction of the play of private sectors of higher education in various national systems. Occasionally profit-making, private higher education for the most part appears as a distinctive segment of the Third Sector. Why it develops strongly in certain countries and not in others becomes a fascinating question of the interplay of that sector with state and market alternatives. In seeking explanations, Geiger places historical development on an equal footing with the logical and virtually ahistorical analyses of mainstream political economy. For example, the issue of who gets there first—the private sector as in the United States, the public sector as in Japan—determines who may seize the commanding heights of prestige and condition the thought and practice of all that follows. In the development of a new and promising set of interdisciplinary ideas, this study is the type of inquiry that is needed to give careful consideration across sectors of society as well as across nations.

This volume was initiated within the efforts of the Yale Higher Education Research Group, which I had the good fortune to chair between 1974 and 1980. It grew out of the evolving capacity of that research group to compare national systems of higher education in their division of academic work, the foundation of academic beliefs and values, the distribution of authority in academic systems, the ways in which academic change takes place, and finally, the relations of such systems to the state and the market.[3] The study was completed within the Program on Nonprofit Organizations, a part of the Yale Institution for Social and Policy Studies, which has become an important national center for the study of the Third Sector.

As a study in comparative higher education, this research report developed in tandem in the late 1970s and early 1980s with a second project that pursued the public-private distinction throughout the many countries of Latin America.[4] Together, these two major investigations provide description, analysis, and interpretation that can inform the conventional wisdom, as well as scholarship, on why private sectors exist, what they do, and what differences they make in the all-important domain of higher education.

Such systematic, cumulative research serves us well. It gives impetus internationally to a new branch of social inquiry. It enlarges our understanding of an opaque, complex sphere of human affairs. Professors, administrators, students, and members of the general public should find this explication of higher education worth their close study.

Burton R. Clark

Contents

Chapter 1

Comparing Private Sectors in Higher Education

In 1980 almost 2.5 million students enrolled in some 1,500 private colleges and universities in the United States, thereby comprising the world's largest private sector of higher education. So large, in fact, that it virtually constitutes a world of its own. It is organized into a number of national associations that look after the interests and publicize the virtues of their member schools. It is largely preoccupied with a set of issues that are peculiar to American conditions, including omnipresent anxiety over maintaining several forms of income, competing with the public sector for students, perpetuating the American interpretation of a "liberal education," and preserving independence in the face of governmental regulation.[1] As important as these issues are for the everday existence of American private colleges and universities, they nevertheless appear somewhat parochial in an international context. The American private sector is not only the largest in the world, but, as will be examined later in this volume, it is perhaps the most unusual as well. Judgments drawn on the basis of its unique features, then, are unlikely to be an adequate guide to understanding the phenomenon of private higher education throughout the world today.

To take just one significant issue: the relative shrinkage of the American private sector from one-half of total enrollments after World War II to less than one-quarter today has created a widespread perception that private higher education is undergoing a secular process of inexorable decline in the face of ever-growing government activity. Yet, the international record of private sectors in the postwar era provides no basis for such a judgment. While Sweden and Canada have gone much further than the United States, incorporating almost all private institutions of higher education into the public sector, there are still numerous countries that can be entered on the other side of the ledger. Japan, the Philippines, and Brazil have all depended primarily on private institutions to expand participation rates in higher education. Private-sector predominance in these countries thus presents a kind of mirror image of the public/private distribution in the United States. In Spanish-speaking America private colleges and universities have been capturing a significant and growing minority of enrollments since the 1960s. Even in western Europe, motherland of the welfare state, private sectors sometimes have a role to play. In Belgium, privately controlled universities have increased their share of enrollments, despite the founding of new public institutions. Portugal, following its modernizing revolution, changed its laws to permit the formation of a private sector. And, in both the United Kingdom and the German Federal Republic, public-sector monopolies over university education have been ever so slightly cracked by the recent creations of singular private exceptions.

These illustrations should suggest several things about private sectors viewed internationally: they form a significant component of many national systems of higher education; they differ markedly from one country to another; and their recent developments have been shaped by rather different forces. In fact, the single rubric "private higher education" stands for a broad range of institutional forms and educational functions that have yet to be analyzed outside of single national systems of education.[2] The purpose of this volume is to begin the process of filling this lacuna—to gain a greater understanding of private higher education by examining it in an international context. This means, first, examining the principal structural forms of private sectors and the functions associated with them in the contemporary world. Second, it requires imposing some kind of order on this profusion of institutions and purposes. Third, to the extent that the evidence allows, some generalizing is necessary regarding the attributes and consequences of privateness in higher education.

The initial task, then, is to present the types of private sectors that exist outside the United States. To this end, the three chapters that follow are devoted to analyzing three basic structural configurations of public and private sectors. Where public higher education is restricted in size and somewhat selective in intake, private sectors become the agency for meeting the general social demand for higher education. The result is "mass private sectors" that usually contain the majority of a country's enrollments. Where public and private institutions have equivalent status and functions, the two sectors may be said to be "parallel." And, where government chooses to have the public sector dominate the principal tasks of higher education, private institutions are left with only "peripheral" roles to fulfill.[3]

The choice of the countries to be studied here was dictated by the desire to include conspicuous examples of these three kinds of private sectors, and also to elucidate those systems having features of intrinsic interest for private higher education in general. The strategy has been to begin building a knowledge of private sectors by making comparisons between structurally similar systems. The multifarious demands for higher education are refracted quite differently through the conditions and circumstances of each society to produce widely divergent institutional arrangements. In each country unique patterns of historical development, government powers, legal arrangements, cultural fault lines, and more, all contribute to different divisions of tasks between publicly and privately controlled institutions. Because this produces far-reaching differences between national systems, the most meaningful initial comparisons can only be made between countries with similar structures. For this reason, at least two examples of each structural type were needed.

The most important example of a mass private sector is clearly provided by Japan. That country now challenges the United States for the mantle of most highly educated society on the globe in terms of the schooling patterns of the current generation of students.[4] The remarkable growth of Japanese higher education has largely taken place within private colleges and universities—just the opposite of the process that occurred in the United States. Since no other developed nation possesses a mass private sector like Japan's, it was necessary to turn to a developing nation, the Philippines, to find a basis for comparison. The mass private sector of the Philippines is proportionally the largest of any major country. It is also the only private sector included here in which proprietary institutions assume importance alongside the usual nonprofit forms of organization.

Although private higher education is not prominent in western Europe, Belgium provides an exception by enrolling a full two-thirds of its university students in private institutions. This situation has been due to the conscious maintenance of parallel and equivalent public and private sectors. This type of structure, and the social relations it expresses, exists in somewhat similar form in the Netherlands. The Dutch private sector is distinctive in having been almost completely assimilated with the public sector, thus making it in some ways the least private example in this study.

Peripheral private sectors by definition have less numerical weight and generally less salience than the cases just mentioned. As an advantage for this study, though, they present the operation of private sectors under less favorable conditions. Their limited size also permits the analysis to descend to the institutional level. In the three countries examined here, emphasis has been divided between the relationship of peripheral private sectors with dominant public ones, and the individual cases of quite singular private institutions. France is often taken as a prototype of a centralized state, and there centralization has entailed consistent support for public-sector hegemony in higher education. The rigid division worked out a century ago between state universities and institutions sponsored by the Roman Catholic Church has essentially endured to this day. One exceptional case is provided by the Ecole Libre des Sciences Politiques, which for several generations monopolized an educational function that is usually reserved for public institutions and closely scrutinized by public authorities. Sweden is the smallest system of higher education considered here, but it provides a classic case of the process by which growing government responsibility for higher education led to the gradual absorption of a private sector. Today, only the Stockholm School of Economics remains as an independent university-level institution, and its survival thus presents another important case of a singular private school. The evolution of higher education in the United Kingdom presents another variation of the peripheral pattern. Over the course of the twentieth century Britain's semiautonomous universities have gradually been fused into a publicly funded and publicly directed system. Largely in reaction to this trend, a group of academics in the late 1960s launched a movement to found a private university. The fruit of these efforts received a Royal Charter in 1983 as the University of Buckingham, Britain's only private, degree-granting institution and, for present purposes, an intriguing example of a singular institution in a peripheral private sector.

The perspectives provided by mass, parallel, and peripheral private sectors allow the large and complex American private sector to be seen in a comparative perspective. While private higher education in the United States has elements in common with each of the other basic types, it is unique with respect to its pluralistic sources of revenue, and especially the reliance of many institutions on private giving. These features are analyzed here in order to separate American private colleges and universities into smaller and more homogeneous groupings. Private research universities, liberal arts colleges, and urban service universities are distinguished by the mix of revenues that they typically receive, and by the activities that these revenues represent. Within these three groupings, then, the amount and source of voluntary support establish meaningful subgroupings. The taxonomy of the American private sector produced by this approach allows groups of American private colleges and universities to be compared with their counterparts in other countries. The final two chapters, then, are based upon comparisons of all eight countries across structural types.

Chapter 6 concentrates on the topical and practical issue of government support for independent institutions. In almost all the developed nations considered here the rising costs of higher education have at some point led to a decision to provide government subsidies to the private sector. Each country has adopted different means to accomplish this. It thus becomes possible to compare the different forms of government assistance and to evaluate the consequences that each form entails for institutions of higher education.

In the final chapter, comparisons are pursued on a more general level in order to elucidate some fundamental attributes of private higher education. First, it is pointed out that a consistency exists within each national system on three levels: the values underlying the rationale for a private sector, the structure of that sector, and the general conduct of private higher education. Second, the degree to which private universities are integrated into the academic systems of their respective countries is found to be an especially significant variable for private colleges and universities. Finally, the trade-offs involving the advantages and disadvantages of privateness in higher education are weighed in light of the experiences of these eight national systems.

In essence, then, this study proceeds in an *a posteriori* fashion, initially presenting cases of seven private sectors that conform to three basic structural types; next utilizing this material in part to break down and analyze the eighth and most complicated case; and then drawing on this empirical base to conduct a comparative exploration of significant dimensions of private higher education.

The subject of private higher education is almost self-evident—but not quite. Technically speaking, the focus here will be on nongovernmental, postsecondary educational institutions. An effort will be made to avoid that phrase, however, not just for aesthetic reasons, but also because the simpler designation (*private*) connotes an essential feature of the subject. Educational institutions not under state control have a slightly different status in each nation. In France, where the definition of state authority is quite explicit, they are definitely *privé;* but in neighboring Belgium, under a different political tradition, they are conventionally designated as *libre.* In

Sweden every institution must act in accordance with socially defined responsibilities, so that private control in higher education, even though existing for all practical purposes, in fact requires a high degree of public-mindedness. At the opposite extreme of the spectrum, higher education in the Philippines is so overwhelmingly private that it is conventionally discussed in terms of the more meaningful subdivisions of proprietary, sectarian, and nonprofit. The word *private* has definitely fallen from favor in the United States, where spokesmen have chosen to emphasize the public services of privately controlled colleges while, not coincidentally, making claims for greater public support.[5] The array of organizations that assist, coordinate, promote, and lobby for these institutions have been accordingly rechristened with *independent* in their titles (or *I* in their acronyms), as this became the preferred usage. But both terms are in fact relative. Independent colleges and universities actually depend considerably upon the government, just as they depend upon their private constituencies. *Private* will be the preferred term throughout this study, not only because it seems to invite somewhat less misinterpretation, but also because it conveys important aspects of the origins and social roles of nongovernmental higher education.

Higher is also an appropriate description for the type of education that will be considered here, because the emphasis will be predominantly upon university-level institutions. Other forms of postsecondary education have proliferated, especially since the 1960s, and this has sometimes provided an area in which privately controlled institutions have had considerable scope to operate. But, the configurations of these nonuniversity sectors vary more widely and more randomly from country to country than do universities— which themselves are not easily matched for purposes of comparison. Moreover, the sphere of nonuniversity postsecondary education has few discernable boundaries, shading into secondary education on one side and into completely nonacademic activities on another. This is as it should be, considering the fluid nature of this enterprise; but it greatly complicates comparative study. Where called for, private institutions in this segment of the education system will be discussed, but for the most part universities and their equivalents will provide a more congenial and more important subject. Universities, in particular, are committed to creating as well as transmitting knowledge, and this task is inevitably a fundamental source of their vitality and their prestige. Where this commitment is attenuated, as it inevitably is in parts of all large systems, this fact in itself becomes a significant point in characterizing institutions. Universities are involved with international disciplinary communities in ways that nonuniversity institutions are not, and this facet allows judgment to be made about the elusive matter of institutional quality. Higher education is distinctive in other ways as well.

Private education of course exists at all instructional levels, but there are several reasons why privateness in higher education has special characteristics in the modern era and deserves separate consideration. As a very broad generalization it could be said that the basic knowledge and skills imparted at the primary and secondary levels have a general social utility. This has been universally recognized by modern states, and officially promoted through the setting of legal obligations for minimum levels of schooling. In contrast, higher education is far more closely related to actual positions in the work force, both because of its profession-related content and because it is the final stage of the educational process. It is therefore undertaken at the discretion of individuals largely in expectation of personal betterment.

Higher education also is heavy with cultural content in a way that differs from lower levels of education. If the mission of primary and secondary education is to transmit and inculcate a particular culture, the function of higher education is to define, articulate, and extend that culture. When more than one culture are in competition within a society, the importance of these different roles becomes manifest. Where the issue of control over education involves mass allegiances, divisive political conflict will usually reach higher education *last,* as was the case at different times in France, Belgium, and the Netherlands. Where cultural conflict originates with an elite or intelligentsia, as in the national awakenings of central and eastern Europe, struggles tend to occur in the universities *first.* The role of higher education in protecting and preserving certain cultures, and its role as a means for personal achievement, in fact represent two different kinds of private interests. Both of these interests have been involved in the origins of private sectors.

The private sectors under study here are by-products of the development of the modern secular state. They consist of privately controlled institutions offering educational programs equivalent to those given in public institutions. A private sector thus implies the existence of a public one, and before the nineteenth century there was no such distinction in Western countries.[6] Examples can be found of private instruction, especially in light of the large role played by tutors, but in advanced formal education, public and private features were jumbled together in each sovereign territory. Before the modern era, the existence of established state churches gave governments an arm for dealing with spiritual and intellectual matters. The intermittent historical conflict between churches and monarchs tends to obscure the fact that they both were quite in accord that educational institutions not beholden to either one of them were decidedly unwelcome. Significantly, in places like Germany, where church-state linkages remained strong into the twentieth century, no private sector ever emerged. But, in those western European countries where a secular state and a secularized educational system deprived the Church of its university forum, the usual result was the creation of private institutions under Church auspices. Religious organizations, however, have not been the only social groupings that have felt compelled to pursue their interests through private institutions of higher education. Cultural goals, from rationalism to nationalism, have served as inspiration for the private foundings of colleges and universities. Furthermore, the collective interests of such economically defined groups as businessmen have also prompted the establishment and continued support of private schools.

All of the above factors have an important bearing on a fundamental question underlying this study: why do private sectors in higher education differ so markedly from one country to another? The answer, generally speaking, lies both with the pursuit of private interests and with the distinctive attributes of higher education. That is, individuals have the discretion to choose where to seek their educational or professional goals among alternatives that may or may not include public institutions. And, groups within society will act to guarantee their collective interests through higher education in ways which, once again, may or may not involve the public sector. Thus, the public/private division in higher education represents the sum of these actions within the structural possibilities that society permits: individual demand and preferences for higher education, the collective interests of special groups, the state provision of higher education, and, to be sure, the feasibility of providing private alternatives. These four phenomena are useful categories for conceptualizing the forces involved in the constitution of private sectors, but clearly they do not operate independently of one another. Instead, there are recurring patterns between these four variables, and it is these patterns that provide the key to understanding the differences between these eight private sectors.

Because each private sector constitutes what first appears to be an almost arbitrary section of its respective national system of higher education, the literature that focuses on the relation of educational systems to social variables offers little guidance on public/private patterns. More helpful is the theoretical literature concerning voluntary nonprofit sectors. With a few significant exceptions, almost all of the private institutions considered here are nonprofit organizations. They are situated organizationally on an ambiguous middle ground between for-profit firms, which are assumed to take their character from the discipline of market forces, and agencies of the state, responsible indirectly to the popular will. Explanations of the existence of nonprofit sectors reflect the fact that they face in these two directions, and must be distinguished analytically from the spheres of both for-profit and governmental activities.

One interpretation of the role of private nonprofit organizations is based upon the inability of free markets to operate effectively in certain types of industries.[7] This may be due to difficulties regarding consumer information, lack of comparability of products, and/or the absence of conditions for meaningful price competition. Under these conditions consumers are likely to seek providers whom they can reasonably trust not to exploit these inherent supplier advantages when they seek services that are difficult for nonexperts to evaluate, that entail large and lengthy commitments not easily withdrawn, or that include important considerations of quality that are not reflected in prices. This is often the situation with regard to education and human care, and the preceding remarks about higher education should make it evident that nonprofit forms are especially appropriate for its special circumstances. The organization of higher education reflects the fundamental fact that it is an industry based upon knowledge.[8] There is an inherent ambiguity facing potential students concerning the nature of the knowledge that they will be offered and what its occupational consequences are likely to be. Furthermore, the open-endedness of knowledge makes quality a crucial consideration in the operation of higher educational systems, even though the higher costs of quality cannot be captured in its price.[9] Conversely, the cases where certain forms of higher education are successfully offered on a proprietary basis tend to be exceptions that confirm these distinctions: proprietary schools generally offer fairly uniform products aimed at rather definite goals, and the absence of incentives for quality competition allow minimal services to be offered at a price that will cover costs.[10] The market-failure interpretation of nonprofit organizations, however, offers little guidance on the division of tasks between private nonprofit and government institutions.

A second important interpretation of nonprofit sectors sees their basic function as supplying those collective goods and services that governments fail to provide.[11] It is assumed for these purposes that a government would be willing to supply a service such as higher education at a level approximating the wishes of the majority of its citizens. It follows that the greater the heterogeneity of demand—i.e., the more people disagree about the kind and the amount of the services they desire—the greater the scope for the voluntary sector.

As plausible as this hypothesis may appear, it encounters some immediate difficulties with higher education in the countries considered here. Heterogeneity of demand stemming from cultural pluralism would seem to account in general for the private sectors of Belgium and the Netherlands, but not for the fact that the Dutch, with considerably greater religious diversity than the Belgians, have considerably less private higher education. Even more worrisome, the two countries that are, without question, internally most homogeneous culturally and socially—Japan and Sweden—are polar opposites with regard to private sectors. On the other hand, in the most emphatically heterogeneous nation—the Philippines—the types of private colleges and universities bear little relation to its numerous cultural fault lines. Clearly this perspective needs to be refined if it is to be of use in comparing private nonprofit sectors of higher education.

Above all, it would seem to be necessary to recognize that there are different forms of heterogeneity, and that they each imply quite different relationships between public and private sectors. Where governments intentionally restrict their provision of higher education to a fraction of the amount demanded, the private sectors' essential task will be to provide *more* higher education to meet the excess general demand. Where cultural groupings in society have the power to insist upon separate and equal educational institutions under their own control, the private sector will embody culturally *different* traditions. And, where the state endeavors to be the dominant provider of higher education, niches are likely to remain for private institutions to serve those minorities who demand and will support their own *distinctive* forms of higher education.

This list does not fully exhaust the possible reasons why voluntary private efforts might supplement the public provision of higher education,[12] but these three rationales do correspond to the mass, parallel, and peripheral private sectors that will be analyzed in the next three chapters. In each of these cases the pattern of individual and collective demands for higher education, the mandates for the public sectors, and the terms set for the existence of private sectors all conform to a different logic. In those chapters the different national systems are presented as exemplars, or paradigms, in the sense in which Thomas Kuhn originally used this term.[13] That is, the patterns found in the principal exemplar, and then confirmed through a second case, allow for generalizations about theoretical relationships that will be applicable to similarly structured systems. The general features of these paradigms that will thus be isolated include aspects of their historical development, current modes of operation, and likely points of stress and future change— in short, the essentials of structure, function, and change in private higher education.

Paradigms pertaining to social knowledge, it has been widely recognized, lack the same degree of certitude or authoritativeness that Kuhn expected of natural science paradigms. Nevertheless, it is by no means clear that social inquiry should always aspire to approximate the natural science model. Charles E. Lindblom and David K. Cohen have argued in *Usable Knowledge* that the "authoritativeness of propositions may be of less importance than other aspects of the task that need further study before they are well sorted out and understood"; and, furthermore, that social inquiry may be "capable of clarifying man's understanding of the social world" even without developing testable scientific propositions.[14] This would especially seem to be the case with respect to comparative analysis in certain areas, such as private higher education, where no theory currently exists. In such situations, it has been suggested, comparative analysis should properly aim for enlightenment, or the generation of new hypotheses and concepts.[15]

Certainly, one essential task of this study is to bring order and coherence to a body of knowledge that has hitherto been fragmented and unorganized. This endeavor is basically pursued in two stages, involving first the elaboration of three paradigms of private sectors in higher education, and then the application of these concepts to other topics. From the perspective thus developed, new dimensions of the American private sector become evident, patterns of government subsidization of private higher education can be related to the nature and structure of private sectors, and, finally, the significance of attributes closely associated with private higher education (such as diversity, innovation, and privateness itself) appear to vary within different types of private sectors. Ultimately, then, by furthering an understanding of the familiar and superficially understood phenomenon of private higher education, this study is intended to expand the knowledge base of the nature of educational systems and the partition of services between public and private sectors.

Chapter 2

Mass Private Sectors

Mass private sectors essentially fulfill the role of accommodating the bulk of popular demand for higher education. They complement public sectors that are relatively small, predominantly selective, and to a large extent oriented toward the elite tasks of higher education. The defining feature of mass private sectors consequently lies in the public-private relationship rather than the relative sizes of the two sectors. The two examples that will be considered here are both very large—the Japanese private sector enrolling 78 percent of the country's university students, and that of the Philippines accounting for about 85 percent. The private sector of Brazil also fits this type with two-thirds of the total enrollment, but the Belgian private sector, with the same proportion of students, is clearly not a mass private sector.[1] The hallmark of mass private sectors in the postwar era has been the capacity for extremely rapid enrollment growth. As a result they have typically supplied educational opportunities for the masses in developing countries that have experienced a rather abrupt growth in the demand for postsecondary studies. Nevertheless, the nature and structure of these private sectors was evident in their origins and early development.

For analytical purposes, three types of institutions can be identified in the early stages of these systems. Most prominent would be a single national university, created by the government and supported generously with public funds in order to serve specific national purposes. The national university is intended to provide a locus for research and a conduit for advanced foreign learning, to serve as a kind of national outpost on the frontiers of knowledge. Its other chief function is to train the leaders of the learned professions and, in particular, to fulfill the needs of the government itself for highly educated civil servants. These are broad purposes, but in such circumstances they are narrowly conceived: just one of these exceedingly costly institutions is, at least initially, presumed to be sufficient for the needs of state. The private demand for advanced education at this juncture is no concern of the government, and is consequently left to private institutions.

The private sector is likely to originate from a mixture of specialized vocational schools and culturally oriented colleges. The former type arises to offer narrowly focused instruction for specific occupations to students who pay full cost for their education. The breadth and the depth of this instruction are likely to be the minimum necessary for the end in view. This type of training is almost ubiquitous in modern society, and in some places is offered on a for-profit basis. Most of it was not originally considered to be part of higher education; however, in mass private sectors conditions exist for it to grow into a larger and more significant role. Most culturally inspired colleges are founded by religious organizations, and for them both vocational considerations and academic scholarship tend to be subordinated to the goal of offering a fairly general education grounded in their own spiritual values. The economics of these colleges are different as well. In most cases a portion of the costs are covered by, or through the auspices of, the sponsoring organization. This type of education also has particular attraction for affluent families who can afford a relatively high rate of tuition. For a few of these colleges, then, income may exceed the minimum necessary for instruction *per se,* thus allowing greater spending on desirable educational and overhead expenditures, such as better buildings, small classes, libraries, and the like.

A system consisting of these three types would be highly compartmentalized in its initial stage, but it would be unlikely to remain so given the dynamics of rapid enrollment growth. The fixed point in the entire system would undoubtedly be the original national university and its subsequent clones, secure in both academic prestige and assured government support. There nevertheless seems to be a long-term secular trend for such restricted public sectors to expand. The definition of national educational needs through the political process inexorably grows, and many of these needs cannot be met by private institutions. Hence, a less prestigious and less costly stratum of state colleges would follow in order to train agricultural specialists, teachers, or engineers. Still, during periods of rapid growth the secular expansion of the public sector is likely to be dwarfed by increases in the private sector. Such growth periods offer great opportunities for specialized schools to expand their programs and enhance their status. The development of cultural colleges is likely to depend upon the resources at their disposal. Those with external or endowment income and an upper-class clientele—conditions that usually go together—will tend to emphasize academic attainments and selectivity. But colleges with limited means will experience the pull of market forces, and may add vocational programs to their original cultural mission.

Given such a development the original compartments tend to dissolve into a single academic hierarchy with the national university at the top, other institutions arrayed beneath it according to relative prestige, and at the bottom numerous institutions which, compared to the others, are newer, smaller, and more limited in scope. Such hierarchies are always complex: it may be quite pointless, for example, to attempt to compare the rank of a women's Christian college with that of a state agricultural university. Nevertheless, in contrast with other types of systems, one of the most salient characteristics of mass private sectors is a widely recognized institutional hierarchy. Differences in selectivity of students, student/teacher ratios, library size, and campus amenities become embodied in institutional reputations; these reputations, in turn, become generally known and, more significantly, faithfully mirrored in family choices for their children and employer preferences for graduates. Viewed in this way the academic hierarchy would appear to be self-perpetuating, but this is not entirely the case. The institutional competition implicit in these hierarchical relations in combination with other characteristics of mass private sectors create a high degree of internal dynamism.

One of the most basic features of mass private sectors during their developmental period is an extreme reliance upon tuition revenues, even though they depend predominantly upon a student clientele that is by no means wealthy. Only a very few of the cultural colleges are likely to be at once small, selective, and prestigious. For the majority of private institutions getting better means getting bigger. New divisions, capital improvements, and additional faculty ultimately must be financed through increased tuition revenues, and in the long run this can only be brought about through enrollment growth. Institutions of course differ greatly in their capacities to exploit opportunities for expansion. Those in large urban centers have the most potential due to the proximity of both potential students and graduate employment opportunities in the modern sectors of the economy. This condition has a tendency to produce pronounced urban concentration in mass private sectors. In Japan and the Philippines it has also led to the development of a few mammoth private universities. At the start of the 1970s, for example, the largest of this type in the Philippines enrolled more students than the entire public sector. The eagerness of private universities to grow is obviously one important reason for the expansionary ten-

dencies of mass private sectors as a whole. Probably of equal significance is the relative openness of higher education in these societies
to new institutional entrants. New schools are able to begin on a
quite modest scale because they are usually just single faculties of
commerce, or domestic science, or whatever. Another typical en-
trant would be a secondary school that expanded upward by adding
a junior college, and then a four-year college division. Thus, as the
more successful private institutions grow into multifaculty universities, the lower tiers of the academic hierarchy have been continually refilled, at least until recently, by a steady stream of
newcomers.

The expansionary capacities of mass private sectors are all the
more remarkable when seen in comparative perspective. They alone
among the world's systems of higher education have been able to
supply the space to meet the great postwar surge of demand for
higher education in private institutions and at private expense. The
remarkable degree of access to higher education thus achieved has
nevertheless had its negative aspects. While some of the private
institutions in mass private sectors are comparable to the best that
the state can offer, the bulk of the additional student places are of a
decidedly inferior quality. This widely acknowledged problem invariably seems to induce countervailing efforts on the part of the
state ministry of education. Considering the vocational- or second-
ary-school origins of many private institutions, their often thin financial foundations, and the questionable qualifications of their
teaching staffs, the government's natural concern to uphold minimal standards frequently results in close control over curriculum,
degree programs, and many more minor aspects of the educational
process. As a result of this extensive government regulation, mass
private sectors exhibit considerable conformity in educational programs, despite the wide variety of institutions represented there.

In the cases that follow it will also become evident that the
great growth of mass private sectors was a temporal phase in their
developments that could scarcely be sustained. However, natural
limits to growth manifested themselves rather differently in Japan
and the Philippines, in part due to their markedly different levels of
economic development. Both have depended upon their private colleges and universities to attain a remarkably high level of attendance in higher education. Japan, only one generation removed
from the overwhelming tasks of postwar reconstruction, now vies
with the United States for the distinction of being the most highly
educated society on the globe. The Philippines, the only industrializ-

ing nation considered in this study, for a time surpassed the higher education enrollment rates of western Europe. Together, they provide an instructive contrast for elaborating and qualifying the general characteristics of systems that rely upon private institutions to satisfy the popular demand for higher education.

Japan's Mass Private Sector

Education has played a central role in the modernization of Japan. The remarkable success of the Japanese in "borrowing" knowledge from the West and utilizing it in industry has become legendary, but the antecedents that made this possible were deeply rooted in the country's strong educational traditions.[2]

In the middle of the nineteenth century, while Japan was still in the twilight of a feudal regime, nearly half the males were acquiring basic literacy through temple schools. Advanced education was still the nearly exclusive prerogative of the aristocracy—the samurai—but they were conditioned by a centuries-old tradition of intellectual and aesthetic cultivation. Samurai were educated to varying degrees in official schools of the feudal domains or in private academies. Although by the end of this era commoners might also be found in some of these schools, education was nevertheless explicitly based upon class. When the political and social revolution of the Meiji Restoration (1868–1912) abrogated the privileges of the samurai, it also undermined the existing system of schooling. The old institutions rather quickly underwent closure or metamorphosis. More importantly, as the Meiji regime created the foundation for a new state system of education, it heralded a society in which education would take the place of class and birth in determining individual life chances.

The new state institutions clearly led the transformation in higher education, but in their wake came new and different types of private institutions to replace the schools of the samurai. This private sector has evolved through four broad stages in the past hundred years. At first a variety of private institutions offered specialized instruction at a level that was advanced but officially inferior to that of the national universities. Eventually, these institutions were allowed to attain university status, although their limited resources kept their stature well below the universities of the state. The reorganization imposed by the American occupation completely altered the structure of higher education, and these changes were compounded by a prolonged period of rapid enrollment growth. The result was a third stage in which a mass private sector was fully developed. The consequences of this evolution propelled the Japanese private sector into a fourth stage in the 1970s, when the scope and responsibilities of private higher education became too great to remain solely a private matter. The current state of affairs, which will be considered below, thus represents the latest phase of a larger evolutionary pattern for Japanese higher education.

The new leaders of Japan following the Meiji Restoration set as one of their foremost goals the acquisition and dissemination of the advanced learning of the West, but the funds they could spare for this purpose were exceedingly meager. Intellectual aspiration and fiscal limitation were the two conditions that determined higher education policy for the new regime during its initial stage of development.[3] Immediately after the Meiji Restoration the educational system was quite amorphous, but within two decades a definite pattern crystalized. Institutional models from different European countries and the United States were tested during these years. Western scholars were brought to Tokyo to lecture at European-style faculties of letters, sciences, and medicine, as well as in American-inspired schools of engineering and law. Some Japanese students were sent to the West to be trained as future professors. These efforts alone were extraordinarily burdensome: in 1873 both types of exchanges consumed 32 percent of the total national budget for education.[4] A small elite of Japanese students studied Western languages intensively for three years beyond secondary school in order to prepare themselves to learn Western subjects in the university. They were largely destined either to fill important government posts, or to disseminate Western knowledge further in the state educational system. The latter effort was particularly vital in order to escape from the temporary dependence on foreign language instruction. When the separate Tokyo schools and faculties were finally united into the Imperial University (1886), the founding ordinance articulated the rationale for this entire policy:

> The purpose of the imperial university shall be to provide instruction in the arts and sciences and to inquire into the mysteries of learning in accordance with the needs of the state.[5]

The number of Imperial Universities eventually grew to seven as the definition of national educational needs gradually expanded. The original establishment of a national university nevertheless dictated the basic structure of Japanese higher education by separating the educational priorities of the state from the tasks that would be left to private institutions.

The emphasis placed on Western learning during the formative period of Japanese higher education resulted in a two-tiered structure. The Imperial Universities alone taught the advanced curriculum, and entrance was allowed only after three years of postsecondary study in what were called "higher schools." The rest of higher education took place in three-year institutions known as *senmongakko*. The term literally means "special school," but originally it also stood for Japanese-language schools. Both meanings are pertinent, since most of these institutions consisted of single specialized faculties which, unlike the universities, taught only in the vernacular. This form included a broad spectrum of institutions. The state created *senmongakko* in engineering, commerce, and medicine as less costly alternatives to the universities, but the bulk of these institutions were private.[6]

The private sector that took form in the first two decades of the Meiji era contained *senmongakko* for law, medicine, foreign languages, and even fine arts. Some schools sought to emulate Western liberal arts, while Buddhist and Shinto institutions were formed to stress native traditions. Toward the end of the century the creation of women's colleges added another distinctive type. Many individual institutions have endured to become contemporary universities, and several have played key roles in shaping the contours of the private sector. The spirit of Western learning, in either its secular or its Christian form, was the inspiration for several important schools.[7] One of the most single-minded apostles of free inquiry in the Western style was Yukichi Fukuzawa, who began propagating Western learning in his own school as early as 1858. The *senmongakko* he created grew into Keio University. The Tokyo Senmongakko, which later became Waseda University, was founded in 1882 by Shigenobu Okuma to provide a center of independent thought not beholden to the government. A third dedicated founder, Jo Niijima, returned from a Christian education in the United States with a gift of five thousand dollars that proved sufficient to launch the future Doshisha University in Kyoto. The fact that these three universities have been the perennial leaders of the private sector has not been accidental. Their dedication to a liberal conception of learning contrasts with the vocationalism of most other *senmongakko,* and it led them to strive for a degree of quality and breadth of education that distinguished them from their competitors. A group of legal *senmongakko* gained considerable success by following a different course. Willingly or not, they were induced by the circumstances of the existing structure into becoming inferior alternatives to the Imperial University. Students who failed to enter the university preparatory schools could thus study similar subjects in a *senmongakko* to qualify for second-rank positions in the civil service.[8] That such opportunities represented desirable careers is apparent from the vigorous development of these schools into many of today's largest private universities.

During their first decades of operation many *senmongakko* led precarious existences. Their total dependence upon tuition revenue conditioned many of their activities. The utilization of part-time instructors kept costs low, as did limiting the curriculum to inexpensive subjects in humanities and social science. Special courses for students not qualified for the regular programs brought in extra tuitions. But survival could still be a problem. Lack of funds, for example, led Fukuzawa almost to the point of closing Keio in 1879.[9] The steadily rising demand for higher education gradually strengthened the established schools, and in time allowed them to upgrade their offerings. By 1890 Keio had already established departments of literature, economics, and law in a quest to become a full-fledged university. After the turn of the century Waseda became the first private school to establish programs in engineering. The continued qualitative improvements of the more vigorous private *senmongakko* created pressure to relax the two-tiered structure. By 1900 the Imperial Universities were no longer the only places capable of offering education on the highest level, and the private schools accordingly demanded a formal equalization of status. A step in this direction was made in 1903, when *senmongakko* were allowed to offer an additional year of work in a "university division" course, but full university status had to wait another decade and a half.[10]

The University Order of 1918 inaugurated the second stage in the evolution of the Japanese private sector by allowing the existence of full-fledged private universities.[11] The same 3 + 3 structure for higher education was retained, only now single-faculty state *senmongakko* (schools of commerce, institutes of technology, etc.) and some of the privates were permitted to operate on the advanced, university level. The Ministry of Education possessed the power to authorize university status, and during the interwar years only some twenty-five private institutions were so-recognized. The government's intention was undoubtedly to maintain close control.

New departments and all teaching appointments had to receive ministerial approval, as did the amount of tuition, the number of students, and virtually every other aspect of school operations. There were capital requirements to guarantee the financial solvency of the institutions, including a substantial deposit held by the ministry. In actuality, though, the new private universities were far more constrained by the circumstances of their existence than they were by the government.

The new private university sector was largely a response to a burgeoning demand for higher education that tripled the number of university and *senmongakko* graduates from 1920 to 1930.[12] This expansion was certainly necessary for the new private universities to broaden and upgrade their programs, but in other ways it did not work to their benefit. State-supported higher education also grew steadily during these years, and a new class of institution joined the public sector as municipalities began sponsoring universities. In contrast to these relatively well financed competitors, the private institutions faced a continual problem just making ends meet. Their tuition, for example, was held approximately equal to the national universities, and supplemental sources of revenue were not easily produced. The principal function of the new private universities came to be the training of white-collar workers for Japan's private enterprises. The education of *sarariman*—the Japanese coinage for "salaryman"—was an inexpensive type of instruction that they could afford to offer. Every private university consequently sprouted a faculty of economics or commerce for this purpose, although law or political science would do just as well. The pressure of market forces gradually shaped private universities into an identical mold. Even in the liberal institutions that had risen to distinction during the previous period, the intellectual ideals of the founders tended to be engulfed in a tide of careerism. It is symptomatic of this transformation that the Imperial Universities of Tokyo and Kyoto, rather than any independent universities, became the last spokesmen for academic freedom against an increasingly militaristic regime.[13]

The evolution of Japanese higher education after 1918 produced many of the distinctive features that characterize the present system. By the 1930s the public and private sectors roughly divided the task of supplying higher education. Public institutions, however, offered subsidized, high-quality instruction that led to the most prestigious occupational opportunities. By the 1930s these jobs included *sarariman* positions in the largest corporations. Entrance into the state universities consequently grew increasingly competitive. During these years the phenomenon of *ronin* first became conspicuous. *Ronin,* which literally means a masterless samurai, were students without universities who spent one or more extra years cramming for university entrance examinations. For the most part, those who could get accepted chose public-sector institutions; the remainder had to content themselves with places in the largely unselective private sector. So, even before it became a true "mass private sector," Japanese private universities existed on the overflow demand that could not be accommodated in public institutions. Thus, the achievement of legal equality for the privates resulted in a system of informal ranking—an institutional hierarchy in which most of the private schools were inferior to most of the public ones. The picture was naturally complicated by the dual structure of three-year *senmongakko* and essentially six-year universities. Nevertheless, institutional stratification was to outlast the old structure as one of the permanent features of the Japanese system.

Postwar Reconstruction

At the insistence of the American Occupation Authorities, Japanese education was restructured to fit the pattern familiar in the United States. Secondary education was lengthened to six years and divided between middle and high schools. The two distinct segments of higher education were combined and shortened into a single, four-year unit. In the resultant reorganization all different types of private institutions were transformed into four-year universities. Within a short time the need for junior colleges was recognized as well, but this detail followed the general reorganization. In those prefectures that did not already have national universities, existing *senmongakko,* teachers' colleges, and technical institutes were somewhat artificially lumped together in order to create one. The number of national universities thus rose in one year (1949) from twenty-three to seventy; various municipal institutions were reborn to add eighteen more universities; and the number of private universities suddenly jumped to ninety-two—with more to come. Thus, the third stage of development brought an entirely new face and structure to Japanese higher education.

For the private sector the conditions of existence changed completely in the postwar world. The regulatory powers of the Ministry of Education were considerably curbed, and a new policy of virtual laissez-faire was embodied in the Private School of Law of 1949.[14]

The residual powers of supervision that the ministry did retain were to be exercised only after consultation with the Private University Council, where the schools themselves were strongly represented. The fact that university charters were liberally granted and never revoked typifies the spirit of the new regime. The legal basis of the sponsoring entity was altered to give private universities a more "public" character. A large board of trustees, auditors, and an elected board of councillors were all required. Within this framework, though, private administrators had considerable leeway for setting school policy. During the period of postwar reconstruction, however, almost all had to face the realities of widespread needs and scant resources. As in the past, the fate of private institutions depended heavily upon the interplay between the public and private sectors.

The Japanese educational authorities were less than enthusiastic about the new structure imposed by the Americans. The creation of seventy nominally equal state universities, accompanied by American encouragement to equalize funding across institutions, presented them with two paramount problems. Given a scarcity of public funds for many pressing purposes, they had to rehabilitate and protect the high academic standards of the former university sector, while at the same time raising standards at the newly created institutions to an acceptable university level. How these goals were reconciled largely determined why Japanese higher education developed the way it did, rather than like the American model toward which the Occupation Authorities had seemingly steered it.

To resolve the first issue, the ministry soon reverted to the prewar funding pattern for the former national universities. This assured Tokyo University a disproportionately large share of government expenditures for higher education, followed in the pecking order by Kyoto, the next five former Imperial Universities, the other eleven prewar universities, and finally the fifty-two newly created state universities.[15] In keeping with this pattern of financing, only the prewar universities were allowed to offer the Ph.D. With inequality thus reestablished, the second goal could only be realized through prosperity. By 1956 the Japanese economy had reached its prewar levels; from that point on its development was breathtaking. The skewed pattern of funding was perpetuated, so that each state university depended upon the expanding economic pie for its additional resources. The decision to preserve the research function of the elite universities thus reaffirmed the institutional hierarchy of the Japanese system. However, the policy of relentless upgrading caused by the rather premature and unwelcome postwar expansion was pursued at the expense of growth in the public sector. From 1952 to 1970 the national universities nearly doubled their enrollments, but this supplied only 150,000 additional places. Over the same years the private universities supplied 820,000 additional places while more than quadrupling their enrollments. The government policy of limiting the number of national universities and only moderately increasing their enrollments, then, was the negative condition behind the emergence of a mass private sector.

If the unequal competition with the public sector before the war tended to minimize institutional differences in the private sector, the hothouse conditions of growth prevailing after the war soon emphasized inherent inequalities. In the immediate aftermath of the war all private institutions found themselves in straitened circumstances. Besides the destruction and dislocations caused by the war, the attendant inflation had rendered their endowments worthless. The private schools were consequently more than ever dependent upon student fees to acquire the buildings, books, and faculty considered proper to university status. Growth thus became a necessity. Except for a handful of colleges receiving foreign support, Japanese private universities literally could not afford not to grow. Nevertheless, as in the public sector, an inherent ranking was evident. The prewar universities obviously had a more substantial base to build upon than former *senmongakko;* the latter, in turn, had some advantages over institutions starting from scratch. The established private universities in major cities clearly presented the most desirable alternatives in the private sector—and were in many ways more attractive than the remote, new national universities. They were able to exploit this attractiveness not only to expand to optimal size, but often to increase their standards of admission.

This last element, selectivity, provided the key to the gradations of the private sector. The more students wanting to attend a particular faculty, the higher quality of student body that could be recruited through the faculty's entrance examinations. (Students are admitted to a specific faculty, not to a university, in Japan.) Potential employers, influenced more strongly by the screening function of Japanese universities than by their educational mission, preferred graduates of the more selective institutions. Employer preferences then influenced future students, thus reinforcing the desirability of the most selective faculties. The effect of this vicious circle was to produce both uniformity and differences within the private sector. The uniformity came from the singular model of academic prestige established by the leading universities and imitated throughout the rest of the system. Universal acceptance of this model, however, led to wide disparities between institutions. The prestigious universities could grow large enough to support the overhead expenses of graduate programs, research commitments, and faculties in the hard sciences; while at the other end of the spectrum new universities could do little else but offer inexpensive subjects in crowded facilities taught by part-time instructors. The widespread recognition of this stratification tended to assure that students would find places with peers of similar tested abilities. The self-perpetuating features of this system made it difficult for an institution to better its position. The implications of this academic stratification will be explored in greater detail below. Here it is essential to note that the apparent stasis of the system in fact generated one of the dynamic elements in the postwar development of higher education. Under conditions of rapid growth few private universities could be complacent; they had to expand and improve their facilities and faculty merely to maintain their existing niche. These efforts accentuated a disequilibrium within Japanese higher education that eventually led to the crisis of the late 1960s.

The Crisis of the Japanese Private Sector in the 1960s

A basic disjunction existed in postwar Japanese higher education between the role thrust upon the private sector and the means available for its fulfillment. The conditions that produced a mass private sector were in part the result of political forces acting upon conservative governments and ultimately upon the Ministry of Education.[16] Throughout this period the demand for more university places was in tension with the ministry's constant concern for improving academic standards. An effort in the mid-1950s to tighten requirements for new university charters was soon overridden as a result of pressure from middle-class parents, the business community, and influential educators eager to upgrade their own institutions. Chartering standards were first eased, and then virtually ignored during the 1960s, when baby-boom cohorts and dramatic increases in personal income together produced an unprecedented leap in the demand for higher education. From 1962 through 1968, 128 applications for university charters were approved out of 159 submissions (81 percent). Given the prevailing conservative policies toward taxation and social expenditures, little could be done to assist private universities. Some loans to improve facilities were provided through the Private School Promotion Society, a state funded independent body established for this purpose in 1952.[17] The amount of available government funds each year varied, but never rose above 3 percent of private university income. During the 1960s aid was specifically designated for expanding science and engineering education, and hence concentrated in a minority of private institutions.[18] Basically the Japanese private sector had to generate funds as best it could to educate the ever-growing numbers of students.

Although the Japanese private universities have always been tuition-dependent, the revenues derived from students have never covered much more than half of their total budgets.[19] Students are made to pay in numerous ways. Entrance examination fees, to begin with, are a significant source of income, and a hefty entrance fee for new students currently averages more than half of annual tuition. Contributions to the building fund and other miscellaneous fees likewise add up to better than half of the official tuition.[20] But, this still leaves more than 40 percent of expenditures to be met by other means. Only a few exceptional institutions can count on significant donations or endowment income. A variety of related activities, from hospitals to university presses, might yield operating surpluses. However, where capital expenditures are involved, the recourse has been to loans, either from the Private School Promotion Society, when possible, or otherwise from commercial banks. Student revenues and loans, then, comprise the bulk of university income, and each of these sources can only be manipulated within definite limits. These limitations have largely determined the financial health of private universities in the postwar era.

In the two decades from 1955 to 1974 the expenditures of private universities increased by a factor of thirty-seven.[21] Every year brought more students, but each of those students also paid more than the year before. Educational costs during these years were rising more than 60 percent faster than the consumer price index.[22] Of course the Japanese were becoming more prosperous as well, so that the significance of these different factors only becomes evident in relation to each other. One such analysis has revealed that through 1965 tuition at private universities was increasing more rapidly than family income.[23] By that date, first-year tuition and fees at private universities averaged 21 percent of the median family income. At this point serious student protests began to occur at the leading private universities, and the high level of tuition was a prominent issue. In the most notorious case, the decision of Waseda University in December of 1965 to impose a large tuition increase provoked a determined student reaction that paralyzed the university for six months, eventually forcing the resignation of the president and trustees.[24] In effect, notice was served that the limits of family sacrifice had been reached. For the next nine years (1966–74) the burden of private tuition relative to family income consistently decreased, bringing the cost for a median family down to a more manageable 13 percent of annual income. This trend appeared to reverse in 1975 and 1976, for reasons that will be explored in the following section. More germane here is the way private universities compensated for the contraction of their chief source of revenue.

A surge in institutional borrowing followed closely after the period of rapid tuition escalation. With private university enrollments more than doubling from 1962 to 1968, loans were the principal source of capital for the expansion of university facilities. In this process the private universities, as a whole, clearly overextended themselves. In 1965 loans amounted to 29 percent of their income, while debt service on previous borrowing was consuming 19 percent of expenditures. Five years later, probably as a result of the constraints against tuition hikes, the amount required for debt service was larger than the income from new loans.[25] The Organization for European Cooperation and Development [OECD] examining team that evaluated Japanese education in 1970 concluded that the private universities were essentially bankrupt; only the voluntary restraint of the banking community sustained their existence.[26] The deteriorating financial condition naturally could not help but affect the performance of their function.

Figure 1 starkly depicts how the growth curve of per-student expenditures in private universities was abruptly deflected after 1965, and was unable to resume its expected path, given inflation and the need to improve conditions, until government financial assistance arrived in the 1970s.

Still, there can be little doubt that during the first two decades of the postwar regime many Japanese private universities, particularly the large and prominent ones, gradually improved their academic standards. For the private sector as a whole this development was partially offset by the many new institutions entering higher education with minimal pedagogical and physical resources. During the 1950s increases in teachers and buildings seemed to outpace the implacable rise of student numbers, but as enrollment rates shot up in the early 1960s the ratios moved in the other direction.[27] As a result of these two trends the private universities were doubly

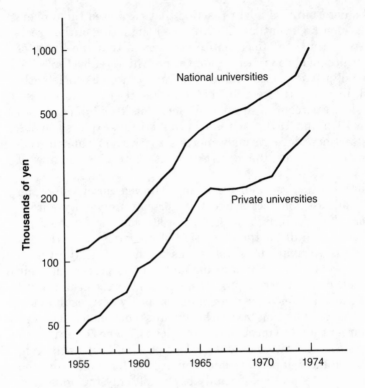

Fig. 1. Per-student expenditures at national and private universities in Japan. *Source*: Compiled from Hiromitsu Muta, "Sources of Expenditures for Higher Education," in *Allocation of Educational Resources in Japan*, ed. S. Ichikawa, pp. 56, 62.

cursed on the issue of academic standards. The constraints upon increasing revenues left them little choice but to squeeze more students into existing classrooms, and by doing so to worsen objective indices, like the student/teacher ratio, which constituted the conventional measure of academic quality. At the same time the standards of comparison were becoming more stringent. The gap between the level of per-student expenditures at national and private universities widened dramatically during the last half of the 1960s (see figure 1). The legacy of this period was a very large absolute disparity between spending levels in the two sectors. Of course, much of the difference is due to inflation; however, a regression analysis of the components of expenditure growth during this period has found that twice the proportion of these increases (13.4 percent) can be associated with qualitative improvements in the national universities as compared to the private universities (6.7 percent).[28]

By the end of the 1960s, then, the crisis of Japanese private higher education was evident to all concerned. The financial situation was clearly untenable, and the gap in standards between public and private sectors was becoming intolerable. In public discussion the issue was most often couched in terms of equity. Private university students were paying nine times more than their public counterparts, and receiving a decidedly inferior education in return. The OECD examiners that visited Japan early in 1970 condemned the low overall investment being made in higher education, and specifically recommended that the national government accept part of the responsibility for financing private universities.[29] In doing so they merely added some force to a consensus that had been slowly building within the country. The private universities had already been lobbying for state subsidies for a number of years, but in the late 1960s they managed to win the support of the Ministry of Education as well. An important committee of the Central Council of Education was formed in 1967 to consider educational reform, and it quickly endorsed the notion of subsidizing private higher education.[30] Support from the Ministry of Finance was more grudging, but eventually achieved. In 1970 the Diet passed the Private School Promotion Law, which for the first time provided regular government financial support for the operating expenses of private institutions of higher education. This reform was probably facilitated by the general discredit into which the government's higher education policy had fallen as a result of the intense student rebellion of the preceding years.[31] Nevertheless, it portended an enduring change in the relationship between the state and private higher education.

The Private School Law of 1970 signaled that the third phase in the evolution of Japanese private higher education was closing, but it took another five years for the new era to take definite form. The Private School Subsidy Law of 1975 completed and finalized the work that the earlier law had begun. Its passage changed the situation of private universities in three fundamental ways. First, government subsidies were increased and regularized on the basis of a permanent formula. This development stabilized the finances of most institutions, thus alleviating the prolonged fiscal crisis of private higher education. Secondly, regular government subsidization formally ended the implicit dualism that had governed Japanese higher education in the modern era. No longer would the "needs of the state" and the educational aspirations of individuals be treated as if they could be segregated into national universities and private ones; there was now an explicit recognition that the mass higher education provided by the private sector also contributed to the collective good of society, and could thus make a legitimate claim for public support.[32] But with public support came public responsibilities. Thus, the third important change was that henceforth private institutions would be subject to an overall effort of national higher education planning. These are important themes that will loom large in the section to follow, where the dimensions and dynamics of the contemporary Japanese private sector will be considered in greater detail.

Structure and Dynamics of Private Higher Education in the 1970s

The nature of the postwar expansion of Japanese higher education caused the private sector to gather an ever-increasing share of total enrollments. Starting from a level of about 60 percent in the early fifties, the proportion of students in private universities rose steadily until 1970. When enrollments stabilized in the last half of the seventies, the private sector's share leveled off as well at 76 percent of the total. Essentially the same process occurred among junior colleges, although they were more heavily private from the outset. Since 1975, 91 percent of these students have attended private institutions. If both these categories are combined, it could be said for comparative purposes that, as of 1979, the private sector of Japanese higher education comprises 78 percent of enrollments.[33]

The expansion of the private sector was accomplished both by the growth of institutions and a growth in the number of institutions. The latter process was facilitated by the long-established tradition of small, specialized institutions. Almost all Japanese colleges and universities (*daigaku*) had their origins in, and the majority still remain, single-faculty institutions. The classification of institutions in table 1 shows 193, or 61 percent, in that category. Although taken together they only enroll something like 17 percent of university students, their singular tasks make them a convenient point to begin to describe the institutional structure of Japanese higher education.

The liberal arts colleges include not only those specializing in letters, literature, or humanities, but also colleges of education, fine

TABLE 1. Japanese Universities by Number of Faculties, Authorized Class Size, Graduate Programs, and Date of Founding

		Authorized Size of One Class					Graduate Degrees	Founded					
	N	30–100	101–300	301–1000	1001–2000	2000+		to 1918	to 1939	1940s	1950s	1960s	1970s
Single faculty													
Liberal arts	43	14	22	7			15	5	6	4	10	13	5
Social science	32	6	15	11			3	1	1	2	7	15	6
Science and technology	35	1	12	22			10	0	3	2	3	20	7
Women's college	48	17	26	5			9	4	8	6	14	16	
Medical													
Medicine	14	11	3				15	2	3				9
Dentistry	8		8				8	1		1		1	5
Pharmacy	13	2	7	4			8	2	5	1		1	4
Total medical	35	13	18	4			31	5	8	2		2	18
Total single faculty	193	51	93	49			68	15	26	16	34	66	36
Two faculties	51		17	28	6		29	5	12	7	8	14	5
Three faculties	22			16	6		14	2	7	3	4	6	1
Four faculties	13			5	8		12	2	4	1	3	2	1
Five faculties	10			5	3	2	10		3	2		4	
Six faculties	8				2	6	8	6	1	1			
Seven to nine faculties	8				2	6	8	5	1	2			
Ten to fourteen faculties	9					9	9	6	2	1			
Total	314	51	110	103	27	23	158	41	56	33	49	92	43

Source: Compiled from Directory of Japanese Colleges and Universities, 1979–1980 (Tokyo: Saikon Publishing Co., 1979).

arts (9), and theology (3). Of those teaching liberal arts *per se,* a number are Christian colleges directly inspired by American models. Others are largely oriented toward women students, who outnumber males 3:2 in the humanities. In this respect they are little different from explicitly women's colleges (see below). It might be said of most of these institutions that they either would not or could not grow. In the latter group would be many of the postwar creations, often in outlying areas, that sprouted from existing high schools or junior colleges. Given limited means, the only feasible areas for them to enter were liberal arts or certain programs in the next category, social science.

The social science colleges are those teaching economics, commerce, political science, law, and those subjects related to social services—programs that account for 41 percent of undergraduate enrollments. The first four of these subjects together form what can be regarded as a single recruitment pool for unspecialized positions in private industry. It is quite natural, then, that most of these colleges were founded during the boom years when the lure of *sarariman* careers was a driving force behind enrollment growth. In this competitive area, most of the single-faculty schools are the latecomers that entered at the bottom of the hierarchy (see table 2). In fact, none of these colleges teach law or political science, which seem to be concentrated in more affluent and prestigious universities (see figure 2). Instead, most offer economics or commerce (business)— programs that are more similar in a Japanese context than in American colleges.

In the area of science and technology a large majority of the one-faculty colleges are engineering schools. Five of the thirty-five have specialities relating to agriculture, and only one, the Okayama College of Science, teaches pure science. There are a number of factors at work restricting the role of the private sector in these fields. Most important is obviously cost: the expense of providing facilities to teach science and engineering is significantly greater than that for social science or letters. This is reflected in student tuition, which is 40 to 50 percent greater for these courses. Then, too, demand is limited by the number of students with aptitudes in these areas. Finally, there is the competition from the public sector, where expanding the training of scientists and engineers was one of the highest priorities during the 1950s and 1960s. As a result, science courses in national and municipal universities outnumber private offerings by more than 3 to 1. The private sector plays a much greater role in engineering education (72 percent of total engineering enrollments). The fact that the technical faculties are on the average significantly larger than other types would seem to indicate that they are able to take advantage of economies of scale. A few have had the advantage of being directly sponsored by private industry. The Daido Institute of Technology, for example, was founded by and retains close links with the steel company of that name. Government has helped as well: the fact that the majority of these institutions were established in the 1960s is certainly due in part to the subsidies designed to increase the supply of engineers. In this case the objectives of public policy seem to have been achieved at minimal cost by stimulating private initiatives.

The situation in the medical and dental colleges shows the private sector responding to quite different kinds of incentives. Although there were a few such faculties of long standing, most of the single-faculty colleges were created during the early 1970s as a result of the intense demand for entry into the medical professions and a temporary easing of Ministry of Education requirements for chartering. As admissions into the established medical schools became extremely competitive, many sons of practicing physicians or dentists found themselves blocked from pursuing their fathers' profession. The new schools were founded largely to serve this small but affluent clientele. Not only could they afford the exceedingly high tuition charged by these faculties—typically about $40 thousand for a first-year medical student and $45 thousand in dentistry, but in one case as much as $75 thousand—but their desperate families could often be induced to make additional "gifts" to the college.[34] It is widely believed that such gifts in effect purchase admission in certain cases for students whose examination scores fail to qualify them. If true, such purchases have not always been wise. Graduates of the new medical colleges have compiled dismal records on the state medical examinations that confer the right to practice.

The remaining type of single-faculty colleges, those for women, cannot validly be discussed in isolation, because it comprises just one facet of the entire subject of higher education for women in Japan. The postsecondary educational paths of Japanese women are above all shaped by the predominant pattern of family formation. A large majority expect, and are expected, to work until their mid-twenties, marry, procreate, and then devote themselves exclusively to raising their families. These expectations effectively exclude women from most graduate careers involving a continuous, lifelong commitment. Educational choices of Japanese women consequently tend to reflect the likelihood of a limited participation in the work force. More female than male secondary school graduates actually enter higher education, but three of every five choose a junior college. For those who enter four-year colleges, sex roles continue to be influential: 76 percent of these women study in predominantly female faculties—humanities, arts, home economics, education, and nursing.

The role of junior colleges is obviously crucial for female higher education, even though they were not originally intended for this purpose. When established in 1950 they were explicitly tailored after the American example, but like so many borrowed institutions in Japan they rather quickly assumed a unique form in their new environment. For men, junior college degrees never became particularly valuable credentials. Colleges wishing to retain their male students consequently had a strong inducement to seek charters as four-year institutions. For women, however, the junior colleges possessed some clear advantages. They offered a modicum of cultural finishing, perhaps some preparation for their future domestic life, vocational credentials for certain feminine careers, and (compared to four-year programs) an extra two years in the work force. For this last reason it is now commonly said that employers prefer female junior-college graduates to university women. Although conventional wisdom can be a dubious guide, the existence of this belief probably indicates that it is true for certain industries. Some predominantly male technical junior colleges remain, but the vast majority of two-year institutions have become female and terminal.

Of the women studying in four-year institutions, roughly one in four attends a women's college. Some of these are selective schools with serious academic programs—a few of the older colleges even grant the doctorate; others are noted for their recruitment from the upper social strata; and many could be included under the derisory rubric of "bride's colleges." The latter would include most of those schools offering domestic science or home economics: their principal difference from junior colleges being simply a matter of duration. In recent years the attraction of distinctive women's colleges seems to have receded. None have been founded since 1968, and several existing women's colleges have lately become coeducational. The president of one of the more distinguished schools has lamented that students choose the institution only because of its selectivity, rather than out of any commitment to the concept of women's education. It would seem that the most able women students attend regular universities where at least some of them prepare for working careers. While most good business careers are virtually precluded for women, areas like publishing, teaching, and more recently, the civil service, are more accessible. Because bright and ambitious women can earn admission to selective universities, a relatively high percentage of women students has, ironically, become associated with academic prestige. Female students, then, tend to gravitate toward the top or toward the bottom of the academic pyramid.

Most of the seventy-three universities that consist of two or three faculties could be classified in the same single-function categories used for one-faculty colleges. Not surprisingly, they are on the average older, larger, and more selective. When one moves down table 1 to universities with four and more faculties almost all are multiple-purpose institutions; that is, they include faculties in more than one of the categories already discussed. It is difficult to generalize about these forty-eight universities—Japan's largest and best known. While there is considerable resemblance between each type of faculty from one school to the next, almost every one of these medium and large universities represents a unique combination of faculties. What is more important about these universities is not their similarities, but their differences. And, the most significant difference between them is their relative institutional prestige as indicated in student selectivity.

Most national systems of higher education possess some degree of institutional hierarchy, but Japan's is the most explicit in the world. Furthermore, because employers abide by this hierarchy, and because first jobs tend to be lifelong jobs, its effects may be more consequential for life chances than in any other system. The general reasons for this phenomenon have already been noted in the historical development of the system, but its specific features are a consequence of the nature of the admissions process.

Each faculty of each university conducts a competitive entrance examination to select the students it will admit.[35] In recent years the various exams for the national universities have been amalgamated into a single series, and most private colleges admit a few outstanding students on the basis of their high school records. It has been suggested that a national system of testing would be an improvement upon the current anarchic system, but examination fees provide a significant source of income that private schools would not forego without a struggle.[36] In fact, a high degree of order has been imposed upon this decentralized system by private testing companies. They offer high school students administered examinations that simulate those of the faculties. By correlating the scores of these mock exams with the actual attainments of their students on real entrance exams, the companies are able to state with considerable precision what scores correspond with admission into which university. These scores are adjusted for the degree of competition, and the resulting number is a proxy of sorts for the prestige rank of the faculty. These rankings plus a great deal of other information about each faculty and its admission requirements are published in magazines or college guides and sold in bookstores all across Japan. Using this information, high school graduates can quite accurately gauge their relative chance of admission to different faculties. The rankings of social science faculties by one of these companies, Obunsha, have been used in figure 2 and table 2 to illustrate several aspects of the private sector.

The most striking feature of figure 2 is that a large segment of the private sector is equivalent in prestige with the public sector. The faculties of law and economics of the University of Tokyo stand above the rest in a class by themselves, but elsewhere above the median the private university faculties, which are generally larger in size, are just as selective as their public equivalents. Only a few years earlier this was not the case. In 1972 the top sixty faculties in these fields were two-thirds public; in 1980 they were virtually half-and-half.[37] The gains of the private sector in this case do not seem to have come at the expense of public universities, since Obunsha ratings for both types of institution have been rising. A number of factors might have some bearing on this shift, including an increase in the number of able students, restriction of size by the best private faculties, and the lure of the Kansai and Tokyo areas where the large privates are concentrated. This kind of profile would naturally vary from subject to subject. Government universities are decidedly more prestigious in engineering, but only in dentistry do all of the public faculties rank higher than all privates. With these exceptions the configuration of figure 2 can be regarded as fairly typical, chiefly because prestige is associated quite closely with universities, despite the considerable autonomy of their faculties.

Below the median line in figure 2 almost all the faculties are private. This, of course, represents a different facet of the Japanese private sector. As shown on table 2, these are the faculties of smaller and newer (cf. table 1) universities that were created in response to mass demand for higher education.

Table 2 reveals a linear correlation between university size and faculty prestige; table 1 demonstrated the same kind of relationship between age and size (and hence faculty prestige as well). A

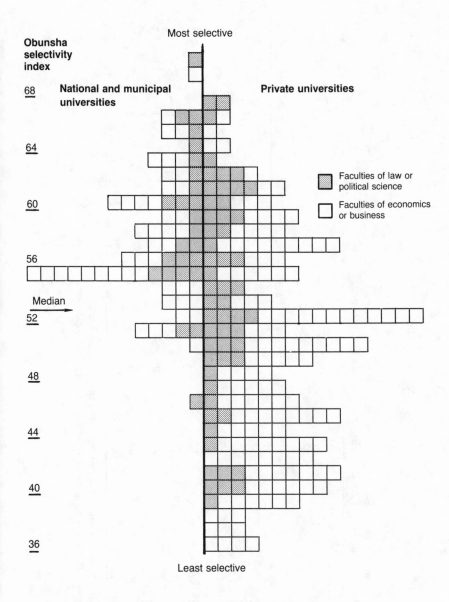

Fig. 2. Relative selectivity of various Japanese public and private faculties, 1980. *Source*: Compiled from *Keisetsu Jidai*, August, 1980, Supplement.

TABLE 2. Rankings of Japanese Universities with Faculties in Economics and/or Business by Number of Faculties (In Approximate Quintiles)

	Most Selective 20%				Least Selective 20%	
	57.0–66.6	51.0–56.9	46.0–50.9	42.0–45.9	41.9–36.2	Total
Total faculties	27	27	29	29	29	141
One faculty	0	0	0	8	15	23
Two faculties (social science)	0	1	0	3	6	10
Two faculties (mixed types)	0	1	3	4	1	9
Three faculties (social science)	0	0	3	3	1	7
Three faculties (mixed types)	1	1	3	1	2	8
Four faculties	2	2	4	2	1	11
Five faculties	1	4	2	2	0	9
Six faculties	3	1	1	1	1	7
Seven to nine faculties	3	3	2	0	0	8
Ten to fourteen faculties	3	4	2	0	0	9
Total universities[a]	13	17	20	24	27	101

Source: Compiled from Keisetsu Jidai, supplement to the August, 1980 issue.

[a]For universities with more than one faculty of this type the average ranking was used.

third factor of undeniable significance is location in one of the two major population centers of the country—the Tokyo and Kansai (Osaka-Kyoto) areas. The capital region is naturally dominant: besides Keio and Waseda, the acknowledged pacesetters of the private sector, Hosei, Meiji, and Rikkyo are distinguished universities of long standing. Together with the University of Tokyo these universities form the "Tokyo Six," a baseball league with intense interschool rivalries. Three other Tokyo universities, Sophia (also called Jochi), Gakushuin, and Aoyama, have also secured places near the top of the rankings. The cream of the Kansai area are Doshisha, Ritsumeikan, Kansei Gakuin, and Kansai universities. Together these dozen universities monopolize the first eighteen positions of the rankings of private faculties of economics or commerce. In fact, for the top 25 percent of this particular list only Seinan Gakuin University in Fukuoka is not located in one of these two population centers.

Size, age, and centrality do not by themselves confer institutional prestige, but rather are manifestations of more fundamental forces at work. At the root of the notion of prestige are the closely interconnected phenomena of academic quality of universities and employer preferences for graduates. A consensus seems to exist in Japan that colleges with the best scholarly reputations will attract the brightest students, and that this screening can be relied upon in hiring the most able employees. The process of prestige determination, then, actually has two poles, one in the universities and one in the labor market. The advantages of centrality seem to be largely determined by the latter. The largest firms, which are also the most desirable employers, are located and do their recruiting in the Tokyo or Kansai areas. Organizational size is associated in Japan with strength, stability, and security, and is thus highly prized. It has been a common practice, only recently officially discouraged, for the largest firms to restrict their recruitment to a handful of elite universities (*siteiko*). The fact that the recruitment process depends heavily upon self-perpetuating networks gives a further advantage to the well-established prewar universities.

The same factors affect the academic potential of universities. Over time, successful institutions are able to accumulate the physical resources, libraries, and teachers upon which scholarly reputations depend. Centrality is also important in attracting and retaining scholars, given their needs to remain in touch with their peers. Academic strength, however, is also the result of explicit choices made by an institution. A recent classification of Japanese higher education considered the existence of scientific faculties, doctoral degree programs, and a relatively high percentage of graduate students, all to be correlated with institutional prestige.[38] Each of these factors is associated with a capacity for scholarly research. There are thus strong institutional incentives for colleges to increase overhead expenditures on research, become more selective, and grow in size. Not only are these goals to some extent mutually contradictory, but, in the competitive environment of the Japanese private sector, relative progress toward reaching any of them could be difficult. Two somewhat extreme examples can at least illustrate the range of possibilities.

Nippon University (f. 1904), with its main branch in central Tokyo, has for some time been Japan's largest university by a wide margin, but far from its best. With over 88,000 students in 1976, it was more than twice the size of the next largest university, Waseda. This position was achieved by deliberately endeavoring to provide education as efficiently as possible to as many students as possible. In doing so, Nippon has become a vertically integrated empire, with a network of junior high and high schools to feed into its university. Although a nonprofit organization like all private universities, Nippon is apparently efficient enough to divert part of its annual revenues into its sizeable endowment, and for this reason it is often disparaged as "Nippon University Incorporated." Despite the disdain of the academic community, the size and centrality of Nippon apparently count for something. In the Obunsha rankings the Nippon social science faculties fell just below the median, in the fifth decile. Fifteen years ago, during the height of its expansion, Nippon's faculties of economics and commerce were located down in the second decile.

Jesuit Sophia University (f. 1913) was a rather late starter compared to the other major privates, but after World War II it launched a determined effort to rise to the top ranks of Japanese universities. In doing so it attacked each of the variables in the complex equation determining academic prestige. To improve its student body Sophia actively recruited top high school seniors, and granted them admission without an entrance exam (a practice now widely imitated). To raise their academic standing they recruited famous professors, but the payroll was kept manageable by mixing them with large numbers of inexpensive priests and foreign visitors. To improve the prospects of their graduates a placement office was established and special efforts were taken to secure placements with large, prestigious firms. These efforts were undeniably fruitful. In 1966 the Sophia faculties of law and economics were ranked by Obunsha a very respectable twenty-fourth and twenty-fifth; however, by 1980 they were respectively fourth and fifteenth.

Social Distribution of Private Higher Education

If the academic hierarchy affects the behavior of institutions, its influence upon the actions of individuals has proven to be far more predictable. During a period of weeks each spring known as "exam hell," high school seniors take the faculty entrance examinations in an attempt to gain admittance to the highest ranking institution that their capabilities will permit. In no other democratic society is this initial postsecondary sorting so consequential for career chances. Given this powerful motivation, along with the intense and single-minded efforts put forth by most of the students and a rather efficient market for matching students and colleges, this system might be expected to produce a fairly just and meritocratic distribution of educational opportunities. In the real world, however, things are usually more complicated. In fact, these crucial college entrance examinations cast a shadow that extends deep into the anterior stages of schooling. Along the way there are several critical factors that can be and are manipulated in the attempt to gain valuable ground in the meritocratic race.

The preparation for university entrance exams could be said to begin in lower secondary school. Students with high academic ambitions would, in the seventh grade, most likely start attending private *jukus* (special review schools) for supplementary classes after school and on weekends. The chief purpose of these classes is to help them clear the first crucial hurdle, securing admission to an academically strong secondary school. Because education is compulsory in Japan only through the first nine grades, both public and private high schools select their students on the basis of school records and competitive examinations. High schools, as a result, are sharply stratified according to their ability to place students into universities. A study of two urban prefectures found 14 percent of the students attending high schools that sent more than 80 percent of their graduates to college; at the other extreme 40 percent were in schools sending on less than 20 percent of their graduates.[39] As the fateful university entrance examinations draw near, high school students may supplement their supplementary *jukus* with private tutors and testing services like Obunsha. Finally, if all these efforts fail to secure entrance to a desired college, a student (usually a male) may choose to become a *ronin,* spending an additional year or more at a specialized private "cram" school (*yobiko*). In recent years about one-third of all university entrants have been *ronin,* but the percentage is considerably higher for medical and dental faculties. No stigma is attached to this practice; if anything, *ronin* are admired by the Japanese for their perseverance.

These factors taken together cannot help but have some impact upon the social distribution of opportunity for higher education. While *jukus* are not terribly expensive, a year at a *yobiko* definitely is. There is no escaping the fact that wealth plays a role in this ostensibly meritocratic competition. Location is a less obvious factor; yet, the most precious educational opportunities are in the population centers and nearly monopolized by local inhabitants. Given these effects, it is remarkable that the social origins of Japanese students are not more skewed toward the affluent.[40]

Social origins data on Japanese students are readily available, yet not so easily interpreted. Information compiled by the Ministry of Education from its student surveys has an adequate base, but is suspected of having a bias toward greater equality than actually exists. A different series gathered by the Bureau of Statistics is highly accurate, but, when used for information on college students, has a rather narrow base.[41] Both series consequently contain anomalous findings that must be viewed suspiciously in the absence of additional corroboration. Also, given the importance of seniority in determining salaries in Japan, family income groupings are only a meaningful basis for comparison when they are restricted to family heads old enough to have college-age children. Figure 3 is offered as a probable approximation of the social origins of Japanese students in recent years. For the first four quintiles it shows aggregate participation increasing only moderately with income; however, participation nearly doubles when one moves to the highest quintile. Moreover, the role of the private sector in accommodating the demand from high-income students is evident: six of every seven students from this group attend private colleges. This produces the unusual situation where recruitment to the far more selective public sector has a more egalitarian profile than that to the less selective private sector. It should be added, however, that more fragmentary evidence strongly suggests that high-income students are considerably overrepresented in the top universities of both sectors.[42] In sum, Japanese college students are drawn from a broad social base, but high-income families are apparently particularly zealous in maximizing the educational attainments of their chil-

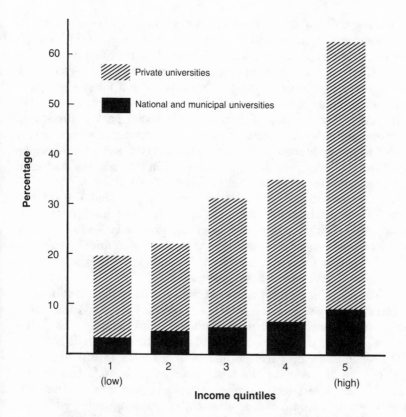

Fig. 3. Rate of enrollment in Japanese higher education institutions, by family income quintiles (household heads aged 40-59), 1975. *Source*: Adapted from Jyoji Kikuchi, "Access to Education and Income Redistribution Effects," in *Allocation of Educational Resources in Japan*, ed. S. Ichikawa, p. 183.

dren. Thus the system exhibits both egalitarian and inegalitarian characteristics.

The egalitarian tendencies owe more to the nature of Japanese society and the lower-school system than they do to higher education. To begin with, the degree of economic inequality in Japan is among the lowest for any industrialized democracy.[43] Furthermore, Japan possesses an extraordinary degree of cultural homogeneity, which includes a high valuation placed upon education. The public system of elementary and lower secondary schools endeavors with great success to educate each student up to a common standard of competency; and both the content and the quality of education during these years is quite uniform throughout the country.[44] Through the years of compulsory schooling, then, Japan probably provides more equal educational opportunities than any of the Western democracies. The intense academic competition that follows brings to light the advantages of high social position. Secondary schools are highly stratified by ability, function, and social backgrounds; and the decision to devote a year or more to improving one's placement in the academic hierarchy is more easily arrived at by high-income families. The large representation of *ronin* in the entering classes of the elite faculties thus assures an overrepresentation of the affluent. There is widespread apprehension in Japan that the intense level of competition has been making the best universities increasingly socially exclusive.[45] Even though this type of inequality is one of the undesirable consequences of a hierarchical structure, there is another facet of hierarchy that tends to counterbalance the advantage of overrepresented groups.

It should not be forgotten that the returns to higher education fall off markedly as one descends the academic hierarchy, and that a large number of high-income students are perforce relegated to the lower reaches of the system. Many of these students might be *ronin* who needed extra preparation just to find a place in higher education, or possibly to enter the best attainable college.[46] In the past decade a few less-selective colleges have acquired reputations for catering to an affluent but academically undistinguished clientele, much like a well-known type of American private college. Because of the persistent oversupply of college graduates, the expected pecuniary returns to college education for graduates from the bottom fourth of the hierarchy may be essentially nil.[47] This would not mean that such degrees are useless: they might be a prelude to entering a family business or the fulfillment of parental expectations. But the absence of economic benefits would indicate that differential access to such educational opportunities represents a preference, rather than a privilege.

The Japanese system of higher education seems to be predicated upon two quite different principles. At the top there is a competition truly based on merit. The competition for those university positions that promise prestigious graduate careers is long, arduous, broadly based, and fair. Those who succeed are meritorious indeed. Moreover, this system functions exceedingly well in allocating the most prized career opportunities. There is consequently little likelihood that it will be altered in any major way, despite its imperfections.[48] At the bottom the Japanese system is essentially open to anyone with minimal qualifications desiring a college education. Wide access fulfills an important function in an open society by allowing individuals to pursue their educational aspirations freely. Historically, of course, it has been the private sector that has kept access relatively open by accommodating most of the growth in demand for higher education. Since the upgrading of private institutions that occurred in the 1970s, the private sector has enlarged its part in the meritocratic functions of Japanese higher education as well. However, these divergent roles have produced crosscurrents in the formulation of government policy toward private higher education.

Government Financial Support for the Japanese Private Sector

The 1970 decision, made only after long deliberation, to inaugurate regular institutional subsidies to private colleges was above all intended to solve the deep financial crisis plaguing the private sector. However, employing public funds for this purpose also presaged a new relationship between the private sector and the government. The decade that followed brought a clear fulfillment of the first goal, but the significance of the second change has been unfolding only slowly. As a result there are several aspects of the future role of private higher education in Japan that have yet to be clarified.

The Private School Law of 1970 was passed as a temporary measure in the expectation that a definitive solution to the financial assistance question would follow. It aided private colleges simply by supporting a gradually increasing percentage of teaching salaries. Under these arrangements the government's contribution to the aggregate operating expenses of private colleges grew from 7.1 percent in 1970 to 21.4 percent in 1975.[49] During these years a major planning effort was under way within the Ministry of Education both to devise a permanent subsidization formula and to establish guidelines for the future development of higher education. Some of the themes that emerged from these efforts were fateful for private institutions. It was understood from the outset that accepting government funds would affect the balance of publicness and privateness inherent in the conduct of private higher education. Subsidized colleges would be expected to increase their "public character," but what this would mean in specific terms had to await a definite plan. While this question was under consideration between 1970 and 1975, the percentage of Japanese eighteen-year-olds continuing on to college shot up from 24 percent to 38 percent. In addition, the "oil shock" of 1973 seemed to threaten gravely the prospects for future economic growth. Educational planners, who were concerned at the beginning of the decade about expanding access to higher education, reacted to these developments by opting to curtail future growth. Thus, to remain within existing enrollment levels and to concentrate on raising instructional quality became the public responsibility of private colleges. These two principles were embodied in the Private School Subsidy Law of 1975, both in the formulas for subsidization and in Japan's first five-year plan for higher education.

The remarkable feature of this financial assistance is that it varies according to the degree to which a private college conforms with ministry objectives. Aid is thus intended as a means for shaping the behavior of individual institutions without actually imposing coercive regulation. The calculation of each subvention involves two stages.[50] First the standardized operating costs of a college are determined by adding up allowable expenditures (at rates set by the ministry) in eight categories, including full- and part-time teaching staff, and spending for education and research prorated by the number of students and the type of faculty. This base figure is then divided into four percentage parts of 30, 30, 30, and 10, each of which is subject to a different adjustment. Each of the four portions of the standardized operating budget can be augmented by as much as 30 percent, or diminished by up to 50 percent, depending upon the degree to which the faculty meets the ministry's norms.

For example, the first category, constituting 30 percent of the total, is based upon the ratio of actual students to the officially authorized number of students. A faculty with between 95 and 110 percent of their authorized total would receive 130 percent of the normal subsidy; one admitting between 126 and 130 percent of their total would receive 100 percent; and a highly overenrolled faculty, admitting more than twice their authorized level, would get only 50 percent of this figure.

The other three categories are graded in just the same way according to appropriate ratios established by the ministry. The second 30 percent category is for student/teacher ratio, which is different for each type of faculty. The third 30 percent is the ratio of nonsalary educational expenditures to student-derived revenue: the higher such costs, or the lower the charges to students, the better. Finally, there is a ratio to encourage colleges to keep operating expenditures in balance with revenues ([expenses − revenues] ÷

expenses) where zero is the optimal value (10 percent). As a result, then, those faculties that limit their enrollments and spend liberally on the qualitative improvement of their programs (i.e., fewer students per teacher and more educational resources) will be rewarded by an inflation of the base figure for their subsidy. What portion of that figure the colleges will actually receive in any given year is ultimately determined by the government.

The 1975 law authorized the state to pay up to 50 percent of the operating expenses of private colleges. The Ministry of Finance actually set the rate of subsidization nearer to 40 percent; and, because the private sector as a whole admits about 50 percent more students than authorized, more base budgets have been deflated than inflated by the adjustment formulas. The determination of the total subsidy to private higher education is a complex process in which the Ministry of Education works closely with private colleges through their associations. The latter consistently advocate enlarging the number of items included in the definition of operating expenses. For the 1980 school year, for example, the Union of Private Universities proposed a total subsidy of 330 billion yen to the Ministry of Education. The Ministry of Education, in turn, suggested a figure of 291.5 billion yen to the Ministry of Finance. The figure ultimately approved by the latter was reduced to 260.5 billion yen.[51] This was then the amount turned over to the Private School Promotion Foundation to dispense to Japan's private colleges. This figure represented approximately 30 percent of their actual operating expenses. The sufficiency of this level of subsidization is naturally a continual source of disagreement. However, in a longer view there can be no doubt about the benefits it has brought to the private sector. Since other sources of revenue have been unaffected, government subventions represent a net addition that has stabilized finances and increased the resources available for educational purposes.

With the incentives built into the subsidies providing an effective "carrot," the Ministry of Education has had little reason to resort to the "stick" to get private institutions to conform to its plan. The ministry's most significant regulatory power would be the restriction against the creation of new faculties, although this chiefly affects the less established and less selective colleges still wishing to expand.[52] In practice exceptions have been made where they were compatible with other goals of the plan. The original five-year plan, as well as its very similar six-year successor (1981–86 Plan), sought to diversify higher education offerings, to begin making them available to mature adults through recurrent education and an open university, and to decentralize opportunities away from metropolitan areas.[53] New faculties, and even new universities, that could be justified on these criteria have received approval. Similarly, limited expansion of enrollment has been authorized in some existing faculties. However, such exceptions have not affected total enrollments. Since the inception of the plan the number of new students entering Japanese colleges has been remarkably stable; but then, so has the number of high school seniors seeking admission.[54] So, it would not seem that the leveling of college enrollments has been the direct result of the institutional constraints created by the Ministry of Education. Rather, a cap was placed on enrollments after the pressure for increased access was already spent.[55]

In other ways the planning efforts of the government may have influenced the attendance patterns of private colleges in some unintended and unwelcome directions. One disconcerting development in recent years has been a sharp rise in the tuition and fees charged to students in the private sector, even though an avowed purpose of government subsidies was to keep these in check. The steep increases, as noted above, began in 1974, that is, before the plan went into effect. Then, from 1975 to 1978 the burden of these charges rose by 77 percent (unadjusted for inflation). Furthermore, whereas in 1974 the general revenues of private colleges were roughly in balance with operating expenses, by 1978 revenues exceeded expenditures by 13 percent—an amount, in fact, equal to about half of the total government subsidy.[56] The tuition spiral was thus not a result of dire need, as could be argued for the previous spiral in the early 1960s. More likely, private colleges have been taking advantage of their market position to enhance revenues.[57]

Private institutions were initially placed in an advantageous position as suppliers by the unprecedented increase in student demand during the first half of the 1970s. This advantage was then reinforced as the ministry established incentives for institutions to scale down the discrepancy between actual and authorized enrollments. The incentives for qualitative improvement, on the other hand, gave colleges further reason to increase their revenues. Extra tuition income devoted to expanding library collections, for example, would not only add to the academic prestige of an institution, but would also count toward inflating its government subsidy. Private institutions naturally contend that they have been forced to increase tuition by the rapid escalation of their costs. Nevertheless, the essential point is that a significant portion of these costs, however justifiable or laudable they might be, are self-imposed—a by-product of the official and unofficial incentives to improve institutional quality.

It should be evident from the account of the postwar development of Japanese higher education in the previous section that the Ministry of Education has generally placed greater emphasis on the quality of higher education than on the quantity available. The great postwar expansion was a result of the proliferation of new private schools and the lack of ministerial control over enrollments in existing ones. Since the mid-1970s, however, the ministry's inherent preferences have been bolstered by public concern about the oversupply of college graduates. Hence, a consensus has existed behind the principal government strategy in the first five-year plan: constraining growth and upgrading quality in the private sector. These efforts have met with considerable success—but at a price. Private higher education has become significantly more expensive for both students and taxpayers. For the government, the increasing subsidies to private colleges have been, considering inflation, about what was anticipated. But, the colleges themselves have presented a cogent case that much more is needed to fulfill the ministry's objectives.[58] In the meantime, an increasing financial burden has been carried by students. The demand for higher education in Japan is, by all indications, relatively inelastic. Still, one has to suspect that the sharp rise in tuition has played some role in bringing about the cessation of enrollment growth.

This problem, as important as it is, also exemplifies more fundamental issues raised by the transition from laissez-faire to central planning. The effort of planning in itself is testimony to dissatisfaction with the course of development produced by the play of existing market forces. The thrust of planning consequently must run counter to existing social forces to some extent. An obvious example is the plan objective to decentralize the locus of educational opportunities, despite the increasing concentration of demand in metropolitan centers.[59] In more complex cases the tension between the "ought" and the "is" will tend to produce mixed results that will in part frustrate the planners' intentions. The goal of promoting diversity in Japanese colleges has been successful at the margins by stimulating the creation of unique faculties, but on the whole the subsidization formulas have powerfully induced greater institutional uniformity.

Another difficulty arises when the plan monitors have to rely upon secondary indicators rather than actual educational substance. Here the question of academic quality is again germane. The fact that Japanese higher education is in large measure a device for screening manpower is a considerable impediment to the goal of raising academic quality. The Ministry of Education requirements for individual institutions are not terribly consequential for the actors most involved, i.e., for students, teachers, and potential employers. Thus, it will make little difference if a professor lectures to a class of one hundred or to a class of ten, as long as the prevailing academic culture sustains permissive grading and minimizes intellectual interaction. Nor is that academic culture likely to be threatened as long as employers consider the test scores of incoming students to be the best indicator of the worth of a college's graduates. For these reasons the improvements in qualitative indices that have been achieved under the first five-year plan ring somewhat hollow. The Japanese, it should be added, have not been blind to this situation: they currently regard the search for methods to raise real standards as one of their highest educational priorities. The conclusion, nevertheless, seems inescapable that, to date, these efforts have considerably raised the costs to society of the current method of screening.

It would be quite misleading if this probe of present trends were to leave a negative impression of the capacity of Japanese educational planning. In fact, it is in many ways a most impressive process characterized by deliberate incremental policy formation, broad representation of all concerned, an elaborate information base, and the establishment of consensus on goals. Nor is the efficacy of such planning in doubt: with a minimum of overt regulation the ministry seems to have powerfully affected the behavior of private institutions. There is consequently little reason to believe that changes in the planning process could produce better results. Rather, it is the very existence of educational planning—of significant government funding and, directly or indirectly, significant government control—that would seem to determine the future prospects for the private sector.[60]

Central direction is antithetical to the dynamism, which formerly, for good or for ill, characterized the private sector. Its establishment in the 1970s consequently represents a transformation of the historic role of independent universities in Japan. The vast expansion of participation in Japanese higher education was able to occur because of the wide availability of socially inexpensive, low-quality programs. The same could be said of the United States, except that there such opportunities were provided in the last generation by public four-year and community colleges. Largely as a result of this availability—the ample supply of places in higher education—both countries today constitute the most highly educated societies in the world in terms of the educational careers of the current generation of young people. It now appears, however, that Japan is ready to depart from the structure that has brought this achievement. If the current Ministry of Education policy of containing enrollments and upgrading standards in the universities while expanding postsecondary opportunities in special technical schools (*shenshugakko*) were to be projected into the future, the result would be a binary structure similar to that now found in England and most countries of northern Europe. Japan would have a rather large sector of high-quality, expensive university education, perhaps accommodating one-quarter of college-age cohorts. A lower quality, less expensive, nonuniversity sector comprised of junior colleges and postsecondary technical schools might serve another quarter of the age group. This would not be too far from the situation as it exists today.

The fulfillment of this scenario, or something like it, would change one of the fundamental characteristics of the Japanese mass private sector. No longer would it be the open part of higher education, capable of absorbing surges in demand for additional college places. Instead the private sector as a whole would become one of the more privileged elements in the constellation of postsecondary education, and the nonuniversity, short-cycle institutions (both public and private) would become the locus of new enrollment growth. Whether this would constitute the maturation or the negation of mass private sectors as they have been considered here is perhaps a moot point. When viewed in a larger perspective the trends in Japanese private sector seem to correspond with a functional need for postindustrial societies to control more closely the educational credentials that loom so large in the determination of life chances. Mass private sectors essentially belong to an earlier stage of development. For that reason it is instructive to turn from the unique case of Japan to an example of mass private sector that has remained far closer to the circumstances of its origins.

The Philippines: A Mass Private Sector in a Developing Nation

The Philippines presents some immediate stark differences from Japan both as a nation and as a society. In contrast to the unity and homogeneity of Japan, the Philippines stretches across an archipelago containing a dozen major islands and hundreds of minor ones. The population is similarly divided between eight major languages encompassing sixty or more dialects. Because of the nation's colonial heritage the language of higher education has not been one of these indigenous tongues, but was originally Spanish and is now almost exclusively English. Undoubtedly the most decisive differences arise from the relative poverty of this developing nation. In 1978 the per capita gross national product was $7,280 for Japan, but only $510 for the Philippines. Furthermore, this limited wealth is distributed unevenly over a sharply graded social structure, and social disparities are further increased by the urban-rural dichotomy. In cosmopolitan Manila, English is widely spoken and public education is available for some through the secondary level; however, in the barrios of the hinterland, where only dialect is heard, laborers may earn as little as one dollar per day, and not all children even have the opportunity to complete elementary school. In light of these formidable obstacles the extent of higher education that has been achieved in the Philippines appears quite remarkable.

According to the *UNESCO Statistical Yearbook,* in 1965 the Philippines, with 1,605 students in higher education per 100,000 population, was fourth in the world in this category behind only the United States, Canada, and the USSR.[61] Although that ranking may be due to the inclusion of some nondegree students not truly belonging to this category, and also to the youthfulness of the Philippine population (50 percent under eighteen at that time), the size of its higher education system is nevertheless exceptional for a developing nation. Perhaps a more indicative measure is that during the last half of the 1960s, 20 percent or more of the relevant age group was attending college, a rate that would place the Philippines in the same league as France and Belgium for those years. There are several reasons for this unusually high level of attendance in higher education.

First, the Philippines has a strong, indigenous educational tradition. Education was closely linked with the struggle for independence and national identity against both Spanish and American rule. The Philippine national hero, José Rizal, was an educator who championed independence from Spain. Under present conditions education is a key factor in bringing about the comparatively high degree of social mobility for a developing nation.[62] Filipinos seem willing to pursue advanced education at considerable sacrifice in the hope that it will secure them a niche in the modern sector of the economy.

Second, in a marked departure from normal practice elsewhere in the world, higher education in the Philippines commences after only ten years of lower school instead of twelve. This means that the college-age population consists of seventeen- to twenty-year-olds. The percentage attending college is naturally higher as a result of this practice, although it would be difficult to say by how much. In other respects the pattern of schooling in the Philippines is similar to those in other developing nations. The government's first educational priority is to achieve universal primary education. The greatest attrition of students currently occurs during the higher primary and lower secondary years. The state takes little responsibility for secondary education, and as a result two-thirds of these students attend private schools. Both public and private secondary schools, in any case, depend heavily upon student tuition. For the minority who pass through this level, secondary school is chiefly a preparation for college. Given the weakness of middle-level credentials and the limited resources available for education, the benefits of adding two more years of schooling in order to bring the Philippines into line with other systems seem questionable. Nor do Filipino students appear to be at a significant disadvantage when they transfer to other systems. Nevertheless, one result of the ten-year pattern is that higher education bears a larger share of the total educational burden.

The third reason for the high enrollment levels of the Philippines has been the existence of conditions that allowed the development of a mass private sector. Being unable to meet the demand for college places within its own institutions, the state placed few obstacles to the proliferation of private schools. The result has been the private provision of higher education at minimal cost. By 1970 the private colleges and universities of the Philippines were serving 92 percent of the nation's students—the most of any private sector in the world.[63] The Philippine case is unique in another respect: only one-third of the private sector's students were in schools set up as nonprofit organizations. The rest were in colleges and universities that operate as for-profit corporations. These two characteristics of the Philippine system, then, represent an extreme of privateness in higher education.

Historical Development

The University of Santo Tomas, founded in 1611, was organized in Manila by the Dominican order. With charters from both the papacy and the Spanish Crown it represented the combination of publicness and privateness typical of premodern universities. These twin sources of support allowed it to fend off potential competitors and nearly monopolize higher education in the Philippines until the end of Spanish rule. In the late nineteenth century Santo Tomas was known informally as "the University of the Philippines," but an effort to actually secularize it was successfully resisted by the Dominicans. The development of true private and public sectors had to wait until American rule was established at the conclusion of the Spanish-American War (1898).

After the Philippine independence movement was subjugated by American military forces, a civilian government embarked on an ambitious education plan for the islands. One of the foremost domestic objectives was to establish English as the common language of the country. This, of course, could only be accomplished through primary education. The primary level thus became, as it is today, the chief educational priority of the Philippine government. Other institutions were necessary as well. A normal school (for teacher training) was founded as early as 1901, and in 1908 the Philippine Assembly decreed the establishment of the University of the Philippines (UP). The model for the UP came from American state universities. In the Philippine context the flagship university had to be "the highest seat of learning [and] to set the highest standards in the most important professions," while also providing the knowledge and the leaders for national development.[64] The UP in the Philippines, then, like the University of Tokyo in Japan, was a special priority of the government with first claim to available educational resources. Despite the venerable traditions of Santo Tomas, the UP was designated as the apex of higher education in the Philippines.

The lifting of clerical control over education at a time when the educational horizons of Filipinos were rapidly widening led to diverse private initiatives in founding schools. Almost all of these ventures began as elementary or secondary schools and subsequently developed into colleges or universities.[65] The desire to preserve Philippine culture against the threat of Americanization inspired the founding of Colegio Filipino in 1900 (National University, 1921), Centro Escolar in 1907 (university, 1930), and the Instituto de Manila (university, 1921). Other educational endeavors were no doubt made possible by the American presence, such as the Presbyterian Silliman University (f. 1901; university, 1935) in Dumaguete City and the Baptist Central Philippine University (f. 1905; university, 1953) in Iloilo. American influence also probably hastened the acceptance of higher education for women: the Philippine Women's College was founded in 1919, and became a university in 1932. Roman Catholics maintained their influence during this period despite the loss of their educational monopoly. Both the Christian Brothers of Belgium and the Augustinian Fathers started schools during these years that grew to include institutions of higher education. For this group of schools the overriding motivation for founding was cultural, even though some were owned and controlled by one individual or family. In the next wave of private school foundings, more practical motivations were apparent.

By the 1920s the growing economy of the Philippines was creating opportunities for graduates with practical commercial and industrial skills. The schools that sprang up to meet these needs had little difficulty meeting the lenient state chartering standards when they chose to become officially recognized colleges. José Rizal College (f. 1922) was organized by Vincente Fabella (the first Filipino certified public accountant) to teach commerce, finance, and accountancy. A similar Institute of Accountancy was opened in 1928, and shortly blossomed into Far Eastern University (1934). It soon added institutes for law and technology, and by the end of the decade was the largest private university in the Philippines. Other schools of this type developed less purposefully. For example, Tomas Mapua, chief architect for the Manila Post Office building, established a school to train workers on that project, in 1925 the school officially became the Mapua Institute of Technology.[66]

Whatever the origins, Philippine law required that all private schools be incorporated as either stock or nonstock corporations.[67] The sectarian institutions naturally organized as nonstock, nonprofit entities, committed to reinvesting any surpluses back into their schools. Many private individuals who founded schools saw that it was expedient to establish educational stock corporations, whether or not they ever envisioned making a profit. Perhaps the organizers of the fast-growing Far Eastern University were motivated by pecuniary returns, but they were probably the exception rather than the rule among prewar schools. Some other schools, like the Mapua Institute of Technology, were largely intended to serve local industry. The incentives for owning and operating a college, however, are best understood in relation to the close family ties that characterize Philippine society, and their relation with the economy and politics of the nation.[68] Controlling a college could enhance the social prestige, the political influence, and the patronage power of a family. For substantial families these benefits were in all likelihood more telling than the admitted advantages of controlling the institution's cash flow. In any case, this type of closely held, family-run corporation, which probably includes the great majority of the nonsectarian colleges, did not have to produce a profit or declare dividends in order to further the interests of its owners.

Before the Philippine Islands were engulfed by World War II the basic structure of higher education was already well established. In the public sector the state employed the limited means at its disposal to set a high standard in academic and professional subjects, while providing for basic national needs in such areas as agriculture, forestry, and sanitation. This was accomplished through a single state university, the University of the Philippines, enrolling about 7,500 students in sixteen schools and colleges. Other state institutions like the normal schools had not yet attained postsecondary status. The remaining demand for higher education—some five-sixths of the total demand—was met by a diverse collection of private institutions. Eight universities and eighty-four colleges had a combined enrollment of over thirty-six thousand students. In the aftermath of the war the Republic of the Philippines, independent and prostrate, would have to depend even more heavily upon the private sector to meet the growing demand for higher education.

The disruptions of the war years caused many Filipinos to postpone their educational plans, and this pent-up demand produced a surge in college enrollment as conditions gradually returned to normal. When it reached its peak in 1951 this postwar wave of students pushed enrollments to five times their prewar level.[69] But even as this wave subsided, an even larger one was gathering force. As the government drive to expand educational opportunities progressed, an ever-increasing number of children finished primary, and then secondary schooling. The impact of this development began to be felt at the postsecondary level in the mid-fifties. From that point the participation rates of seventeen- to twenty-year-olds shot up to the extraordinary level of 20 to 21 percent in the last half of the 1960s. In addition, an underlying population growth rate of 3 percent meant that student numbers kept rising even after participation rates reached that plateau. The result was an increase in higher education enrollment from 182,000 in 1954 to 621,000 in 1969—a rise of 340 percent in just fifteen years.

Growth of this magnitude obviously affected every type of institution, however, the expansion of the public sector before the

1970s was both relatively smaller and rather irregular. The first postwar necessity for the government was to relocate and rebuild the University of the Philippines, which had been devastated in the battle for Manila. After this lengthy and costly task had been completed it became government policy to direct further expansion of the public sector outside of the capital area. This was undoubtedly a sound policy on many counts, but it did not relieve the concentration of demand for higher education in the greater Manila area. The largest market in the country thus remained, except for the highly selective UP, virtually the exclusive preserve of private institutions.[70]

Proliferation of Private Institutions

In the hothouse conditions of the postwar years private colleges and universities grew in every conceivable manner. Colleges sprouted from existing secondary schools, or began from scratch; vocational schools became colleges, then blossomed into universities; and existing institutions ballooned to many times their prewar size. The two most notable trends in this expansion were the growth in the number of institutions and the increase in magnitude of a few. Regarding the first, the immediate postwar surge of enrollments stimulated a doubling of the prewar number of private colleges and universities by 1951. Then, in the following wave, their numbers grew from 184 in 1956 to 617 in 1969. The new institutions were divided nearly evenly between religious and nonsectarian schools, but the latter captured about two-thirds of the private enrollments. As of 1970 the 40 largest private institutions contained 60 percent of the private sector students.[71] This meant that the average size of the remaining 577 private schools was less than 400. Clearly the proliferation of private colleges left a large number of tiny and marginal institutions. At the other extreme the extraordinary growth of the college population created a few behemoths as well.

The epitome of the behemoth type began in 1946 as a review course for the government accountancy examination. The next year it became the College of Commerce and Business Administration; and in 1950, when colleges of arts and sciences and education were added it was rechristened as the University of the East (UE). Its initial success was due in part to the high placement of its graduates on the accountancy exam, and the business school still remains its most prestigious component. It continued to spawn degree programs, especially from the late 1950s onward; and in the 1960s it surpassed Far Eastern University as the largest in the Philippines. In fact, by the end of the decade it had more students than all the state colleges and universities combined.

Feati University is a similar case. It originated after the war as an aeronautical school for Far Eastern Air Transport, Inc., but when that company was taken over by the Philippine Airlines the school became a separate entity bearing the acronym of its parent. Starting even later than UE, it became an undisputed behemoth in the 1960s, at times ranking as the country's third largest university.

Among proprietary schools, the three institutions mentioned above (Far Eastern, UE, and Feati) represent a distinct class of capitalist universities. Their stock is relatively widely held, and at times is traded over the counter on the Manila Stock Exchange.[72] All indications are that they are also the most profitable of the proprietary institutions.[73] Their guiding principles would seem to be keeping volume high and costs low. The University of the East, for example, in 1979 enrolled almost sixty thousand students on a campus of twelve buildings located in a crowded business section of Manila.[74] These facilities are utilized almost around the clock, with classes beginning at 7:30 in the morning and ending at 10:30 in the evening. Full-time faculty are required to teach twenty-four hours of undergraduate courses per week, while part-time teachers, who teach 40 percent of the courses, are paid by the number of hours they are in the classroom. Fifty-four percent of the faculty in Arts and Sciences had master's degrees, but only 4 percent had Ph.D.s. In the university's largest school, business administration, the student-faculty ratio was 75 to 1. The university libraries claimed a total of 129,000 volumes, or fewer than three per student. Higher education on these terms can be supplied cheaply enough to be affordable to a large clientele. Tuition for a full load at the University of the East was just $42.00 a semester in 1979, plus another $7.50 in miscellaneous fees. Yet, even at this price, 90 percent of the students chose to pay on an installment basis. Most of the students were employed, a large proportion of them full time. Thus, although the education offered by the UE is minimal in many respects, it would seem to be all that most students can afford.

The University of the East does not charge the lowest tuition in the Philippines, although it does fall near the bottom of the range for the Manila area. Elsewhere proprietary universities charge, if anything, slightly less; and one could undoubtedly find lower tuition levels among many of the hundreds of colleges scattered throughout the country. Compared to the more marginal of these colleges, the educational resources of the UE would seem superior by virtue of size alone. Aside from the behemoths, the other proprietary universities of the central Manila area charge approximately 20 percent higher tuition than the UE, and this extra revenue would seem to allow them to maintain a somewhat better student-faculty ratio. With this would go a higher percentage of day students, and perhaps fewer students in vocational majors.[75] However, these are differences of degree, not of kind. In general, the paucity of resources at the University of the East is representative of higher education institutions in the Philippines.

Among the sectarian colleges and universities the variation between institutions is considerably greater. Two Catholic universities in Manila, Ateneo de Manila and De La Salle, are recognized as having some of the strongest academic programs in the private sector. They are also the most expensive schools, charging tuition and fees more than four times those of the University of the East. These differentials are manifest in more highly qualified faculties, lower student-teacher ratios, and far superior educational facilities in general. In these two cases educational quality is achieved by cultivating an affluent clientele. The students of these schools are overwhelmingly drawn from the Philippine upper and upper-middle classes, who not only can afford the cost, but also set the social and sartorial tone of the campus.[76] Both schools are selective, but their selection process includes such subjective features as personal interviews and recommendations.

In contrast, several of the other better sectarian universities are committed to providing quality education to a wide constituency. This is certainly the case with the venerable University of Santo Tomas, which has grown in recent years to more than forty thousand students, but it would also apply to such provincial institutions as the University of San Carlos and Silliman University. Each of these schools is moderately selective, sets its tuition near or below the prevailing averages, and offers a limited amount of financial aid. With restricted revenues, then, these schools attempt to maintain the broad course offerings, graduate and professional programs, and at least a token commitment to academic research. Their success is relative: these three schools, and others of this type, are generally superior academically to proprietary schools. It is doubtful if the same could be said for most other sectarian colleges. The economic realities of higher education in the Philippines dictate that they can only charge what the market will bear, and they can only spend on their educational programs as much as they receive from their students.

The colleges and universities of the Philippines form a hierarchy with a very narrow peak and a very broad base. At the summit is the University of the Philippines, almost completely funded by the government as the country's only world-class university. Next would come the types discussed in the preceding paragraphs: elite liberal arts colleges and then the larger sectarian universities. The fast-developing system of state colleges would probably belong to the next tier. Although their funding increased rapidly during the 1970s, their selectivity has remained low. The remaining colleges and universities of all different types make up the broad base of the hierarchy. In spite of gradations of quality, differences in organization, size, or mission, all of these schools are essentially constrained by the amount of tuition their mass clientele is able to pay. The disparities in the resource levels for different categories of schools appear in table 3. In the public sector the UP spends almost four times more on each student than do the state colleges and universities. In the private sector the sharply higher level of expenditures in capital-area sectarian schools reflects the presence of several elite institutions. Otherwise, all types of institutions confront similar situations and have similar levels of expenditure. This is certainly one important factor explaining why proprietary higher education has been able to flourish in the Philippines.

Higher Education for Profit

The most surprising feature of the Philippine private sector is the extent to which proprietary institutions have been able to infringe upon areas usually monopolized by public or nonprofit institutions.

TABLE 3. Educational Costs per Student by Institutional Type, Philippines, 1976 (In Pesos)

	Public		Private		
	University of the Philippines	State colleges	Foundation	Proprietary	Sectarian
Metro Manila	3,585	1,047	497	498	951
Nonmetro Manila		899	477	345	411

Source: Adapted from "Financing of Private Higher Education," FAPE Review 10 (July 1979): 120, 128, 141.

In the literature of economics the higher education industry would be characterized as a segmented market. Proprietary institutions are often able to capture some of the more minor segments of this market. Such fields are generally distinguished by the fact that consumers can reasonably judge the utility of the instruction that is offered. Either there is a valuable credential involved, as in the cram courses for professional certification examinations; or there is promise of specific employment, as in vocational education, and especially education in business; or the knowledge being taught is evident to the student, as in language schools. When the ends of education become less immediate, the consumer becomes less confident in his or her judgment and has to rely increasingly upon trust. As one moves along this continuum the advantage of institutions sponsored by government, cultural groups, or professional organizations grows accordingly, because they can, at least in theory, be trusted to act in a disinterested manner regarding the sale of their services.[77] This pattern of incentives has usually precluded proprietary institutions from selling instruction in such areas as liberal arts or the natural sciences, but this has not been the case in the Philippines.[78]

The aggrandizement of proprietary schools is exemplified by the development of the University of the East. It began as a cram school and then expanded into a college of business—activities that are commonly organized on a proprietary basis. Upon this base it then added colleges of liberal arts and education (1950), law (1953), and a few years later more expensive programs in science and engineering. The first condition of this expansion was the enormous demand for higher education after the war. The abundance of available students allowed UE to erect a physical plant for its business school, and then utilize those facilities for other programs. The next area it entered was education, which at that time led to a credential with almost automatic employment value. So popular was teacher training in the late 1960s that education degrees comprised 54 percent of all degrees awarded in the private sector. Teacher education overlapped considerably with arts and sciences programs, thus helping to sustain that college. The first scientific degree offered by the UE, for example, was a bachelor of science in elementary education (1956). After this rudimentary scientific capability was in place, programs followed in engineering, premed, and finally pure science. The UE, then, like a good capitalist firm, developed its base in the largest and most profitable areas, and then gradually expanded into complementary adjacent fields.

In theory one would expect nonprofit schools to be able to provide education at either lower cost or better quality than proprietary schools. In the latter a student would have to pay the unit cost of instruction, plus an increment for return on investment; but in the former the charge should be the unit cost, minus a prorata share of other revenues. These variables, however, appear to be muted in the Philippines. For one thing, the nonprofit colleges benefit from few "other revenues."[79] Secondly, the proprietary institutions have been quite successful in keeping their unit costs extremely low. They do so in part by pitching their appeal to the large numbers of potential students at the lower end of the student market.[80] The proprietary schools tend to emphasize the practical and the inexpensive. Their programs are tailored to working students who predominantly study in evening classes, and their enrollments are heavily weighted toward business and other vocational subjects. The sectarian and foundation institutions, by way of contrast, cater more to full-time, day students. They also have a greater proportion of students in liberal arts and preprofessional majors where future rewards are less tangible. And, of course, the sectarian colleges are attractive to parents who wish to see their sons and daughters educated in a religious ambience. Thus, there is a perceptible differentiation of function between nonprofit and proprietary institutions: the nonprofits tend to be more attractive where nonvocational subjects are involved; and, when the opportunity costs of higher education are taken into account rather than just the direct costs, the proprietary institutions are decidedly the low-cost producers in the industry. But even though the actual overlap between these two forms of organization turns out to be less than was originally apparent, it remains greater in the Philippines than in any other nation. This is not a situation with which the Filipinos feel comfortable.

The combination of an elevated demand for higher education and relatively low levels of personal income has meant that the majority of students were located in the segment of the market dominated by proprietary schools. The growth and apparent prosperity of these institutions, however, was accompanied by an undercurrent of public distrust concerning the incompatibility of profit motives and educational ends.

If the critique against proprietary schools stemmed partly from normative opposition to "commercialism" in education, the specific accusations focused on exorbitant profits, low standards, and the overproduction of graduates.[81] The latter two conditions of course cannot be wholly attributed to proprietary schools; in fact, they tend to be common in many less developed nations with relatively high enrollment levels. There was nevertheless a disquieting amount of truth in the charge that these schools exploited their students by providing minimal or insufficient training without any regard for eventual employment opportunities. In fairness to the proprietary schools, it should be pointed out that the alternative—no higher education at all for this class of students—was generally not considered by the critics. The charge of excess profits is more difficult to judge. An economic analysis undertaken at the end of the 1960s determined that proprietary schools were yielding a return on equity of 17.3 percent.[82] This may appear generous, but this figure represented a sample of Manila area schools (the most lucrative market), during what was undeniably a boom period for the education industry. Furthermore, this return was only moderately higher than that for all manufacturing industries (14.9 percent). Several structural features of the education industry should tend to limit the possibilities for excessive profits: the market for higher education is both decentralized and competitive, and under Philippine conditions there is a significant degree of price elasticity as well. It should consequently be difficult to overcharge. College proprietors also must temper their efforts to maximize profits with a concern for the legitimacy and long-range prospects of their enterprise. To some extent, then, the charges against proprietary schools would seem to be normative in nature. They certainly seemed so to the former president of UE when he stated in apparent exasperation

> we are sick and tired of being told that profits are evil, that we should not make a profit at all as if we could operate meaningfully at a loss, as if suffering a loss would make us better schools.[83]

This climate of distrust nevertheless affected government actions toward proprietary schools. However, to be properly interpreted these actions should be seen in the context of overall government relations with the private sector.

Government Policy and Private Higher Education

The Philippine Constitution states that all education is under the regulation and supervision of the state. In higher education only the UP and the state universities are autonomous under their own boards of regents; all other institutions are directly answerable to the Ministry of Education and Culture. Although the ministry's actual ability to supervise has been limited, its zeal to regulate has not. The ministry has consistently attempted to compensate for the admitted problem of low standards through tight control over all aspects of instruction. For example, the curriculum for every degree program is rigidly prescribed, in some cases down to the last course; until recently all course books had to receive the approval of the Board of Textbooks; and a requirement of compulsory attendance dictates that student attendance in each class be recorded and reported to the ministry. The *Manual of Regulations for Private Schools,* published in its seventh edition in 1970, decrees standards for every facet of the operations of private schools, often with little regard for the schools' capacity to meet them.[84] An absence of government sympathy for proprietary schools in general is indicated by a 10 percent tax on net income. Private educators often point out that the government is willing to subsidize gold mining and tobacco growing, but not private schools.[85] The regulatory environment, then, is harsh to begin with, and an absence of insulation from the political process can make it more intrusive still. When students in the Manila university belt demonstrated against overcrowded facilities in 1969, for example, the ministry responded by freezing enrollments in the affected schools. In this vein, then, the prevailing antipathy to proprietary schools elicited a series of government actions designed to curb "abuses" in the private sector.

In 1969 the Philippine legislature expressed its preference for nonprofit over for-profit schools by passing an act that encouraged the conversion of educational stock corporations into foundations. Few institutions, however, have actually changed their status.[86] The following year under the impact of an economic crisis more far-reaching measures were enacted.

The devaluation of the Philippine peso during these years caused a rapid inflation of living costs and a decline in real wages. Private universities, with the majority of their budgets committed to salaries, repeatedly increased tuition in the face of strident and often disruptive student opposition. Largely to appease this opposition a bill was passed in 1970 to regulate the tuition and fees of private educational institutions.[87] Its principal provisions specified that

- tuition and fees could not be increased by more than 15 percent in any year;
- such increases could be appealed by student representatives;

- tuition could only be expended for instructional costs, and other fees for their stated purpose;
- private educational corporations could earn a maximum of 12 percent of net worth.

With this law education became a regulated industry, restricted in its price setting, internal budgeting, and return on equity.

Outside of political expediency there would seem to be little to recommend treating educational institutions like public utilities. True, they are intended to perform a public service, but they do not require a monopolistic structure to do so efficiently. On the other hand, distorting the market for higher education has had several drawbacks. Free enterprise in education had the benefit for the Philippines of mobilizing resources not otherwise available for educational purposes, thereby increasing the places available to meet the extensive private demand. Price regulation instituted by the tuition law may have temporarily sustained the existing quantity of higher education by keeping the cost artificially low, but doing so discourages further private investment. The return on equity for proprietary institutions in the 1970s shrank to about 6 percent—well below what would be considered a fair return for a utility.[88] At least part of the reason for this was political. The government's involvement, directly or indirectly, in setting tuition levels was not something from which it could easily be extricated. In 1979, for example, it acquiesced to student pressure and froze tuition and fees at the previous year's level. Under these conditions it has been virtually impossible for private schools to fulfill such pressing needs as improving instructional facilities or attracting and retaining competent faculty. Thus, the government's approach to tuition would seem to have gravely compromised the hopes of improving the quality of private colleges and universities.

In a quite different area the government has implemented a significant change that would seem to have potential for positive benefits. This is the National Collegiate Entrance Examination (NCEE), which was decreed by President Ferdinand Marcos shortly after the imposition of martial law (September 21, 1972) and first administered in 1973.[89] The primary concern behind this step was to rectify a persistent manpower imbalance resulting from too many underemployed college graduates and too few workers with vocational skills. A general scholastic aptitude test was imposed upon everyone wishing to enter a four-year college program. The cutoff point for qualification was placed at the twenty-fifth percentile the first year, and subsequently raised to the thirtieth and then the thirty-fifth percentile. Nonqualifiers, it was hoped, would choose to enroll in two-year technical courses, which were assumed to be more relevant to the country's manpower needs. And indeed, the NCEE seemed to produce this result. Ministry of Education figures show the vocational schools' share of first-year matriculants rising abruptly from 37 percent in 1973 to 44 percent the next year and thereafter.[90] This has clearly had some effect upon college enrollments as well.

Raising academic standards was also proclaimed as an important goal of the examinations, although it could also be interpreted as an indirect consequence. The hurdle of the test, in any case, would tend to exclude some of the clientele of those schools with the lowest academic standards. Enrollment levels are affected by a number of factors, but the impact of this step can nevertheless be discerned. Outside of the Manila area the imposition of the entrance examination seems to have caused a 5 percent decline in enrollments for all types of private colleges—proprietary, sectarian, and the few foundation schools.[91] However, the proprietary schools were somewhat less successful than the sectarian in recouping those losses, and their share of enrollments contracted slightly in the next three years. In Manila the proclamation of martial law and the delayed opening of schools in 1972 apparently interrupted the educational plans of the more marginal students in proprietary schools. A quarter of these enrollments disappeared from 1972 to 1973, so that the effect of the entrance exam the following year was not immediately detectable. In the longer run, though, the Manila proprietary schools also experienced a loss in their share of the student market.[92] It seems likely, then, that the NCEE has served to depress the enrollments of those institutions that were most open to all comers, but since most of the proprietary schools also include noncollegiate vocational programs their losses need not have been total.

Enrollments in the private sector during the 1970s have been chiefly sustained by the ever-larger cohorts of a rapidly growing population and an increasing rate of graduation from the expanding secondary school system. From 1973 to 1979 the number of high school seniors increased from 379,000 to 584,000; in that same interval the number who qualified for college by passing the NCEE rose from 241,000 to 381,000.[93] Thus, despite the efforts of the Ministry of Education to limit student numbers through the NCEE, the pool has inexorably grown. The government has increased its

share of total enrollments by more than doubling the capacity of the
state colleges and universities during the decade, yet ultimately
most of these additional students have had to be accommodated in
the private sector. Due to the disorganization of official bookkeeping, precise enrollment data for the decade is lacking. The evidence
that is available, however, suggests the following picture:[94] from
the end of the 1960s to about 1976 there was almost no growth in
the private sector because of the successive impacts of the economic
crisis, martial law, and the establishment of the NCEE. But since
1977 the sheer weight of numbers has caused all types of higher
education once again to undergo rapid expansion. Under current
economic conditions the meaning of this is inescapable: the Philippines will for the foreseeable future continue to rely upon its mass
private sector to meet the demand for higher education. It is against
the backdrop of this reality that the developments of the 1970s
should be evaluated.

The Current Predicament

In the Philippines, just as in Japan, the public presence in private
higher education has grown considerably during the 1970s. The
most significant difference, of course, is that government subsidies
preceded and to some extent justified a measure of government control over private institutions in Japan, whereas the Philippine government has not been in a position to commit public funds for these
purposes. Its private sector nevertheless presented problems for the
nation that the government could hardly ignore. Its response was
two policy initiatives quite different in nature and, as the preceding
discussion suggested, producing quite different results. Regulatory
actions sought to directly affect the conduct of institutions by fiat.
In addition to the *Manual of Regulations for Private Schools,* the
principal landmark was the tuition law that determined what
schools could charge and how they were to employ their revenues.
The results for the private sector were to weaken the financial basis
of many institutions and to make needed additional investments
less likely. The other major policy of the 1970s was environmental
in its approach. The NCEE, by reducing the numbers eligible to
enter college, changed the environment of private higher education
while leaving institutions free to adapt as they might to the new
conditions. Despite certain difficulties,[95] it has marginally improved conditions in the private sector: low-quality schools have
been prevented from recruiting those students for whom the bene-

fits of college are most dubious; the net effect has been to favor sectarian schools at the expense of the distrusted proprietary schools; and, by retarding the enrollment growth curve, it has to some extent shielded the weak market for college graduates.

If in these cases the environmental approach has produced more positive results than the regulatory, this is probably because it is more compatible with some of the underlying conditions of Philippine private higher education. To describe the situation in starkest terms, the country's mass private sector was able in the past to adapt to a wide and diversified demand and to mobilize sufficient resources to provide an extraordinary quantity of low-cost higher education. The negative side of this achievement was the poor quality and inequitable distribution of that education. By taking a regulatory approach to these problems the government indirectly tended to nullify the positive attributes of the private sector. Curricular uniformity lessens diversity; bureaucratic uniformity stifles adaptive innovation; and financial controls obstruct access to additional resources. The general desirability of substituting environmental policies for at least a part of the regulatory apparatus seems clear, particularly in light of the facts of higher education in the Philippines.

Given existing economic conditions, colleges and universities are likely to be woefully underfunded for a number of years to come. At the same time the high prevailing level of demand and the swelling number of high school graduates assure that there will be a continued need for even more college places. Thus, the proprietary schools that now enroll half or more of the nation's students will remain a necessary component of the system, with the persistence of low standards a concomitant result. Since efforts to upgrade the entire system would seem doomed, perhaps more limited and selective improvements would be a more feasible short-term goal. Specifically, an attempt to accentuate the inherently hierarchical character of mass private sectors and the natural segmentation of the education market would tend to strengthen the few existing, and many potential, middle-level institutions. The preconditions for such a policy would be the restoration of pricing freedom and greater independence over curricula. The former would allow the better schools to charge a premium for their programs, and the latter would mean that those programs would no longer be on paper identical to those of their less costly competitors. A certain class of institutions would then be able to compete on the basis of quality to the extent that the market allowed. The proprietary schools are not well suited for such competition. Over time they could be expected to lose ground to nonprofit institutions in those academic programs for which quality considerations are most crucial. Although their function of supplying mass higher education at a rather low, market-determined price would remain indispensible, the proprietary schools would be likely to concentrate their teaching in vocational areas. Greater segmentation of the market might allow a balanced compromise between attainable improvements in quality and the maintenance of quantity in Philippine higher education.

The antecedents for such an approach already exist. The Philippine private sector has a well-developed independent superstructure that is committed to promoting qualitative improvement. Most important are the Fund for Assistance to Private Education (FAPE), established as a trust fund in 1968, and the private accrediting associations. FAPE employs its endowment income, various grants, and a small subsidy from the government to provide a number of services to the private sector.[96] It endeavors to improve faculty development and graduate training, provide leadership in education planning, and encourage accreditation. This last area is critical for recognizing and rewarding qualitative differences between schools. A Presidential Commission recommended in 1970 that accreditation be used as a criterion in the government's treatment of different schools, and in some cases certain restrictions have been eased for accredited institutions.[97] The oldest agency, the Philippine Accrediting Association for Schools, Colleges, and Universities, has been in operation since 1957. In the 1970s it was linked with other such associations in the Federation of Accrediting Associations of the Philippines. The precedent and the machinery thus exist for the Ministry of Education to transfer the responsibility for encouraging academic standards into private hands.

Many would undoubtedly be concerned that the removal of controls on tuition would exacerbate the inequality of access that already exists, but this might be countered in a number of ways. Financial aid requirements for private colleges could force more affluent students, in effect, to subsidize their poorer classmates.[98] Such an approach might be preferable to the current situation, where the benefits of artificially underpricing higher education accrue overwhelmingly to the middle and upper classes.

There are other obstacles to relaxing control over the private sector that present greater difficulties. The inertia of bureaucratic regulation is certainly one. The fact that the strongest private schools—financially and academically—are the most socially ex-

clusive, combined with the presence of low standards and merce-
nary motives in the proprietary schools, has created a climate of
distrust that strongly sustains these regulatory activities. Furthermore, higher education policy faces larger and even more intractable political questions. Existing arrangements involve vested interests in numerous and complicated ways, including the potential
threat that the wrath of angry students can pose to an authoritarian
regime. Such considerations, however, lie beyond the issues of the
structure and the dynamics of the Philippine mass private sector.
Speculation about the possible benefits of "decontrolling" private
higher education are nevertheless germane to this analysis. While
the developed nations covered in this study may choose, like Japan,
to make their private sector more like the public sector, or like
France, to exclude the private sector from certain tasks, or even like
Sweden, to practically abolish it, the Philippines does not have the
luxury of such a choice. For a long time to come Filipinos will have
to rely upon private education and private resources to educate a
large majority of the country's college students. Under these circumstances it seems appropriate to ask how they might maximize
the advantages that a private sector can offer, while also making
the best of its attendant drawbacks. Otherwise, the possibility certainly exists of reaping the worst of both the public and the private
modes of control in higher education.

Mass Private Sectors: Paradigm and Actuality

If in any system of higher education there is an inherent trade-off
between quality and quantity, then the most salient characteristic
of mass private sectors is the provision of a large volume of instruction with low average standards. The experiences of Japan and the
Philippines in the twentieth century indicate that both these conditions carry unwelcome consequences. Low quality education, of
course, must always be lamented, but too much access to such programs tends to cause the inflation of educational credentials that
can threaten the value of all college degrees. Concerns such as these
are a continual inducement for state intervention, but this is only
one of the dynamic elements propelling the evolution of mass private sectors. The original and preponderant dynamic springs directly from growth; from the remarkable capacity of groups, institutions, or individuals in such systems to mobilize private resources to
accommodate student demand for higher education.
    Although the origins of modern higher education in Japan and

the Philippines were quite different, their stages of development since about 1900 have been roughly comparable. During a formative period before World War II both private sectors experienced the entry of numerous advanced specialized schools and upgraded secondary schools, some of which were able to elevate themselves into multifaculty universities. Next came a period of explosive growth commencing in the aftermath of the war and accelerating during the 1960s. Finally, the past decade in both countries has witnessed attempts to contain enrollment growth and place additional controls upon private institutions. Within the broad context of this evolution it is possible to distinguish some general features of the nature of mass private sectors—the content and character of private education, the social consequences of this structure, the interaction of institutional finance with institutional quality, and the changing relationship between private higher education and the state.

Diversity and innovation are commonly regarded as attributes of a vital private sector, but it would seem that these qualities are inhibited when private institutions are responsible for the bulk of a nation's higher education. The independent creation of numerous new institutions during the sector's formative period has the initial effect of producing diversity, but as the system matures the dominant trend is toward greater uniformity. From without there are constraints produced by government regulations as ministries of education attempt to standardize degree programs. Internal forces for conformity are present as well. The existence of an institutional hierarchy encourages the emulation of more prestigious schools. In particular, this produces convergence on the multifaculty university model. Lack of discretionary resources can be even more constraining. Where the available means are minimal, as in many Philippine colleges, the nature of instruction is likely to be similar regardless of the type of control. Of course, a considerable degree of superficial variety persists within mass private sectors, but it is accompanied by less functional diversity than would otherwise be expected.

The judgment on adaptive innovation would have to be similar to that on diversity. Standardized degree programs eliminate much of the scope for experiment and change. On the other hand, the strong incentives for institutional expansion tend to produce market responsive behavior, particularly during the stage of rapid growth. This does not necessarily stimulate innovation, but it does mean that a successful new program, like physical education faculties in Japan during the 1970s, will be widely replicated. While the private sector of the Philippines remains essentially market driven, Japan has developed some different incentives for innovation since the advent of planning in 1975. Because new colleges or faculties are only approved under exceptional circumstances, sponsors must develop unique programs if they hope to win government charters. This had produced at least a few distinctive new colleges. Thus, a source of innovation exists at the periphery of the Japanese private sector, the bulk of which is probably becoming increasingly monolithic.

Another aspect of this issue is embodied in the notion of pluralism, the capacity of private sectors to fulfill the many different, and often contradictory, demands that are placed on higher education. Japan is certainly a poor example in this regard. The extraordinary homogeneity of its population and the value placed on conformity in its culture leave a small role for pluralistic alternatives. Those that do exist, such as women's colleges and Christian colleges, have been seen to be declining in importance. In the Philippines Catholic institutions still play a large role in its educational system. But even there the importance of pluralism is diminished by the heavy vocational emphasis in much of higher education. Where vocational credentials are at stake, the cultural orientation of schools becomes far less important. In liberal arts colleges, on the other hand, the Catholic schools are dominant. In sum, it would seem that pluralism may or may not play an important role in mass private sectors, but, in contrast to the structures that will be considered in the following chapters, it is not the primary justification for privateness.

The most conspicuous achievement of mass private sectors is supplying far more higher education than the state is willing or able to provide itself. However, a hierarchical structure assures that the opportunities thus made available are unequal in value, while the decentralized nature of these systems guarantees that they will be inequitably distributed. In this respect private sectors merely reflect social conditions in the societies that spawn them, but they are particularly ill-suited to affect those conditions. Students who secure places at the peak institutions will have excellent chances for high-status careers; for those who study in undistinguished schools the real competition for success will lie in the world of work. In the rigidly meritocratic Japanese system, of course, students must earn their places. But, those from educated, affluent families adopt ambitious educational strategies from an early age; and should they fail in their first attempts, they can afford a second or third try. The situation is far bleaker in the Philippines where the population of secondary school graduates is already a select group. Then, high tuition and explicit social selection for the elite private universities reserve the benefits of these quality schools for a privileged few. These realities, however, should not obscure the value of the wide opportunities provided by mass private sectors. Even if college credentials prove a cruel disappointment for some, for many more they open the way to respectable semiprofessional careers, and for a significant few they are the precondition for considerable success. Mass private sectors, for all their obvious shortcomings, are associated with greater opportunities for social mobility than comparable societies with more restrictive systems of higher education.

No feature of mass private sectors is more fundamental to their nature than reliance upon student-derived revenues. This limitation, of course, restricts the level of educational spending and virtually precludes many of the expensive, high-overhead activities that are generally associated with academic prestige. One can readily point to the formidable costs of modern laboratories, computing facilities, adequate libraries, and other capital goods that seem indispensable for the advanced pursuit of knowledge. Of more immediate relevance to the needs of these private colleges, however, is the difficulty of securing and retaining competent teachers. Advanced degrees, especially research degrees, are investments in human capital that require a return in the form of decent salaries. Another significant expense relates to faculty time as represented in reasonable teaching loads and opportunities to pursue individual scholarship. The weakness of mass private sectors in these respects leads to comparatively weak disciplinary organization and a correspondingly weak institutionalization of academic values. Contributing to this condition are such relative factors as the isolation of the research community in a few national universities and the powerful influence of employment markets upon the educational process. Still, the nature of some private institutions is also a significant factor. The proprietary colleges of the Philippines, in particular, would seem antithetical to the development of an academic culture. Many of Japan's nonprofit universities operate in a manner that is inherently little different. The resemblance between the giant universities of Japan and the large capitalist schools of the Philippines is striking. Less apparent is the fact that many Japanese universities are governed autocratically by powerful leaders who founded or developed them. The result in both private sectors, then, is that faculty ties to their own institution far outweigh the bonds that theoretically connect them with colleagues in their discipline or with a larger academic community. Recognizing this condition points toward another conclusion: although academic quality cannot be achieved without ample discretionary funds, it cannot be simply purchased even when such funds are available. It takes time, as well as resources, to develop the infrastructure of values, habits, and institutions upon which academic standards are anchored. From this perspective it becomes possible to explain the apparent inconsistency of the preceding analyses that suggested that tuition may be too high in Japan but too low in the Philippines. Since the advent of the current subsidization formulas in Japan, the most serious impediments to enhancing quality lie with this infrastructure rather than with the level of expenditures. But, given the penury of private colleges in the Philippines, more resources could bring some immediate improvements despite the existence of similar basic weaknesses in academic life.

Governmental regulation in private higher education should be regarded as another inherent trait of mass private sectors. During the rapid-growth phase of their developments these two private sectors were allowed considerable license within the regulatory context, but unrestrained growth eventually produced its own limitations. Underemployed graduates, impoverished insitutions, low standards, and student unrest were all factors that provoked greater government involvement in the 1970s. On this issue national differences become pronounced. The Japanese possessed the wealth to bail out their private sector with public funds. Although this course scarcely seemed feasible for the Philippines, that country acted in the opposite sense by curtailing the ability of private schools to support themselves. Both systems have endeavored to raise standards and protect graduate labor markets by placing global limits on the number attending college. Although a continuing government presence in these systems would seem ineluctable, the nature of the government's role is still an important consideration. The Philippine enrollment policy and the Japanese subsidization policy generally have sought to achieve their ends by manipulating the environment in which institutions operate. Unlike direct regulation, this approach allows private schools to retain their independence and to adapt as they see fit. Without dismissing the difficulties that have accompanied these policies, their relative success indicates that the private institutions of a mass private sector best fulfill their public responsibilities by acting independently.

Chapter 3

Parallel Public and Private Sectors

Anyone familiar with the system of higher education in the United States will find nothing unusual in a situation where independent and government-controlled institutions fulfill roughly the same educational tasks. However, it was seen in the previous chapter, and will be evident again in the next, that it is far more common, and in a sense more natural, to have a significant differentiation of function between public and private sectors. Whether a national government commits itself to shouldering the entire burden for the provision of higher education, or concentrates instead on some limited, vital roles, its legislative and financial powers can preclude a significant degree of competition by privately controlled entities. Yet, in the parallel private sectors of Belgium and the Netherlands almost the opposite has occurred: government powers in these two states have been employed to guarantee that private universities will for all practical purposes be equal to their counterparts in the public sector. It took rather special circumstances in the historical origins and social context of these two systems to produce parallel public and private sectors.

Two preconditions for the development of this pattern are the legal right to establish private schools and the establishment of officially equal national degrees. The first is an identifiable legacy of the nineteenth-century liberal state. The second largely arose as a means for government control over the freedom of education that had been granted. In the initial period of university development the states employed various means to oversee examinations and to certify the validity of degrees, but eventually the private universities were accorded the right to confer on their own authority degrees equivalent to those given in state faculties. Far more was required for this arrangement to survive into the age of the welfare state. Now the assumption prevails in these countries that higher education should not only be freely given, but that it should be freely, or nearly so, received as well. This means that the state must provide most of the financial resources if independently controlled institutions are to be able to educate their students virtually without charge. Arrangements such as these inevitably depend upon decisions taken in the political arena. Thus, the key element in the evolution of parallel sectors has been the standing in the polity of private university sponsors.

Belgium and the Netherlands are both societies with a high degree of cultural compartmentalization. They manage to function as nations through a process described as "consociational democracy."[1] Parliamentary governments are formed by shifting "grand coalitions" representing different segments of the polity. Each subcultural group in such a system is guaranteed the protection of its minority rights, a large degree of autonomy to run its own affairs, and proportional distribution of government resources and benefits. The private universities owe their origins to the sponsorship of these particular groups, and their current situation results from the play of consociational politics. The same would be true, although perhaps less dramatically, for the wide variety of nonuniversity institutions of postsecondary education in each country, although they will receive little attention here. The case of Belgium will be considered first and in greatest detail because it exhibits the pattern of parallel sectors in starkest clarity. The Netherlands also contributes to an understanding of this phenomenon, particularly the assumptions underlying this development. Arrangements that were produced through bitter conflict in Belgium were more often the result of cooperation and accommodation there. The private universities in these countries have obviously sacrificed some of their independence and some of their distinctiveness in return for complete support from the state. The final section of this chapter will explore the differences that still remain between public and private sectors, and the remaining distinctive roles for the private institutions that have become totally dependent upon the state.

Belgium

The Revolution of 1830, which severed an independent state of Belgium from the Kingdom of the Netherlands, presented the new nation with the opportunity for an entirely new start in higher education.[2] For several years successive government commissions pondered whether and where to create one or two universities to supplant the three shuttered Dutch institutions, but private initiatives finally proved more decisive. Belgian Catholics were the first to take advantage of the constitutional guarantee of freedom of education. In 1834, after securing the authorization of the Pope, they officially opened a "free" Catholic university. The rector's opening address left no doubt about its guiding principles: the university "would struggle with all its power . . . to gain acceptance for all doctrines emanating from the Holy See, and to repudiate everything not originating from that august source." Only two weeks later, liberals and Freemasons in the capital countered by opening the Free University of Brussels (Université libre de Bruxelles, or ULB) as a "counterweight to the so-called university of the Catholics." This free university would "combat fanaticism" and prevent the Church from extinguishing the enlightened spirit of the times.[3] Goaded by these actions the Parliament voted the following year to resurrect as state universities the former Dutch institutions in Ghent and Liège. The inchoate nation thus abruptly found itself with more universities than it had anticipated or desired, yet each institution had a special relation to the principal cleavages in Belgian society.

With a free-thinking university in the capital and its Catholic counterpart scarcely twenty kilometers away, the private universities were strategically located in the political and geographic center of the nation. The state universities were pushed into largely regional roles as a result. Liège in eastern Wallonia and Ghent in western Flanders originally drew their students and defined their service missions from their respective regions. When Ghent became a Dutch-language institution in 1930 their roles were defined even more specifically with respect to the two linguistic communities. The private universities, however, were more nearly national entities, not just because of their central locations, but also because they were oriented along a crucial ideological fault line. Although Belgium is nominally a Catholic country, the Flemings as a whole have retained closer links with the Church than have Walloons. The French-speaking bourgeoisie, in particular, was strongly affected by the rationalism of the Enlightenment and the secularism spread by the French Revolution. Given the restricted suffrage based on the property ownership, the political influence of this group, although never preponderant, far surpassed their relative weight in the population. It was this same elite, of course, that was likely to be concerned about higher education, and they provided a barely sufficient base of support for the Free University of Brussels. Urban, secular, rationalist, and self-consciously progressive, the ULB functioned as an intellectual beacon for political liberalism in the nineteenth century, and to some degree for social democracy in the twentieth. The university bore the unpopularity of its advanced views with considerable pride through much of its early history, and was only able to survive Catholic and government hostility through the efforts of its backers and the city of Brussels.

The Catholic university was installed after a slight delay in the Flemish city of Leuven, which is known internationally by its French name, Louvain. There it assumed the mantle and the mission of the medieval University of Louvain (1425–1797) that had been closed after France conquered the region. Created and ultimately controlled by the Bishops of Belgium, who appointed both rector and professors, the Catholic University of Louvain (UCL) became the natural center of Catholic higher learning in the country. The faculties of theology and canon law soon regained the international recognition formerly accorded the ancient university. With the large Catholic majority as a base of support and recruitment the UCL has historically been the largest Belgian university, at times even surpassing the combined enrollments of its three rivals.

Independent higher education poses an inherent problem regarding the nature and value of the credentials it awards. From the outset the Belgian solution was advantageous for the private universities. The basic law on higher education (1835) established a set of national degrees with fixed curricula along with official "central juries" to conduct examinations. Students from the private universities therefore were examined for national degrees on the same footing as those from state universities—or, for that matter, anyone else who felt qualified to take the examination. This arrangement left the field quite open for more modest private initiatives in higher education. Jesuits in the Collège Notre Dame de la Paix in Namur offered advanced instruction in philosophy and letters on this basis from the time the basic law was passed, and in 1858 the Institut Saint-Louis in Brussels began doing the same. When the regime of the central juries was supplanted in 1876, the private universities retained parity under even more advantageous arrangements by being accorded the authority to grant national degrees directly. And deservingly so; in their first forty years of existence the private universities had demonstrated that they could be trusted to maintain academic standards and for the most part to keep ideological passions somewhat removed from course contents. It might be added that they had acquired a measure of influence as well: the Minister of the Interior who introduced the new law on higher education was also a professor of law at Louvain. (This situation would recur with important university legislation in the twentieth century.) The national degrees could be complemented by institutionally defined degrees, called "scientific" degrees, offered by the universities in subjects for which there were no set curricula. The central juries were retained and, indeed, exist in modified form today. They were particularly necessary for the Collège Notre Dame de la Paix and the Institut Saint-Louis, both of which did not receive the right to grant national degrees until 1929.

The enlarged institutional autonomy created by the 1876 law marks the opening of the modern era of Belgian university history. For the private universities the near century that stretches from this date to the transformation of the 1960s can be broadly characterized by a shift from ideological to institutional competition. During the nineteenth century the call for "free inquiry" at the ULB meant the rationalistic rejection of all religious dogma, while the "search for truth" at Louvain implied acceptance of inquiry within the context of a Catholic world view. These and similar phrases were rallying cries that evoked the respective organizational sagas of the two universities. Until well into the twentieth century new students at each school had to sign pledges attesting to their personal belief in the respective institutional philosophies. Over time this ideological sharpness became less strident, less vituperative toward its rivals, and more ritualized within the universities. But the competition that it engendered had a continuing and largely beneficial effect upon higher education as a whole. First, both universities were stimulated to maintain rigorous standards, since the quality of their graduates reflected upon the correctness of their ideology. When the impact of German science began to be felt in Belgium in the last two decades of the nineteenth century, the focus of competition was shifted toward scholarly excellence and scientific research. This was a development that clearly affected all the Belgian universities, but the independent universities possessed the flexibility to establish new programs or institutes, either to keep pace with the advancement of science or to serve new clientele. Private institutions can by no means claim credit for every innovation, but they interacted with public actions in numerous ways to spur the rate of academic change.

The Catholic University of Louvain was clearly the leader in establishing a myriad of institutes and research centers. With its natural emphasis on theological studies it overshadowed the other universities in the humanities. By the 1930s the Louvain Faculty of Philosophy and Letters alone could boast of twenty scholarly periodicals. The Free University of Brussels harbored a special penchant for the social sciences from its earliest years when they could only be taught as optional subjects. It was after the ULB, and also Louvain, established schools of social and political science that the state created national degrees in these subjects and introduced them into the state universities (1898). At times, however, private efforts followed government actions. A decree of 1896 creating "scientific" licenses in commercial science at the state universities was soon duplicated, not only by the private universities, but also by specially created schools of commerce in Mons (1896), Liège (1898), and Antwerp (1901). These last two examples demonstrate how institutional competition introduced subjects into the Belgian universities that were often resisted out of academic traditionalism elsewhere in Europe. The influence of the independent universities here must be regarded as decisive. They not only wished to excel within the framework of their own philosophies, but they also wanted to extend their influence as widely as possible. Thus, even while the UCL was striving for scientific leadership through newly formed institutes, it was also able to incorporate an *école supérieure d'agriculture* (1878), and shortly thereafter another school for brewing. New programs, however, required additional resources. It was the misfortune of the ULB to be constrained by lack of funds until the 1890s, when a series of benefactors led by the industrialist Ernest Solvay provided the capital to greatly expand the university's scientific capabilities. Competitiveness in the Belgian context of compartmentalization produced a tendency toward isomorphism, as each institution felt the need to duplicate the programs of its rivals.

Until World War I the private universities were able to function on their own resources, that is, on student tuition, support from their patrons, and extraordinary gifts. Indeed, as the Solvay example would indicate, large gifts were typically required whenever the university was faced with significant capital expenditures. In 1911, both independent universities were granted the status of civil personalities in order to facilitate the building of endowments. Their financial circumstances, however, were profoundly affected by the war. Many of Louvain's university buildings, including its world-famous library, were casualties of the fighting; and Brussels desperately needed to replace its scattered buildings with new facilities in order to accommodate a doubling of its prewar enrollment. Inflation, meanwhile, had shriveled those assets held by the universities. Private charity mobilized sizable efforts to meet these needs, but in the end proved insufficient. The American Committee for the Relief of

Belgium gave higher education top priority, and ultimately donated most of its unused funds to the universities (public and private) for endowment. A native Belgian philanthropic effort, the "Brussels-Louvain Committee," also helped to meet the capital requirements of the independent universities, although its more noteworthy contribution was the unprecedented cooperation it inaugurated between the two antagonistic institutions. It soon became apparent that a state subsidy would be required to allow the private universities to continue operating at their accustomed level and scale. Beginning in 1922 they were each assisted with an annual grant of one million Belgian francs (BF), which together represented about one-seventh of the national higher education budget. In 1930 this subsidy was placed on a new footing: three-fifths of the credits allocated to the state universities of Ghent and Liège would be divided by Louvain and Brussels. No state controls were included, but henceforth the financing of both public and private universities were inextricably linked.

In the years after World War II annual student tuition at the ULB (BF 3,500, or about $100) covered about one-quarter of the university's operating costs (equal to BF 12,000 per student), and the balance was met largely through the state subsidy. As the needs of the private universities grew, both to accommodate more students and to keep pace with scientific advancement, they looked chiefly to their subsidy as the only expandable source of income. The subsidy formula was revised in 1949 to give private higher education two-thirds the amount of the regular budgets of the state universities—five-twelfths each for Brussels and Louvain, two-twelfths for other private colleges—plus various forms of indexed aid. By 1960 the independent universities were asking for a significantly larger share of the higher education budget, and another complex formula was negotiated: their grant was raised to 44 percent of the base, with an additional 2.2 percent for each fifteen hundred students above five thousand.

On the threshold of the explosive growth of the 1960s the independent universities of Belgium found themselves resting upon a foundation of precedents and assumptions concerning higher education: they were entrusted with performing the identical tasks as their state counterparts; they were therefore providing a necessary and vital service to the nation; and they consequently deserved enough support from the public purse to accomplish this function effectively. Even a national consensus on these principles, however, did not preclude bitter and nearly intractable controversy in the decade that followed. In fact, the current higher educational map and relationship between the private universities and the state were largely determined by the outcome of the two predominant issues of this period. The first was a problem of the form and the financing of university expansion, with the greatest complication being the role of the private universities. The second was the linguistic question, which uniquely affected the two private universities because of their bilingual status.

The Contemporary Belgian Private Sector

Like most other Western countries Belgium experienced an accelerating demand for higher education in the 1960s. A manageable annual growth rate of 5 percent during the 1950s shot up to above 10 percent after 1960.[4] On the whole this development was welcomed, but there was clearly a problem of what to do with the additional students. The private universities, now receiving part of their subsidy on a per-student basis, endeavored to make the most of this opportunity for expansion by aggressively promoting the idea of establishing extension centers. The state universities would have preferred that growth be confined to the existing campuses (although Ghent did have designs for expanding into Antwerp). Cities like Mons and Antwerp, however, that did not have universities, pressured for institutions of their own. How higher education would be expanded, of course, ultimately depended upon what the government would agree to finance. Thus, the formula for subsidizing private universities was called into question once again, becoming an inextricable part of the university expansion problem. Given the underlying assumptions of a parallel private sector, it was entirely logical for the privates to demand government support commensurate with that received by state universities for the unassailable purpose of spreading higher education throughout the nation. As this issue ripened the two private universities took a significant step in order to better navigate the complex political crosscurrents. In 1964 Louvain and Brussels negotiated a private accord concerning projected territorial expansion and the level of subsidization they wished from the government. This act, by subordinating ideology to institutional interest, suggests that the need for government preferment had become the paramount consideration for their development.

The Janne Law of 1965 on university expansion did not disappoint the privates. The Flemish half of Louvain (see below) was allowed to create an extension campus of Courtrai (Kortrijk), and the ULB was permitted to do the same in Nivelles. Existing Catholic schools in Antwerp, Namur, and Mons were elevated to university-level status. In addition, state "university centers" would be established in Antwerp and Mons, offering the first two years of university study. The financial arrangements, however, were undoubtedly most significant. The combined budgets of Ghent and Liège remained the basis of other subsidies, but now Louvain was promised 91 percent of that figure, Brussels 61 percent, with a further 35 percent to be distributed among the smaller private institutions. Government loans for capital expenditures would be offered at a mere 1¼ percent interest. Thus, the direct subsidy to private higher education, which before 1960 had constituted just 67 percent of the combined state universities' budgets, after 1965 would stand at 187 percent of that sum. Moreover, a commitment was made to raise the base budgets of Ghent and Liège by 25 percent in 1966 and 18 percent the following two years. Taken together, these efforts, designed to appease all parties involved in the university expansion question, would have more than doubled the national budget for higher education from 1965 to 1968, without even taking into account the additional capital expenditures. In fact, however, such munificence could not be sustained: the increases in the state university budgets for 1967 and 1968 were reduced to 13 percent and 8 percent instead of the promised 18 percent increase, thus reducing the subsidies of the privates as well. But even with these cuts, Belgium had the highest growth rate in the unit costs of higher education during the 1960s among OECD countries—10.4 percent per year.[5]

The Janne Law was essentially a blueprint for the first phase of university expansion. The generous financial arrangements for private higher education were intended to be provisional until a regular formula could be negotiated. The next phase, however, left no opportunity for lengthy deliberations. Instead it emerged as an outgrowth of a severe political crisis over the language question at the Catholic University of Louvain.

The Language Issue and Expansion
The progress of Dutch-language education at the UCL provides an interesting example of the incompatibility of different organizational goals. Even aside from its location in the Flemish city of Leuven, the bishops of Belgium had an obvious interest in making the university accessible to the pious population of Flanders. Cer-

tain courses began to be offered in Dutch before the turn of the century. Full-degree programs were inaugurated in 1932, just after Ghent became a Dutch-language university. In the years that followed, additional degree programs were created, so that by 1960 virtually the entire curriculum was taught in both languages. In 1962 separate administrations were established, thereby making the Dutch and French halves of the university practically independent of each other. These developments might have been regarded as commendable examples of innovation that voluntarily raised the Flemish to a position of full parity, were it not for the accident of geography that lodged the ancient University of Louvain to the north of the Franco-Dutch linguistic frontier.

The long and rancorous linguistic conflict between Flemings and Walloons was definitively settled in 1963 on the basis that Flanders would be exclusively Dutch-speaking, Wallonia correspondingly francophone, and the Brussels region officially bilingual. The French University of Louvain, although specifically exempted from these terms, was nevertheless a constant source of irritation to the Flemish, especially those in the Flemish half of the university.[6] They well knew from bitter experience that the two languages could not coexist on an equal basis. The French community of Louvain did little to assuage their sensibilities in that respect, and a certain faction was deliberately outspoken and intransigent. Early in 1968 the French half of the university unilaterally announced a plan of expansion that violated the university constitution. The Flemings closed their half of the university in protest, and the ensuing crisis in the relations of the two linguistic communities forced the Belgian government to resign.

As titular leaders of the university the bishops found themselves in a dilemma. The special Catholic mission of the university coupled with its medieval heritage formed the basis of an organizational saga to which Catholic Walloons were deeply attached. Any scheme to move the original French components of the university would detach it from these hallowed traditions and alter the very character of the institution. But, as Flemish opinion became more and more inflamed over this issue, the Church hierarchy found it increasingly difficult to maintain its own leadership. The point had clearly been reached at which the UCL could no longer preserve both its ancient traditions as a French institution and its current mission of service to the Flemish community.

Stating the dilemma in this manner perhaps makes the outcome appear more inevitable than it seemed at the time. In fact it took a national election and a new government to determine that the French would have to leave Louvain. In the end the resolution of this conflict had to be consistent with the acknowledged principle of Flemish cultural sovereignty in Flanders. Once this political decision had been made the bishops quickly bowed to the inevitable. Planning immediately began for transferring the French half of the university to "Louvain-la-Neuve," a new city and campus to be built from the ground up on French-speaking territory south of Brussels. There remained the problem of integrating this development, as well as corresponding changes envisioned for the ULB, into a new overall government policy on the expansion and financing of higher education.

At the ULB events took a somewhat different course, but eventually produced the same result. Despite having a more restricted Flemish constituency, the ULB nevertheless followed the trend toward linguistic parity in higher education. Full-degree courses in Dutch were established in the law faculty in 1935, and by the 1960s many of the university's programs were offered in both languages. In May of 1968, while the Louvain crisis was still unresolved, ULB students were inspired by events then transpiring in Paris to barricade themselves in part of the university. One of their principal demands was the scission of the ULB into independent French and Dutch institutions. In contrast to Louvain's situation, the trustees of the ULB acceded to such a transformation. Its historical mission among the secularized Walloon population, its own progressive image, and the tacit need to remain equal with its Catholic antithesis all made this an easy decision. There were pecuniary interests at stake as well. For several years the university had been negotiating to purchase the Plaine des Manoeuvres, an enormous open area near the main ULB campus. The mitotic birth of the Vrije Universiteit te Brussel (VUB) that ensued thus created a claim for a new campus that exactly paralleled the commitments made to the UCL as a result of their eviction from Leuven. The eventual settlement (the law of July 24, 1969) ceded the Plaine to the two Brussels universities for a price of BF 764 million (or $25 million), to be paid over forty years at 1¼ percent interest; the UCL was granted an identical sum on identical terms to purchase a campus for Louvain-la-Neuve. Once again, parity was maintained at a considerable cost to Belgian taxpayers; however, this was only the first step toward a definitive settlement.

With the university expansion question opened once again, it was only natural that other claims would be made. Antwerp was finally accorded a full-fledged university in a manner that is intriguing for this study. A state institution for second-degree work (third to fourth years) was superimposed over a public and a private first-degree school—the Faculties of Sintignatius and the State University Center of Antwerp—thus producing a peculiar public-private hybrid. Mons, of course, had to receive a corresponding upgrading of its university center to full university status. And, the fast-growing Flemish province of Limburg successfully pressed its claims for a state university center. Finally, in bilingual Brussels, the small Faculties of Saint Louis divided into separate French and Dutch language institutions. In the space of just three years, then, Belgium doubled the number of full universities and added two first-degree institutions for reasons that—except perhaps in the cases of Antwerp and Limburg—had little to do with the higher education needs of the country. The consequences of resolving the expansion problem in this way would soon become evident.

The final act in the restructuring of Belgian higher education was also the culmination of a half-century evolution of public funding for private institutions. The law of July 27, 1971 placed all university-level institutions on ostensibly the same financial footing. A government allocation based upon enrollments was established to cover all costs of teaching, administration, maintenance, and normal research. The per-student grants varied according to the faculty of study. In 1977, for example, they were set at BF 122,810 ($3,684) for each student in the humanities; BF 231,809 ($6,954) in the natural sciences; and BF 375,086 ($11,253) for medical students.[7] This allocation constituted the entire regular operating budget; additional government funds were channeled through a separate capital budget, a budget for student services, and diverse sources of targeted research funds. Income from student tuition (BF 10,000 per year in 1977, or about $300, but since raised) has been inconsequential in comparison. The income from university endowments comprised only 2 percent of a typical university budget, and could not be employed at the discretion of the institution. Special provisions were included in the new financing law to provide generous levels of minimum funding for the smaller institutions, and also to guarantee the existing levels of support at the state universities. At the time, enrollment growth was expected gradually to smooth out these irregularities, but to date such growth has failed to occur.[8] As a result, substantial anomalies in funding have persisted: in 1977 only the three largest privates were funded by the 1971 formulas. Their allocations averaged BF 204,000 per student, compared to BF 252,000 for the smaller institutions invoking minimum funding provisions, and BF 293,000 for the state universities still enjoying their pre-1971 funding criteria. So, equal funding in principle for the private universities has not yet produced equal funds in fact, and this has had an important bearing upon their current situation.

Government Controls
The government largesse toward private higher education was not without its negative features. Foremost among them has been the intricate web of controls attached to the funding formulas. These specified that for certain categories of expenditures, the most important being personnel, the practices of the privates had to be identical to those of the state universities. For other things, maximum or minimum levels were established to restrain expenditures. The latter include faculty/student ratios, the proportion of teaching to research personnel, the square meters of building space allowed per student, and even the number of places in student restaurants.[9] To assure that independent institutions complied fully with these regulations the law imposed on them a "government delegate." This official is charged with guaranteeing the correctness of the number of students claimed, checking that the complex personnel requirements are observed, and generally seeing that the government subsidy is spent in conformity with the law. To accomplish these tasks the government delegate has been accorded powers to intervene in university self-government to an extent unprecedented in Western systems of higher education. He can participate in the meetings of any university body that touches upon matters falling within his sphere of responsibility. Since his charge includes budget, enrollments, staffing, and physical plant, the only topics excepted are those pertaining to the philosophical principles of the institution. He has the power to veto any decision taken by these bodies, thereby appealing it to his superior, the Minister of Education; and he has to countersign for all university expenditures over BF 100,000.

The purpose of these controls is not only to assure equivalent operating conditions in all institutions, but also to place a ceiling upon the government's financial obligations to the universities. Since the state has assumed full responsibility for support, private institutions have an incentive to expand in order to increase their revenues. After the initial implementation of the law these tendencies were discernible in the adaptations of private institutions. Since then, however, a reaction on the part of the government has been evident.

The large increases of public funding for private higher education legislated in 1965 and 1971 were largely the results of laboriously negotiated settlements to political crises. As such they were far more generous than even the prevailing enthusiasm for higher education would justify. It has already been noted that the government had to scale down the commitments made in 1965. Precisely the same fate befell the 1971 settlement, only in this case the effects were exacerbated by a serious weakening of government revenues and a marked decrease in public confidence in higher education.[10] At the institutional level the universities were faced after 1971 with an unexpected stagnation in the enrollments that determined their subsidies. Only a year after passage of the new law, modifications for reducing the government's obligations were enacted in the funding formulas. In 1975 more drastic cuts were introduced, along with additional restrictions upon those university actions that might raise entitlements. Recently annual increases in the rate of subsidization have been limited to the general rate of inflation without regard for cost increases, chiefly in salaries, which are inherent to university operations. Available funds have been further diminished by periodic across-the-board cutbacks of nonsalary expenditures, and by such formula adjustments as tightening the definition of eligible students. Table 4 shows how these measures have succeeded in reversing the growth of real government expenditures on universities. Furthermore, since 1975 successive government austerity measures have exerted continued downward pressure on the real budgets of private universities. The aggregate figures on table 4, however, do not reveal why the budgetary squeeze has been most painful for the large private universities.

Before the advent of full government funding the privates were forced to be more tightly run than their public counterparts. These differences began to disappear after the 1971 law as conditions were supposedly equalized between state and independent institutions. Flexibility was particularly sacrificed in matters of personnel as the privates were obliged to conform to the norms of the civil service. At the same time, they utilized their increased government subsidies to increase their staff considerably. These salary commitments expanded rapidly in subsequent years as raises and promotions were accorded almost automatically on the basis of seniority. The university payrolls, then, have been virtually out of control, while the overall budget has been shrinking in real terms. The result at the UCL, for example, has been that personnel expenditures increased from 60 percent to 75 percent of the university operating budget during this period. Viewed from another angle, one could say that the UCL's entire budgetary increase from 1973 to 1977 was absorbed in salaries, while funds for operations and equipment, remaining stagnant, lost one-third of their purchasing power to inflation.[11] It is indeed ironic that the golden age ushered in by full government financing of the private universities proved to be so ephemeral. They are now more obsessed by financial concerns than perhaps at any time in their past, and also less able themselves to do anything about these problems.

A substantial degree of government control coupled with government-imposed austerity now seems to be the fate of the private universities of Belgium for the foreseeable future. Furthermore, these two conditions have interacted to poison the relations between these institutions and the state. Even from the view of a government delegate, the current system has produced unplanned and unwelcome consequences. It has tended to "transform the financing criteria into obligatory administrative norms, [and] progressively to restrain the margin of maneuver which the university possesses for the utilization of credits." It has consequently restricted the transfer of funds within the budget, dictated the number and type of person-

TABLE 4. Total Basic Belgian Government Grants for Operating Expenses for University-Level Institutions.

	Total Subsidies Current BF (in million BF)	Total Subsidies 1970 BF (in million BF)	Per-Student Subsidies 1970 BF (in thousand BF)
1965	2,956	3,506	87
1966	4,083	4,651	102
1967	4,559	5,049	101
1968	5,025	5,415	99
1969	5,689	5,907	99
1970	6,353	6,353	98
1971	7,784	7,463	107
1972	9,604	8,731	115
1973	10,916	9,274	119
1974	11,967	9,025	114
1975	13,254	8,860	110

Source: Adapted from Conseil National de la Politique Scientifique, Une nouvelle stratégie universitaire (Brussels: 1976), pp. 104–5.

nel, established rigid salary scales, and constrained possible university involvement with other organizations.[12] Before 1971 the differential between the level of government support to private and to public universities was commonly called "the price of liberty." Now that the privates are no longer paying this price, the truth of this phrase becomes apparent. Yet, the fundamental issues for private higher education raised by the Belgian case have scarcely been resolved. How dependent have the independent institutions actually become? What significant differences remain between publicly and privately controlled institutions? And, more generally, will the type of intrusive government regulation that has evolved in Belgium be the ineluctable fate of any publicly supported private university? The development of a similarly structured system of higher education in the Netherlands will be examined in light of these considerations.

The Netherlands

The private universities of the Netherlands, like those of Belgium, owe their origins to the existence of deep cultural cleavages within the nation. Dutch political and social life in the twentieth century has been characterized by highly segmented and integrated substructures. In Dutch they are referred to as *zuilen,* or pillars; the condition that they create is *verzuiling,* or compartmentalization.[13] Although the cleavages have historical roots going back to the Reformation, the *zuilen* have only assumed their modern form in the past hundred years. Their emergence was the consciously intended result of a large-scale social mobilization of first the Calvinist, and then the Catholic minorities. The universities thus created were therefore components in the elaboration of these "pillars," or comparatively minor effects of a far-reaching social phenomenon.

Following the political upheavals of 1848 (to retrace Dutch history no further than is necessary to understand the structure of higher education) the Netherlands became a constitutional monarchy dominated by a liberal and secular bourgeoisie.[14] Their general policy was to keep control of most governmental matters, and particularly education, in the hands of the neutral state; that is, removed from the divisive ideological passions of both Catholics, who formed an overwhelming majority in the two southern provinces, and fundamentalist Calvinists, who were far more zealous than the established Dutch Reformed Church. Higher education was scarcely at issue during this period, being entirely entrusted to the venerable universities of Leiden (f. 1575), Groningen (f. 1614), and Utrecht (f. 1636). The state domination of lower education was the principal grievance precipitating a mass movement among Calvinists. Freedom of education had been part of the new liberal Constitution of 1848, and in 1857 the official encumbrances discouraging private schools were removed as well. The religious communities, however, would be satisfied with nothing less than government financing for denominational schools. Led by Abraham Kuyper, the Calvinists in the 1870s founded the Anti-School Law League, a militant newspaper, and a political party—the institutional beginnings of subcultural separation. They were spurred by the conviction that the success of their movement required isolation from other groups and institutions in Dutch society. It was this logic that led Kuyper to found the country's first private university in 1880—the Vrije Universiteit te Amsterdam (VUA).

The creation of this Calvinist university must surely constitute a unique case: in an era of elite higher education it was initiated and supported by a mass movement. Its purpose, naturally, was to educate leaders for the Calvinist community; but the organizing authority for the university was an association open to all of the faithful. In addition, it was built and sustained during its early years by the meager funds collected each Sunday in the Calvinist churches. For its first twenty-five years the VUA did not possess the authority to grant degrees. Instead, it had to send the students it prepared to the state faculties at Leiden or Utrecht to be examined. By the time it was accorded the right to grant national degrees much had changed in Dutch politics. As early as 1888 the religious forces were strong enough to force the liberals to concede partial support to denominational schools. When the 1905 act gave the VUA equal status with the state universities, Abraham Kuyper, at the head of a coalition of religious parties, was prime minister of the Netherlands.

Unlike Belgium, where the financial exigencies of the universities induced government subsidies, in the Netherlands the issue of full state support for private education was from the outset integral to the strategy of subcultural autonomy. The religious forces finally triumphed on this point when a new constitution was drawn up and ratified in 1917. Article 208 guaranteed complete government financing of all private primary education. Higher education was not included in these provisions, and, strictly speaking, is not guaranteed support even today. However, with the principle of government responsibility for financing education indelibly sealed in the constitution, subsidies began to be incrementally extended to private secondary education, vocational education, and finally higher education as well.

It was only after Article 208 consecrated the principle of separate and equal school systems that the Catholics established a university at Nijmegen (1923). It thus represented one of the final touches in the process of *verzuiling,* rather than an expression of popular fervor like the VUA. This difference between the two universities has tended to persist, with the VUA remaining more consciously committed to its singular mission, and thus more defensive about its privateness. Two other private institutions date from this same period, but they were both schools of economics (a type that will be considered in chapter 4). The Rotterdam School of Economics (f. 1914) was a nondenominational institution set up with the backing of several large Dutch corporations. The Tilburg School of Economics (f. 1927) was founded by the Catholic Church. Because economics was not a university subject at the time of their founding, and since they were narrowly focused institutions, these schools were designated as "high schools" (*hogescholen*) even though their programs were considered to be university level. It was not until 1939 that they received the right to grant national degrees in economics. The status of Tilburg has remained unchanged, and it confines its teaching to faculties of law, social sciences, and economics. The Rotterdam School of Economics, however, was merged with a state medical school in 1973 to form Erasmus University, and thus is no longer privately controlled.

Nonuniversity postsecondary education in the Netherlands is predominantly private, but also reproduces the pattern of parallel sectors. The reason for this is simply that most of these institutions developed out of secondary education. Their relations with the government regarding funding and regulation consequently derive from the secondary rather than the university sector. Their origins also have left them more tightly embedded in the organizational networks of the *zuilen.* This has been an impediment to recent government efforts to rationalize this sector by consolidating many smaller institutions. From the government's point of view, efficiency would seem to be more important than the principle of private-control; but as yet it has not been able to override opposition within the denominational subcultures. As of 1972 there were sixty-nine private colleges training primary school teachers (out of a total of ninety-three) and some twenty private colleges of social and cultural work.[15] The average sizes were only 240 students in the former, and 300 in the latter. Technical colleges were also largely private—twenty-six of thirty schools—but only six of these were under denominational control.

At least one private school in the Netherlands deserves mention because it falls outside of the prevailing parallel structure. The Nijenrode Business Institute (f. 1946) offers a three-year undergraduate education (to the level of *Candidaatsexamen*) to approximately four hundred residential students. The school is primarily supported by student tuition and contributions from private industry. It thus conforms to the type of advanced business education found in peripheral private sectors (see chapter 4). Its heavy dependence upon student tuition and its residential character make it something of an anomaly in the Netherlands. After lengthy efforts Nijenrode has gained official recognition for its diplomas, and it now receives a subsidy from the state.

Current Policies

The pattern of government funding for private universities developed sooner in the Netherlands than it did in Belgium, and with considerably less acrimony as well. The government began providing very limited subsidies to private universities as early as 1905, and these sums were occasionally supplemented by grants from provinces or municipalities. Still, they remained largely self-supporting until World War II. The decisive change came in 1948 when the government formalized the subsidization of private universities at about 50 percent of their operating costs. This support was prompted, above all, by the formidable capital costs facing the universities both for postwar reconstruction and to maintain credible research efforts in medical and natural sciences. This would seem to be another clear case of dependence on government being brought on by extraordinary capital expenditures. Such arrangements, however, seem inexorably to breed further dependence. Universities can always spawn worthy projects that require new chairs and more buildings, especially when the government can be induced to provide the funds required. In 1960 the government commitment to support the private universities became nearly total as subsidies were raised to 95 percent of expenditures. It is interesting to note that this development was not fueled by rising demand for university education. University enrollments in the Netherlands grew only modestly in the late 1950s, and in 1960 just 2 percent of the nation's twenty-one-year-olds were university students.

As in most other European countries, rapid growth in Dutch higher education occurred in the 1960s. In response to this challenge the government chose to minimize the creation of new institutions. New medical schools proved necessary in Rotterdam (1966) and Maastricht (1975), and technological institutes (*hogescholen*) were added in Eindhoven (1956) and Enschede (1964), but the bulk of the enrollment growth was funneled into the existing universities. This naturally meant considerable additional capital spending, and these sums were no longer a trivial component of the government budget. Nevertheless, the private universities, with about a quarter of total enrollments, only constituted a minor part of the bill for higher education. By the end of the decade (1970) the principle of 100 percent funding for private education was finally extended to the universities.

The evolution to full government funding in itself brought little internal change to the private universities. Historically both public and private universities in the Netherlands have enjoyed an extraordinary degree of autonomy. Under a highly traditional structure of academic governance the faculties were run by the full professors; a largely honorific board of regents oversaw the administrative side of the university; and a *rector magnificus* presided over all.[16] The chief legal difference between state and private universities was whether full professors were appointed by the Crown or by private boards of control. The privates have been guaranteed complete freedom in matters concerning their underlying principles, but in other respects they are bound to comply with state legislation. This last obligation was not, at least before 1970, particularly onerous. The Ministry of Education formulated regulations for the universities in close consultation with an Academic Council, made up of representatives of all the universities. University autonomy depended as well upon the ingrained respect for pluralism in Dutch society and the accommodative climate pervading Dutch political life. These things, too, were altered during the 1970s.[17] Since 1970 the government has assumed an increasingly active role in university affairs, and the independent institutions have had to face the full consequences of their dependence on the state.

Democratization
Government interference in the affairs of the independent Dutch universities has, unlike Belgium, been only an indirect consequence of government financing. The initial and most far-reaching govern-

ment action grew out of the Dutch version of the international student rebellion of the late 1960s. The government's reaction—some would say overreaction[18]—was the University Administration Reform Act of 1970. The complex technicalities of this act are beyond the scope of this study, but its general purpose, to "democratize" the governance of university affairs from subject department (*vakgroep*) to University Council, has profoundly affected university life for public and private institutions alike.[19] Although there has been widespread dissatisfaction with this legislation, it would be disingenuous to see it as the imposition of an insensitive government upon helpless independent universities. The Dutch university protest movement was born at Nijmegen, and the other two private universities were among the most radicalized in the country. By forcing the privates to accept university democracy, the government, in effect, rescued them from the wrath of their own students and junior staff. Nevertheless, the effects of this reform still seem to have been most traumatic for the private universities.

Democratization produced such uncertainties in university life that it became difficult for an institution to speak with a single voice. The boards of control became further removed from university affairs; the rector was forced to operate within a protean political forum; factionalism often reigned in the various elected bodies; while at the same time the administrative staffs dealt surreptitiously with the ministry to ensure the orderly operation of the institution. In an important sense the private universities lost a measure of control, not to their students and staff, but to the dominant factions of university electoral politics. They also had to sacrifice a degree of control to the imperatives of standardization. In the most thorough analysis to date of the consequences of the 1970 reform, Hans Daalder has argued that democratization led ineluctably to bureaucratization.[20] The act itself required innumerable rules to govern elections, to specify the relations of the various boards, and so forth. These rules soon bred more rules to cover the internal behavior of the new organizations, the composition and authority of committees, and more. An additional spate of rule making inexorably followed in order to protect newly acquired power positions, or to correct the excesses of the original rules. In sum, regulations rather abruptly took the place of corporate traditions as the basis of university governance. As a result, mountains of information had to be gathered and circulated, and a considerable staff of professional administrators was required to accomplish this. Moreover, this regulatory activity was set in motion even before the state became concerned with what had always been internal university matters.

Increased Government Influence

The government was led to intervene ever more deeply into the universities by three intertwined issues: the obvious need to place some controls on the expansion of student numbers; the strong case for separating national science policy from dependence upon university expansion; and the inescapable problem of containing university costs.

The decisive action on the first issue was taken in 1973 with the establishment of a *numerus clausus* in such faculties as medicine that had excessive demand and high unit costs. Due to deeply divided opinions concerning admission criteria, a national weighted lottery was instituted as a compromise. One effect of this system has been to deny the universities some of their ability to select students. In 1975 another important piece of legislation aimed to make the universities more productive and efficient. The government hoped to accelerate the languid pace of university study from the current six-year course, which actually takes on average more than seven years to complete, to a four-year course with a six-year maximum limit. University opposition was strenuous and repeatedly delayed implementation of the reform. The gulf separating the two camps illustrates perfectly the prevailing state of university-government relations. The faculties, arraying their defense on their strongest ground, have taken refuge in academic standards. The private universities argue that the state has legal authority only to set minimum standards for national degrees, and thus cannot penalize faculties wishing to exceed them by teaching their students more (and longer).[21] Such legalistic logic does not seem likely to prevent the government, in one way or another, from having its way. Not only are Dutch university customs anachronistic in this age of mass higher education, but the state no longer has the resources to tolerate that degree of inefficiency. The universities' inability to reform themselves has ultimately caused state intervention in the curriculum.

The same reform act of 1975 attempted to establish a more coherent science policy for the Netherlands.[22] A minister of science policy was added to the cabinet, and efforts toward long-range scientific planning were initiated. To the extent that scientific research was a by-product of university teaching, however, the national science effort remained tied to student enrollments. To loosen that connection the government endeavored to force the faculties to undertake more teaching and less research. The funds thereby freed could then be reallocated to targeted research projects. The controversy engendered by this policy has produced a consistent demand for greater accountability from the universities. For this reason and others, the work loads of Dutch university teachers are now determined through complicated time budgets that supposedly set the number of hours to be devoted to each task. In 1978 it was seriously proposed that the academic staff be required to be present on campus from nine to five each working day, and that they punch in and out on time clocks to prove it. More recently the Minister of Education has announced the intention of creating an office of Inspector General, much like the Belgian government delegate, for overseeing university operations and assuring conformance with the law.[23]

Underlying all these developments, of course, has been the government's determination to halt or even roll back the steep escalation in the cost of higher education. Since 1978 university expenditures have been held at a level of no real growth. All new programs therefore had to find support in the reallocation of existing resources. In practice this has caused belt tightening in a number of areas, including requirements that faculty accept increased teaching loads. Expenditures on buildings and maintenance have been radically reduced, much as they have in Belgium. The Dutch government also launched a determined effort to contain the expansionary potential of professorial salaries, which are reputedly the highest in Europe. By preventing promotions in some cases, stretching out promotion schedules in others, and reducing benefits, the government hopes to actually lower the average university salary in the future. This unhappy litany might be continued, but the moral is clear: the government has been led during the past decade—by virtue of its own penury, by the dictates of planning and the rational utilization of resources, and by the inability of the universities to manage their own affairs—to introduce controls affecting the governance, student recruitment, curriculum, and professorial work load of universities.

These government interventions into university affairs have applied equally to state and private universities. From the perspective of private higher education, however, the significant issue is that government control followed closely on the heels of full government funding. The private universities did not have the option to accept or reject these measures—to conform with the state universities or to choose a different course. Private higher education must always operate within legal parameters established by the state. But, as the situation has evolved in the Netherlands, those parameters have become so rigid and so all-encompassing as to all but eliminate significant differences between public and the private sectors.

Parallel Sectors: Paradigm and Actuality

The evolution of parallel public and private sectors in Belgium and the Netherlands appears similar enough to suggest a general paradigm consisting of four stages. At the outset, several conditions seem necessary for the establishment of this type of system. It has already been remarked that legally guaranteed freedom of education and the existence of national degrees are essential for the emergence and equal status of private universities. Also of crucial importance is the nature of sponsorship. Most of the private institutions considered here held religious sponsorship. The major exception, the rationalist university of Brussels, derived from an antireligious movement which, especially given its association with Freemasonry, bore a closer resemblance to a religion than most of its partisans would have cared to admit. Religious or quasireligious, the sponsors of private higher education represented significant cultural groupings of their societies and were also significant politically. Finally, as culturally defined groups, they based themselves upon an entire world view that required for its expression a complete institution of higher education. Such a situation stands in contrast to cases where interest groups sought limited objectives by sponsoring specialized schools, or where institutions of higher education were created privately without cultural differences requiring separation from the government. An example of the former would be the business sponsors of the Rotterdam School of Economics; the latter situation often produced the phenomenon of "civic boosterism," where individuals or groups organized a local school.

The second stage in this pattern stretches from the initiation of regular government subsidies to the point where virtually full public financing of private universities is conceded. This development obviously consists of many discrete political decisions, stretching in these two cases over roughly half a century. Still, behind the circumstances of these decisions lay an implacable logic based upon some old and some new assumptions. Initial assumptions would include the recognition that the provision of private higher education was a public service, the legitimacy of the sponsors entrusted with offering this service, and the requirement that the instruction meet certain high standards for national degrees. Given these, the needed extraordinary capital expenditures go beyond the capacity of self-financing or private philanthropy. Reconstruction of war damage, quantum expansion such as that involved in creating a new campus, and the enormously expensive equipment of modern medical and natural sciences—all these have furnished occasions for these capital needs. What various national situations have in common is that a government refusal to assist the privates would constitute an alteration of the status quo—an inability of the privates to keep up with the standards set by government universities having access to public funds. The state consequently comes under heavy pressure to intervene. Once private universities are heavily dependent upon government allocations, the process becomes, for all practical purposes, irreversible. Welfare-state assumptions about equity in education not only preclude the possibility of greater reliance on student tuition, but eventually substitute additional state subsidies for tuition revenues. By their very nature these developments discourage private philanthropy. Even if it were available in the magnitudes needed, few private donors would support burdens that the state is willing to assume. As a result, pluralist modes of financing, and the flexibility that they facilitate, are gradually eliminated, and private universities become completely reliant upon the seemingly ample resources of the state.

The transition to full government funding has characteristically occurred without substantial internal changes in the life of universities. This gives rise to an ephemeral third stage that has been referred to as a "golden age." Here the privates enjoy the best of both worlds as the government meets almost all their needs without yet having developed the means or the desire to intervene in their affairs. This is consequently a period of rapidly accelerating university expenditures. The large degree of university autonomy that prevails permits institutions or individual faculties to pursue internal goals—to vie with one another in building modern facilities, in adding programs, and in expanding staff without regard to national priorities or the pool of available resources. In the Netherlands, golden-age conditions first appeared after 1960; in Belgium, to some extent, after 1965. For both countries the efflorescence of the golden age was the first half of the 1970s. During these years, it is interesting to note, this process seemed to be sustained by its own considerable inner momentum even after public confidence in universities began to wane. A reckoning was bound to come.

The economic downturn of the mid-1970s and the budget tightening that it induced provided the circumstances that brought the golden age to its inevitable end. The fourth and current stage of this paradigm accordingly includes both full government funding and a substantial imposition of government control. The reasons for this are not wholly financial. It should be obvious that the near-exponential growth rates in university expenditures could not be sustained under any conditions. Many of the government controls were intended to curtail the abuses of the golden-age period and to force economies that universities would not otherwise take. Contemporary governments have nevertheless also felt powerful inducements to replace the traditional laissez-faire university policy with central coordination. This tendency was particularly evident in the Netherlands where the government intruded on university life in order to change the basis of university governance, the distribution of students, and the employment of research funds. In the end, the most painful aspect of this stage for the private universities has been adjusting to the passing of the golden age. With bloated payrolls containing built-in annual increments, growing administrative overhead, and extensive facilities to maintain, the private universities have come to feel increasingly impoverished in spite of their massive subsidies. The final irony is that the erosion of their autonomy has left them without the freedom of action to wrestle with their fate. They have become almost, but not entirely, creatures of the state.

The ambiguity of their situation cannot be dispelled, for it is inherent to the current predicament of these private universities. Accordingly, to assess the consequences of privateness in parallel sectors demands going back from the general paradigm to the specific cases. Despite the structural similarities between Belgium and the Netherlands, there are some significant differences as well, and these differences have a bearing upon the contribution of the privates to their respective systems.

Perhaps most obvious is the sheer difference in the size of these two private sectors. In Belgium 69 percent of university enrollments were in private institutions in 1984, compared to only 22 percent for the Netherlands in 1982.[24] Such a disparity should clearly have an effect on government policy. In Belgium considerations of university policy and university finance are largely made with regard to the private sector, and particularly the four large private universities. The Katholieke Universiteit te Leuven (KUL), Louvain-la-Neuve, and the French and Dutch Free Universities of Brussels together account for 63 percent of Belgian university students. In the Netherlands, however, policy is chiefly formulated for the state universities with the assumption that the privates will be obliged to conform. Differences in the political cultures of the two countries extend to the universities. Although both have been described as consociational democracies, the politics of accommodation are decidedly more contentious in Belgium, probably because of the linguistic cleavage. The evolution of university funding in the two countries illustrates this point. The legacy of these struggles in Belgium seems to have produced a deeper sense of rivalry between institutions, and this has accentuated their distinctive identities. A final significant difference relates to university autonomy. All Dutch universities have traditionally enjoyed a high degree of autonomy. The Academic Council has served as an intermediary between the Ministry of Education and the universities. Government funds have been delivered in lump sums for the universities to spend as they please. In Belgium, though, the state universities have always been closely tied to the government. Appointments or new programs have to be decided in Parliament where factors of partisan politics can be involved. For this reason, Belgian privates have been eager to protect their greater autonomy. No one of these three differences may be conclusive in itself, but all of them point in the same direction: privateness seems to be more important in Belgium than in the Netherlands. One crude corroboration of this is the expanding proportion of private enrollments, which during the 1970s rose from 65 percent to 69 percent, in spite of the creation of new public institutions in Antwerp, Mons, and Limburg. The division of students between the two sectors in the Netherlands, on the other hand, has remained stable in the past decade.

But the most significant criteria for determining the relative vibrancy of private sectors remain more subtle and subjective. They come down to, first, whether private institutions are sufficiently different from their public counterparts to enhance the range of student choice, and hence the overall diversity of the system; and second, whether the independence of the privates contributes to adaptive innovation, thus helping the system as a whole to change with the evolution of its social environment.

It has already been seen how government funding and government controls have created a powerful general trend toward bureaucratic standardization. Within parallel-sector universities the pre-

vailing consensus on academic values generates another strong
tendency toward isomorphism in departments and programs. Diversity, where it exists, must transcend these two pervasive conditions.
Originally, of course, the distinctiveness of private institutions was
rooted in their philosophical orientation. Today in the Netherlands,
however, it would seem that much of the rationale for private higher
education has dissolved. The Free University of Amsterdam has
undoubtedly retained the closest links with its *zuil*. Fervent Calvinists would still probably make a special effort to attend there.
But given the broad tolerance for all views within Dutch universities, and the remoteness of religious dogma from most academic
concerns, the orientation of the VUA would no longer discourage
non-Calvinists from also attending. The two Catholic institutions,
which were less doctrinaire from their beginnings, have been in the
vanguard of a general secularization of the Catholic community.
The Dutch bishops were removed from the Boards of Control in
1948, and are now only distantly connected with the universities.
Catholic preferences are still present in these institutions, but certainly muted. Nijmegen remains a center of Catholic theology, but
Tilburg's connection with Catholicism is far more tenuous. When
the government was considering the creation of an additional medical faculty there was substantial sentiment at Tilburg for becoming
a public institution in order to receive this prize. Ultimately this
possibility was rejected by the Board of Control, but the incident
itself reveals how unimportant privateness is within the institution.
A similar transformation was actually effected at the Rotterdam
School of Economics in 1973, when it was merged with a medical
faculty to form a state university. There the rationale for privateness had largely disappeared, and independence was abandoned
for the sake of administrative convenience. The existing private
universities will probably not reach such a point as long as the
religious cultures retain some importance in Dutch society. On the
other hand, unless those cultures actually regain some of their former importance, the private universities are unlikely to make more
than a marginal contribution to the diversity of the Dutch system of
higher education.

Belgium differs from the Netherlands on just this last point.
Belgian Catholicism has not only remained more traditional than
that of its northern neighbor, but it has also maintained its following, especially in Flanders. Fifty-three percent of the Dutch-
language university students can be found in Catholic institutions,
compared to just over 44 percent of their francophone counterparts.

The Catholic institutions in both halves of the country have done exceedingly well in the no-growth decade of the 1970s, probably because they offer some distinctive qualities to prospective students. The Facultés Universitaires Notre-Dame de la Paix in Namur (54 percent growth from 1971 to 1978), for example, offers residential education under the supervision of Jesuit fathers, some selection to assure the quality of the student body, and personalized instruction in small classes. Saint-Louis and Sint-Aloysius in Brussels (51 percent combined growth, 1971–78), also Jesuit but not residential, provide a similar style of education. For certain students these alternatives offer an easier transition from secondary school to the university, improved chances of success in their candidature, as well as a rigorous preparation for their final university years.[25] Although all four of the original Belgian universities date from the country's first decade, Leuven/Louvain undoubtedly possess the richest organizational saga. The KUL has fallen heir to the physical setting of that saga in Louvain, and has stretched its lead as Belgium's largest university (30 percent growth from 1971 to 1978, compared to 18.5 percent for all Dutch language enrollments). It has been a difficult decade for the UCL, trading the historic stones of Louvain for a construction site in an open field—the stuff, perhaps, from which a future organizational saga will grow. They have nevertheless managed 11 percent growth (1971–78) at a time when francophone university enrollments increased by less than 4 percent. Now that they have each other to compete against, as well as their other rivals, Leuven and Louvain have cultivated what are currently probably the strongest overall research efforts among Belgian universities, and this in spite of the budgetary strangulation of recent years.

The Free Universities of Brussels are clearly the type of secular, urban, private universities that elsewhere have been taken over by the state, as will be seen in the next chapter. The battle for rationalism and free enquiry, their distinctive mission, has after all long been won. The ULB and VUB, however, owe their current existence to their historic role as the counterweight to Catholic higher education. At every critical juncture of its development the Free University has benefited from the political achievement of parity with its larger and stronger rival. This is not to deny the importance of its traditions, its saga; but rather to argue that its distinctive traditions of rationalism, cosmopolitanism, and progressivism are only weakly related to independence from the state. The real strength of the ULB and VUB lie in their near monopoly over complete university education in the capital region. Their privateness depends upon the anticlerical current in a Catholic country. This suggests a facet that should not be overlooked. *Not* being something can sometimes be as important a basis for privateness as distinctiveness in a positive sense. Thus, the enmity that occasionally surfaces between Belgian universities, although lamentable for some purposes, is nevertheless testimony of the existence of differences that matter between institutions—a sign that vitality still exists in the private sector.

The relationship between private control and adaptive innovation in higher education depends upon the structure of incentives for academic change. Such incentives have not been particularly strong for the private universities of the Netherlands. Their very nature, as products of the *verzuiling* process, has tended to rule out interinstitutional competition. Their secure financing and elite character have made them responsive, less to the potential needs of their respective communities, than to the ethos of the Dutch academic community. The result has been a rather pervasive academic conservatism which has asked for little more than the extension of disciplinary domains or the duplication of specialties introduced elsewhere. Since 1969 the democratization of the universities has complicated this situation, superimposing a bewildering array of innovations upon this underlying conservatism. A more important and less ambiguous trend has been the emergence of the Ministry of Education as the principal innovative force in Dutch higher education. Specific efforts to reorganize student recruitment, to shorten the curriculum, etc., have already been mentioned. Perhaps most indicative of the recent activism of the ministry was the "Contours Memorandum," an effort to guide the evolution of the educational system of the Netherlands until year 2000.[26] Government reform efforts, whether actual or speculative, have of course been largely resisted by the entrenched academic conservatism of both public and private universities. It seems safe to conclude, then, that the existence of a private sector in the Netherlands under existing conditions does little to enhance the rate of change.

The situation in Belgium is nearly the reverse. There the expansionary impulses of the private universities were traditionally an inspiration for the creation of new programs. Despite considerable compartmentalization a good portion of potential students exercise discretionary choice, and the universities have competed for their preferment. The golden age for Belgian universities probably fortified the omnipresent tendency toward academic conservatism, but for the large private universities this happy time has definitely passed. They now face severe budgetary pressures, and this is perhaps the most compelling incentive for change. Given the mode of government funding, the most obvious way for an institution to increase its budget is to find more students. The private universities have done this about as well as could be hoped with the prevailing enrollment stagnation. Only recently has austerity prodded them to take a step, unprecedented in Belgium, of seeking nontraditional students. The UCL, ULB, and VUB have now established special degree programs on nights and weekends for working students.[27] Moreover, these programs have been implemented despite obstruction from the Ministry of Education. Wishing above all to avoid additional costs, the ministry at first denied allocations for this type of student. As usual a compromise was reached, but this episode reveals precisely the opposite relationship between the universities and their ministry from that existing in the Netherlands.

Another possible course for alleviating the budgetary squeeze lies through internal planning and rationalization. The most concerted efforts in this direction thus far have been taken by Louvain-la-Neuve. In explicit response to their restricted means and spiraling obligations the UCL adopted an institutional strategy in 1978 for controlling finances and personnel. The priorities of their plan were:

1. to keep the operating budget in balance;
2. to free some funds within this budget to create a "margin of maneuver";
3. to break down rigid categories in order to facilitate internal reallocations of funds; and
4. to lower personnel costs by substituting lower for higher salaried positions.[28]

Here too, it might be noted, the university's efforts have been impeded by the administrative rigidities created by government controls. Although the relative success of this policy remains to be seen, in the Belgian system voluntary, internal planning such as this is only likely to take place within independent institutions. Furthermore, universities that successfully implement such processes will be those most capable of adapting to the exigencies of the future.

In a general sense, the evolution of parallel public and private sectors in Belgium and the Netherlands avoided the two principal drawbacks sometimes associated with private higher education. The willingness of these two governments to assume the financial burdens of private universities assured that a high level of quality would be maintained, and that attendance would not become a privilege of wealth. This development, however, unfortunately compromised some of the positive attributes of privateness. This has left the private universities of the Netherlands barely distinguishable from their public counterparts, and just as ill-disposed to change with the changing times. The private universities of Belgium have been deliberately required to become more like the publics in many ways, and in the process have sacrificed much of their former freedom. Still, they seem to have retained the capacity to resist this trend, especially now that the largesse of the government has proven smaller than expected. For that reason, the evolution of private university-state relations in Belgium has probably yet to run its course. The Belgian privates may one day reach the same condition as those in the Netherlands, but for now they still provide a significant degree of choice for Belgian students and the principal source of leadership for the academic community.

Chapter 4

Peripheral Private Sectors

The scope of peripheral private sectors is largely determined by the extent of the higher education terrain occupied by dominant public sectors. Governments are generally able to utilize their legislative powers and financial resources to assume those educational functions that they consider appropriate for state provision. When these functions are defined in an inclusive manner, private sectors are relegated to those tasks that are neglected by the state. They are forced to operate, in other words, around the periphery of the state system of higher education.

Dominant public sectors generally choose to monopolize the university component of higher education either because of the high level of expenditures required to maintain universities according to internationally recognized standards, or because of the importance of university credentials for state and society. Peripheral private sectors are thus commonly left with a variety of tasks which are, or were until this distinction became blurred in recent years, largely associated with nonuniversity postsecondary education. These have included various kinds of advanced vocational education, and especially training for commerce and private industry. The other principal role of peripheral private sectors can be defined in cultural terms. Groups that are excluded from teaching their beliefs in the public sector establish private institutions to serve their particular cultural needs. Such institutions may be similar to universities, but in contrast to parallel private sectors, legal impediments prevent them from assuming an equivalent status. A significant exception to this general pattern is presented by several unique or singular institutions. Of the three that will be considered, one is an historical case, the second is long-established, and the third is new and developing. But even though each has managed to assume university-level, or in the first two cases elite status, they all have found their niche in specialized roles.

The cases that follow reveal two different routes to the establishment of dominant public sectors. Cultural contention between the state and the Catholic church in nineteenth-century France led the government to attempt to monopolize virtually all forms of higher education. The structure of higher education consequently depended upon the balance of political forces in the country. The triumph of the secular state ultimately forced the fledgling Catholic universities to operate at a considerable disadvantage to the state faculties. They were joined in the private sector by a variety of institutions offering diplomas and certificates in areas not covered by the state's academic hegemony. Once established, this essential pattern has persisted to the present day. In Britain and Sweden, however, a broad consensus over the responsibilities of the welfare state caused a gradual evolution toward total state support of higher education. Nevertheless, both systems currently contain, for quite different reasons, single significant private exceptions. In Sweden the Stockholm School of Economics relied upon its established academic eminence and strong external support to withstand the tide of nationalization, even while reaching accommodations with the state system in numerous other respects. In contrast, Britain's recently formed University of Buckingham was established as a conscious reaction against government domination of the state-supported universities. Each case, then, reveals somewhat different facets of private institutions on the periphery of dominant public sectors.

France: Creating a Private Sector

Given the inertia of educational institutions, the underlying structural issues concerning private higher education rarely enter the realm of public policy decisions. Private schools are born under special circumstances, acquire legitimacy by surviving, and gradually become accepted as parts of the matrix of educational activity. Nations consequently are seldom faced with the question of what type of private sector they might need or prefer. Just such an exceptional episode occurred in nineteenth-century France when a controversy extended more than a decade over whether or not, under what circumstances, and with what probable consequences, private higher education should be allowed to exist. The conjunction of forces that produced this debate was also unusual. In higher education the state monopoly designed by Napoleon I was failing to meet the changing educational needs of the times. The status quo was challenged by two quite different groups. Academic reformers, influenced by a strong current of political liberalism, felt that competition from a private sector would reinvigorate French higher education as a whole. At the same time the Catholic church sought the right to offer higher instruction consistent with its own doctrines. The catalyst for this episode was political volatility. The disastrous war with Prussia brought the downfall of the Second Empire in 1870; then a succession of different regimes governed France over the following decade until a secure republic finally took root. This instability caused events to move faster and more erratically than normal procedures ever would have allowed, even in the comparatively insulated sphere of higher education.

Catholics and liberal academic reformers provided two of the three strands of thought concerning private higher education; the other was supplied by those who defended the statist traditions of France. The arguments of each side encompassed issues of structure, conduct, and results of a hypothetical private sector. Starting from quite different first principles, a consensus was quickly established on the desirability of a change in structure that would include the freedom of private groups to offer higher education. The groups disagreed strongly, however, over how this freedom would operate. Thus, the chief arena of conflict became the potential rules of conduct for the system under the new structure. Finally, with regard to possible outcomes, each faction had different expectations regarding the performance of the system that they advocated. A public debate thus ensued over the merits of three alternative models of private sectors.

The state monopoly over education was officially created by Napoleon in 1806, when he announced the formation of a national corps called the Université that would have responsibility for all education in the empire.[1] The ideas behind this action had their roots in the Enlightenment. Ever since the expulsion of the Jesuits from France (1767) there had been those who argued that the state should bear the responsibility for the education of its citizens, and that a national system of some sort should supplant the rather ad hoc arrangements of the *ancien régime*. The immediate stimulus for Napoleon's action came from the dismal record of the existing state schools, produced in part because those opposed to the empire had been shunning its *lycées* in favor of private instruction. The interests of national unity seemed to dictate that they be brought under the tutelage of the state. Napoleon was able to erect few of the institutions necessary for the *monopole universitaire* during the final years of his empire, but in another way the monopoly was effective. Only the Université could grant the national degrees that were required for entry into the learned professions and certain posts in the state administration. This feature of the Université was to persist, as were the perceptions of national interest that lay behind its creation in the first place. Over the next half century its institutional basis was gradually elaborated as well.

By 1860 each educational district outside of Paris possessed a *lycée* for secondary education, accompanied by faculties of letters and science. These latter bodies were integral parts of the Université, but they bore little relation to higher education as it was known elsewhere in the world.[2] Their chief function was to conduct baccalaureate examinations for students who had completed secondary school. That function largely determined their form; and that form was consequently ill-suited for anything else. The faculties of letters and sciences had no real students to teach, and could not even supply the requisite number of qualified secondary school teachers needed in the state schools. Their total preoccupation with the culture of the baccalaureate left them quite remote from higher learning as it was cultivated elsewhere. At a time when the scholarly prowess of German universities was receiving worldwide acclaim, only a handful of scholars in Paris was keeping France from becoming a backwater in the world of modern science.

Reforms of the 1860s

This was the situation that gave rise to the academic reform movement in the 1860s.[3] The chief objective of the scholars responsible for it was to regenerate French science, broadly speaking, to meet the standard then being set by the Germans. What was needed for this, they soon concluded, were true universities that would both unify the branches of knowledge now cloistered within unattached faculties and allow professors and students to pursue advanced learning. For French liberals of the period this idealistic view dovetailed nicely with the concerns being raised about freedom of higher education.[4] Private universities became for them the key to reform. Independent institutions might be the first to raise the standards of French scholarship, but this would in turn force the state to reorganize its faculties into viable competitors. The result would eventually be parallel public and private sectors, each composed of a number of autonomous institutions. High academic standards and fruitful scholarly research would be assured by the competition between these units, much as it then was in Germany. Such a scenario was obviously contingent upon a number of circumstances, including the right of these future private universities to grant legal degrees. Nevertheless, given the liberal faith in human initiative and the free interplay of ideas, this was a compelling vision of the future of French higher education around the year 1870.[5]

French Catholics never accepted the principle of the *monopole*, but their overt opposition waxed and waned with the tide of events. An intense campaign during the 1840s for the right to provide secondary education bore fruit in the Falloux Law of 1850; private schools were permitted, but the state retained the exclusive authority to grant degrees. Higher education was scarcely important then, and it remained of small moment until changing attitudes in Rome deemed otherwise. The increasing militancy of the Church under Pope Pius IX was an essential factor in raising this controversy. In 1864 the Vatican published a "Syllabus of the Principal Errors of Our Time," which condemned, among other things, liberalism, rationalism, and public education. This was followed in 1870 by the declaration of papal infallibility. In between, a letter was sent to all bishops "regretting" state domination of higher education, and asking what could be done "to bring about an appropriate remedy to so great an evil and to assure faithful Christians the benefit of a Catholic education."[6] A campaign was duly launched in France with a petition alleging atheism and materialism in the state faculties (1867). This succeeded in prompting an acrimonious debate in the Senate (1868). Although this rather inauspicious beginning considerably polarized the entire issue, it soon became apparent that liberty of higher education was likely to be enacted in one form or another.

Given the hyperbole on this subject, it is not easy to determine just what kind of private sector the Church realistically hoped to achieve. Certainly it did not want complete liberty, so that socialists, positivists, and other types that the "Syllabus of Errors" called "pests" could expound their doctrines as higher education. And clearly it wanted more than simply the right to open Catholic faculties. Perhaps either of two solutions would have been acceptable to the church hierarchy: a system in which both state and Catholic institutions coexisted, but with Church involvement in the surveillance, control, and degree-granting process for all higher education; or, a more compartmentalized system in which Catholic institutions were free of state controls and could grant their own legal degrees.[7] The first type would have the advantage of allowing the Church to keep noxious theories out of the public faculties, but even more vital was the point of conduct found in both versions: that the certification of education according to Catholic doctrines be kept in Catholic hands. This was the point on which the state was most reluctant to compromise.

By the late 1860s the Second Empire was willing to grant Catholics the same rights in higher education that they enjoyed for secondary education. The Minister of Education suggested legislation to this effect in 1867, only to have it vehemently rejected by representatives of the Church.[8] The ensuing campaign by the Catholics, together with the Emperor's desire for Catholic political support, led to the appointment of a commission in 1870 for the purpose of designing a compromise on the liberty of higher education. In spite of the disruptions of the Franco-Prussian War and the change of regimes, the efforts of this commission carried over to the new National Assembly and provided a basis for considering definitive legislation on this issue. The National Assembly, however, was an exceptional body. Elected in the aftermath of defeat to negotiate a peace and establish a new government, it began with a monarchist majority and decided clerical proclivities. An overwhelming proportion favored liberty of higher education in some form. Defenders of the Université thus found themselves in the unusual position of underdogs, forced to justify continued state control over higher education to unsympathetic opponents.

Law of 1875

Since the state faculties were principally examining bodies, the chief justification for their control of degrees rested on the issue of standards. It was the inherent and inalienable duty of the state, it was argued in countless variations, to safeguard high standards of entry into the learned professions. Competition between degree-granting institutions, from this statist perspective, could only prove destructive by drawing students to the schools with the easiest degrees. Another fear was that a dual system of education would divide the country's elite, contributing further to national disunity. After the moderate Thiers government was replaced in 1873 with more conservative leadership, the expectations of liberal reformers were no longer tenable. It became clear by this time that the sole beneficiary of liberty of higher education would be the Church—the single organization with the resources to sponsor full-scale universities. Moreover, no government with the political complexion of the Assembly would be likely to renovate the state faculties to meet this competition. The issue was thus polarized along clerical/anticlerical lines when the clerical forces took advantage of a slim parliamentary majority to produce a law granting freedom of higher education.[9]

The higher education law of 1875 created a breach in the *monopole* representing the maximum advance that French Catholics could manage against the statist traditions of the Université.[10] It was clearly tailored to their conceptions of a private sector, but even then gave them only partial satisfaction on the principal issues. At the heart of this legislation was a compromise on the granting of degrees. Students of qualified independent faculties could choose to be examined by "mixed juries" containing an equal number of professors from state and independent faculties. To be qualified, an institution had to possess at least three full faculties, not including theology, and it could then also assume the title of university. Catholics were virtually assured of being the only beneficiaries of these provisions. They succeeded in discouraging competition somewhat further, if only slightly, with some weak controls over independently offered courses. Also, by an anterior law in 1873 they were granted representation on the Conseil Supérieur de l'Instruction Publique, which exercised oversight over the entire Université. These conditions, then, were sufficient to bring French Catholics enthusiastically into the enterprise of higher education. At Lille classes were begun in 1874 in anticipation of the new law; immediately following enactment, faculties of law were established in Paris, Lille, Lyon, and Angers; in the next two years enough other faculties were added to constitute Catholic universities in those four cities, with another in the process of formation in Toulouse. But hopes of creating a parallel Catholic private sector were soon dashed. The concessions French Catholics so narrowly won in the political arena were abruptly lost in the same place.

As soon as republicans were securely in control of all levels of government they set about undoing the work of the National Assembly. In 1880 legislation was passed restoring the state's monopoly over degrees. Mixed juries were abolished, and henceforth students of the Catholic faculties seeking national degrees would have to be examined within the Université. External members were also removed from the Conseil Supérieur, restoring it to the status of a corporate body of the Université. And, in a symbolic action with considerable meaning for both sides, independent institutions were forbidden to take the title of university. These changes in the law only affected the Catholic institutions established under the provisions of the 1875 law. Having entered into the enterprise of higher education in the expectation that they could compete with state faculties on nearly equal terms, they were now forced to operate under conditions that they would have rejected as intolerable only a few years before. But where these institutions were already established, closing down was unthinkable as well. Catholic higher education thus persisted in a role it had previously shunned—as peripheral accompaniment to a dominant state system of higher education.

Division of Tasks

The long controversy over freedom of higher education in France and the 1880 law that marked its culmination determined the division of tasks between the public and private sectors in France. By monopolizing the granting of national degrees the state effectively handicapped all competitors to its own faculties. The Université in effect had first choice over the programs and degrees it wished to offer. Thus it naturally continued to dominate the traditional disciplines in letters and sciences, as well as education for the professions of law, medicine, and pharmacy.[11] Everything else was left to the periphery of the Université, the territory where private institutions could operate without handicap.

The development of Catholic higher education in France reveals some of the consequences of unequal competition with a dominant public sector. Considering the rhetoric on the need for Catholic education, and the oaths sworn by professors to teach in accordance with the infallible doctrines of the Holy See, it is somewhat ironic that their course work differed little from that found in the state faculties. Programs for the examinations in law and medicine were sufficiently overloaded to permit little room for additional Catholic material. At Lille a course in Christian Apologetics was worked into the medical curriculum, and the Catholic law faculties found places for Canon Law and Natural Law. Even in letters, where there was much less rigidity, the new faculties offered comparatively few innovations.[12] Presumably, the prescribed subjects were taught in a different spirit within the Catholic faculties, but the contents on which students would be examined nevertheless had to be the same.

During the few years that French higher education operated under the 1875 law it appeared quite likely that a parallel Catholic sector would develop to serve a clientele that only partly overlapped with that of the state. The few letters and science students in the state faculties were preparing for careers in the Université, while their Catholic counterparts were largely recruited from the seminaries. Where they did vie for the same enrollments, as in some law faculties, the Catholic institutions made a promising start. The Catholic law faculty in Paris examined 329 students in 1878, many of whom were undoubtedly attracted from the two thousand plus students in the state faculty; and in Lyon the Catholic law faculty had only slightly fewer enrollments than the faculty hastily created by the government (1875) as its competitor.[13] However, the situation changed abruptly as soon as mixed juries were abolished. The faculties mentioned above promptly lost half of their enrollments. The letters and science faculties, far more marginal operations, in some cases ceased to be viable units. In Paris they were demoted to the status of *école libre,* and in 1889 the Toulouse faculties were forced to close completely. Enrollments in all Catholic institutions fell from a high near 3,000 in 1878 to just 838 in 1884. The only significant exception to this pattern was the Catholic faculties at Lille. That city was the only locale to establish a medical faculty, and thus the only independent organizers ever to group together the components of a full university—five faculties including theology. The Lille faculties found consistent support in the strongly Catholic populace and also benefited from the immeasurable advantage of priority. At the time the Catholic faculties were established, the state faculties of law and letters for the Academy of Lille were located twenty miles away in Douai. Neither moving those faculties to Lille (1887) nor establishing a state medical faculty (1876) were able to threaten the existence of the Catholic institution.

The peripheral status of the Catholic faculties tended to reinforce their original purpose. The religious universities of Belgium and the Netherlands underwent considerable secularization as they became more and more absorbed with disciplinary knowledge, but in France it was precisely those areas that were most effectively dominated by the public sector. The Catholic faculties were consequently continually motivated to emphasize their Catholicism as their chief *raison d'être* and their main source of attraction for students. The faculties of theology thus became the true intellectual centers of these institutions. Being peripheral, then, enhanced the distinctiveness of Catholic higher education and precluded convergence toward a common model. It was this distinctiveness that eventually assured the Catholic faculties of a permanent role in French higher education. In the mid-1880s it seemed that, with the possible exception of Lille, the Catholic institutions without mixed juries had been unable to compete with the state; but from that nadir their fortunes gradually improved. From 1884 to 1913 Catholic enrollments rose by 142 percent compared to a somewhat better 175 percent rise in state faculties. Instead of competing with the state, the Catholic faculties were restricted to a special clientele that sought higher education under the auspices of the Church.

The Private Sector in 1914

That the public and the private sectors in France now had their own distinctive spheres of interest was confirmed in an interesting manner on the eve of World War I. During the anticlerical fervor that swept France in the wake of the Dreyfus Affair, a law was proposed to abolish freedom of higher education. A commission of inquiry established by the Senate took a leisurely twelve years to investigate this issue before reporting that there was no justification for taking such action.[14] The most distinguished and committed *universitaires* testified to the commission that they had nothing to fear from the Catholic faculties. Those institutions served the special purposes of the Church and the faithful, and thus bore no comparison with the universities of the state. Testimony from the leaders of the Catholic faculties carried the same message. Proud as they were of the accomplishments of their institutions, they recognized that the dream of 1875 had not been realized. They had envisioned a set of Catholic universities similar to Louvain in Belgium, but in fact only the faculties of Lille gave any hint of that ideal. For the most part they had lost their lay students to the state faculties. Notably absent in these testimonies were the passions that surrounded the issue of the freedom of higher education in the 1870s. A generation of experience, it would seem, had molded a peripheral private sector that was compatible with the existence of a dominant public system of higher education.

The Senate report of 1914 also provides a convenient, if not exhaustive, overview of the institutions that sprouted in France's peripheral private sector. The Catholic faculties were unique in their ambition to emulate the public sector; all the others limited their scope to specific tasks. Many initiatives proved ephemeral. The report notes that in Paris alone, since 1875, "24 establishments and 56 courses were opened; [but] 8 establishments and 50 courses have since been closed." In the latter category were five courses dealing with skin diseases, part of the many ephemeral private offerings emanating from the Paris Faculty of Medicine. Destined to join this instructional graveyard was an independent school of aerostation, or ballooning. Some institutions clearly served the private purposes of specific groups, such as the religious seminaries that became *écoles libres de théologie*. Then there were certain tasks that the state did not wish to undertake: hence, five schools for notaries (an office of considerable importance in France). However, many of the independent schools were more closely related to the activities of the Université. Municipally backed free faculties of law were established in Marseilles, Nantes, and Clermont-Ferrand to provide a service that the state was unwilling to extend. Three Parisian schools were intended to supplement the Université intellectually in the social sciences (Ecole d'anthropologie, College libre des sciences Sociales, and L'Ecole des hautes etudes sociales). A similar effort, L'Institut Psycho-physiologique, was set up because demonstrations of hypnosis were forbidden in the Paris Medical Faculty. Some tasks managed to straddle both sectors, especially when there was some question about their academic status. Thus, a number of private schools of dentistry were established before the Paris Medical Faculty finally established instruction in this area in 1913. In a different twist, several provincial science faculties established institutes for electricity (*instituts electrotechniques*), but the august Paris Faculty of Science left so practical a subject for three private schools in the capital.[15] Taken together, then, it becomes evident how this diverse collection of offerings compensates for rigidities and lacunae in the monopolistic Université.

Not included in the Senate report were some fourteen *écoles supérieures de commerce* that had been established under the Third Republic.[16] They may have been omitted because they were not considered to be higher education, or possibly because they were not sufficiently private. They are worth mentioning in this context despite their ambiguous status because of their subsequent importance for the private sector. Although the original school of commerce was opened in Paris in 1820, it did not inspire any imitators until the 1870s. Then local notables began to sponsor such schools either through the chambers of commerce and industry (CCI) or as joint stock ventures (and sometimes both). With the partial exception of the Ecole des Hautes Etudes Commerciales (HEC) established by the Paris CCI in 1881, these schools were not on a very high level. They recruited students as young as thirteen for what amounted to secondary schooling, and the final two years of commercial studies were intended for students aged sixteen to eighteen. Nor were they very popular—at least until the military law of 1889. By making commerce school students eligible for the student exemption from military service, that legislation brought to the

schools both sudden prosperity and a large dose of government regulation. Schools now had to recruit their students by competitive
examinations (*concours*) and rank them upon graduation, for example, in order to qualify them for exemption. In the decade following
this law seven additional schools were established, and almost all
had more candidates than places. This bubble burst in 1905 when a
new military law abolished the student exemption. Enrollments
plummeted, and new government regulations reflected this by relaxing entry standards. Proponents of commercial education con-
soled themselves that at least the remaining students were there to
learn the subject. There can be little doubt, however, that the elimination of student exemptions retarded the promotion of commercial
schools to the status of higher education. A detailed international
analysis of this area on the eve of World War I concluded that
France's higher commercial schools were merely advanced vocational training (*enseignment moyen*). The single exception was the
Ecole des hautes études commerciales, which could withstand comparison with the schools of economics of Germany and northern
Europe. By 1913, two-thirds of the students at the HEC were
bacheliers (held baccalaureate degrees), and measures were being
taken to raise admission standards further.[17]

A Singular Institution: Ecole Libre des Sciences Politiques

One private institution in France was able to claim a prominent
place on the higher educational map. The Ecole Libre des Sciences
Politiques was a rather special case whose history reveals some
additional dimensions of peripheral private sectors. *Sciences Po,* as
it came to be known, was the serendipitous legacy of the widespread
liberal belief of the early 1870s in the reform of French higher
education through private initiative. Not only was its founder and
guiding force, Emile Boutmy, a partisan of this view, but he also
recruited other prominent liberals to be among the school's founders.[18] Deeply shocked by the failure of French leadership, so evident
in the defeat by Prussia, Boutmy dedicated himself to organizing an
education for an elite who would set the tone of the nation—"to
remake the head of the people."[19] In the aftermath of the war he
wrote to the Minister of Education asking permission to establish a
"faculté libre d'enseignement supérieur" that he originally envisioned as an alternative to the state faculties. Despite considerable
backing in Protestant financial circles, the resources that could be
gathered privately were quite insufficient for such an undertaking.

Also, the status of freedom of higher education then being in limbo, Boutmy was granted permission only to start an *école,* rather than a rival to the state *facultés.* Accordingly, he chose to concentrate on those areas that were not being offered in the state faculties—diplomacy, recent history, administration, finance, and economics; subjects, in short, that could instruct the present and future ruling class about the actual conduct of affairs of state. On this basis, then, the Ecole Libre des Sciences Politiques opened its doors to eighty-nine students in 1872. That same year an unrelated development profoundly affected the destiny of the school.

In an effort to depoliticize the highest administrative corps of the state, a law was passed requiring the Council of State, the Court of Accounts, the Financial Inspectorate, and the Diplomatic Corps each to organize its own recruitment through *concours.* Students of the Ecole were immediately drawn to these competitions. These *grands corps* of the state administration tended to be the exclusive preserve of the Parisian *haute bourgeoisie.*[20] The Ecole had been from the first explicitly pitched toward this same affluent stratum, and was even placed in their midst near the fashionable Boulevard Saint-Germain. In 1877 graduates of the Ecole won eleven of seventeen places awarded in these *concours,* and Boutmy seemingly awoke to this new possibility for his creation. He added teachers with direct experience in the corps, touted the success of Ecole graduates in the *concours,* and in a few years was declaring that the special purpose of the Ecole was to prepare students for these careers. Boutmy's success was astonishing. From 1899 to 1939, 657 of 716 places filled by *concours* in the four *grands corps* (92 percent) went to former Ecole students.[21] The anomalous feature of this remarkable record was that, given the administrative culture of France, the function that the Ecole nearly monopolized clearly belonged in the public sector.

During the short-lived Second Republic the government had attempted to organize such instruction in a national school of administration (1848–49), only to have it quickly suppressed by Louis Napoleon. A campaign for its reestablishment was waged during the 1870s, and very nearly culminated in the nationalization of the Ecole. A bill to this effect was killed in committee, however, after having passed the Chamber of Deputies in 1881. The quirk that saved the school was its unusual financial organization. It had been set up as a regular joint-stock corporation (*société anonyme*) with the understanding that no profits would ever be distributed. (It was thus a not-for-profit organization in an era before exemption from taxation was an important consideration.) The members of the budget committee apparently saw no reason to reimburse the shareholders for their capital when the school was operating satisfactorily as an independent entity. Although the school continued to be resented for different reasons by the law faculties and by the political left, its independent existence was not threatened again until the Popular Front government of the 1930s. Then another bill to nationalize it (1939) was engulfed by the war. Not until 1945, when the Ecole was badly compromised by its association with the Vichy regime, was the Ecole replaced by the Institut d'Etudes Politiques de Paris (still dubbed *Sciences Po*), and a more advanced national school of administration that prepared students directly for the upper civil service. Ironically, the school that had been created to rectify the failure of French leadership in an earlier war with Germany now bore some of the responsibility for just as grievous a failure in another German war.

Although the Ecole passed out of existence on a rather sour note, and its unabashed elitism has scarcely endeared it to posterity, its accomplishments as a private institution are still impressive. It quickly gained recognition for the distinction of its professors and the quality of its teaching. Many of the men of affairs selected as professors by Boutmy, like the diplomatic historian Albert Sorel, blossomed into acclaimed scholars and teachers. The practice of recruiting eminent figures as adjunct faculty further enriched the offerings. From its outset the school was a striking innovation, and over the course of its history it forged into new areas of foreign affairs, social science, and business education. Finally, the evergrowing popularity of the school was evidence that it fulfilled significant tasks. Enrollment grew to over 250 in the school's first decade, more than 600 by the turn of the century, and upwards of 1,300 in the mid-1920s. In its first fifty-five years more than 16,000 students frequented its courses. Of this total perhaps no more than one in twenty found their way to any of the *grands corps*. These were rather special students, for the most part, who were largely selected on the basis of their family pedigree. They then spent an additional year at the Ecole being individually groomed for one of the *concours*.

The remainder of the Ecole students fall into a number of categories that are themselves indicative of the nature of the school. A significant number of students undoubtedly used the Ecole as a springboard to state administrative posts outside the *grands corps*. This group probably overlapped with the large proportion of the school's population that was simultaneously enrolled in the Paris

Faculty of Law. An association with the Ecole for these students could both complement their legal studies and pave the way for an administrative career. Over time the school also developed close ties with private industry. A separate subsection on private finance emerged as a kind of prototypical business school, and by the mid-1920s it enrolled 40 percent of the school's students. The Ecole was always proud of the attraction it held for foreign students, who at most times provided a significant contingent. And never lacking from its rolls was the clientele Boutmy had originally envisaged—members of the leisure class interested in expanding their knowledge of public affairs. The Ecole thus fulfilled a variety of functions; however, it fulfilled them principally for the constituency for whom it had been created.

The Ecole was completely open to anyone over seventeen years of age wishing to enroll, yet it was also probably the most socially exclusive institution of higher education in France. One must look beyond the stiff tuition (three hundred francs in the nineteenth century; one thousand francs by 1927) to explain this paradox. In fact the school existed within a network of social relations centering upon the Parisian haute bourgeoisie and virtually impenetrable to outsiders.[22] This exclusiveness was embodied in the location of the school, its coldly formal ambience, and the prevailing tone of elitism. But perhaps the most crucial element was the basic purpose of the school itself. A diploma from the Ecole, unlike a national degree, possessed no intrinsic legal value. It only became valuable "currency" when combined with other requisite social attributes. In the case of the *grands corps,* for example, candidates were screened thoroughly on the basis of their social background and political associations before being even admitted to the *concours.* Such family connections counted elsewhere in the administration as well. Private industry was no different. French business firms tended to be dominated by the families that founded them. The scholarships they provided to the Ecole were usually reserved for the sons of employees, undoubtedly in the expectation that they too would join the firm. The Ecole, then, formed the mentality and certified the capacity of those who were already socially eligible to assume elite positions in industry or government. Unlike the Université, it made little pretense of meritocracy; rather it was pervaded by confidence in the inherent right to leadership of the class that it served.[23]

There is little point in criticizing the social exclusiveness of the Ecole simply from the standpoint of contemporary democratic values. Its faults were those of its times and its milieu (to paraphrase one of its inspirational figures, Hippolyte Taine). Its status as an independent institution, however, tended to insulate the school from other currents within French society, and thus to preserve its particular biases. The deleterious effects of such insularity are most evident in the ideology of the school. From its founding the school's curriculum was pervaded by the conservative liberalism of the 1870s: laissez-faire economics; a strong measure of anglophilia, with particular admiration for the British ruling class and their colonial exploits; and, slightly later, the congenial social science of Frédéric Le Play with its emphasis on social hierarchy. All this, when it was not being taught explicitly, was dissolved into the numerous courses covering the then-recent history of international relations, economics, or statecraft. While these doctrines were probably as credible as their competitors during the first two decades of the school's existence, they were becoming decidedly anachronistic by the *fin-de-siècle,* and were virtually antediluvian in the wake of World War I. Only in its last years did the school's ideology begin to shift toward a more technocratic stance. The gradual ossification of the school's doctrines, however, actually meant that it was increasingly failing at its avowed purpose. Rather than providing the French elite with a sophisticated understanding of the political world, by the twentieth century the Ecole was contributing to their isolation: it was powerfully reinforcing their assumptions about society, economy, and polity—and their own roles therein.

It may be natural for private institutions to fortify the values of their sponsors, but what made this case pernicious was the existence of a near monopoly. Given the highly restrictive mode of recruitment to the upper civil service, the ideology of the Ecole became the ideology of the *grands corps.* But even within higher education the monopoly achieved by the Ecole subverted the original intention of its founders. The liberals of 1870 had hoped that liberty of higher education would foster pluralism, competition, and excellence. The creation of the Ecole did succeed in adding diversity to the already rich intellectual resources of the capital. However, its very success stifled potential competitors. The school became another monopolist in the rigidly compartmentalized intellectual terrain of French higher education. The law faculties were precluded from branching out into administration and political science, and only added economics with some difficulty in the 1890s. When schools of economics spread across northern Europe early in the twentieth century (as described in the following section on Sweden)

France remained unaffected: the *grands patrons* of French industry had the Ecole Libre des Sciences Politiques.[24]

The peripheral private sector that developed after 1870 around the fringes of the Université undertook those tasks that the state neglected and catered to constituencies who were ill-served by the state. In the case of the Ecole, however, it clearly preempted one of the elite functions of higher education, a function normally, and in this case ultimately, claimed by the state. Priority was obviously an important factor in this, as was the intimate relationship between the Ecole and the social milieu it served. However, the principle that this example suggests transcends these circumstances: peripheral private sectors are not merely left with the scraps of higher education. There are certain tasks that private institutions can accomplish more effectively and more efficiently, particularly when compared with the large and often lethargic organizational structures of dominant public sectors. This will be borne out by surveying this same peripheral private sector in present-day France, a century after its birth.

Present Anatomy of the French Peripheral Private Sector

The essential character of the private sector in France has changed little from what it was at the beginning of the century, but the topography of the sector has altered markedly. Formerly, its chief feature was Catholic higher education; also highly visible was the unique Ecole Libre des Sciences Politiques. But the other complementary private institutions of higher education were seldom noticed unless one were directly involved in their particular domains. The Ecole, as mentioned, was nationalized in 1945; the Catholic institutions have continued to develop along the track established in the nineteenth century; and a variety of special schools still complement the offerings of the state system. Yet, today, the landscape of private higher education in France is dominated by business education and those subjects closely related to it.

This state of affairs first required that business education be "promoted" into the universe of postsecondary education. For the schools of commerce that had been founded in the nineteenth century this upgrading occurred in the interwar years. Only gradually since the 1950s has the same thing happened to the short-cycle courses that provide technical training. The next step was the expansion in demand for this type of instruction. Finally, the negative condition for this development was the inability, until quite recently, of the public universities to enter this domain. Interestingly, this last condition has changed during the 1970s. Now, for the first time in a century, parts of the state universities find themselves in implicit competition with a viable private sector.

Table 5 breaks down the population of French higher education into public and private sectors by type of institution. These enrollment figures are only approximate: enrollments in religious institutions are estimated, and also include some students counted in other categories. Because of the nature of the French system there is some unavoidable double counting in the state universities as well; and membership in the category of *grandes écoles* is never quite the same from year to year. Nevertheless, these figures give an accurate enough indication of the dimensions of France's private sector. To appreciate what specific tasks this sector has been allowed to fulfill, however, one must look within each type of institution.

The five Catholic institutions that constitute the French equivalent of private universities are the same ones that were founded in the 1870s, including the once moribund institution in Toulouse. They are independent of one another, and over the years have assumed completely different forms and titles. Lille, a university by any definition, calls itself the "Fédération Universitaire et Polytechnique de Lille," while Angers with only a faculty of theology and an assortment of *écoles* and institutes has taken the name "L'Université Catholique de l'Ouest." In their essential functions,

TABLE 5. Enrollments in the Public and Private Sectors in France by Type of Institution, 1977

	Public	Private	% Private
Universities and associated institutes	821,591	32,000	4
Sections de techniciens supérieurs	33,296	15,056	31
Classes préparatoires des grandes écoles	33,539	3,230	9
Grandes écoles (1977–78)			
Engineering	26,719	8,297[b]	23
Commerce	(1,672)[a]	11,199[b]	87
Other	48,930	4,158	8
Total *grandes écoles*	75,729	23,574	24
Total	964,155	73,940	7

Source: Adapted from Ministère des Universités, *Statistiques des enseignements* (Paris: 1978).

[a]Schools of commerce included in universities.

[b]Includes *grandes écoles* within Catholic universities.

however, they are far more alike. Their peripheral status has continued to fortify their bonds with the Church and the Catholic community in France. The academic core of each institution serves those interested in studying subjects connected with religion, or students wishing to pursue secular disciplines in a Christian ambience. Nevertheless, the financial imperatives of institutional survival have combined with the exigencies of peripheral status to pull these institutions in other directions. The search for students and tuition revenue have led them to adopt a variety of service tasks for the Catholic community (social work, teacher training, physical education), for local industry (commerce, engineering, agriculture, technical skills), and recently for nontraditional students (summer schools, language institutes, special courses). Such variety obviously produces an extremely heterogeneous "student body," if one can even use this term. Their clientele ranges from non-*bacheliers* and working adults taking special courses to pupils of elite *grandes écoles* and doctoral students. Because some programs are designed for part-time students, and also because many students use the Catholic institutions to supplement their education in the state universities, a large part of this enrollment represents less than full-time students. Toulouse, the only institution providing this information, reported 56 percent part-time students.[25]

The legal position of the Catholic institutions has not changed since 1880, but their inability to grant national degrees is no longer the handicap it once was. Their development into the service areas mentioned above has largely involved fields not covered by national degrees. Here they either give "certificates of completed studies" on their own authority, or, as in the *grandes écoles,* grant diplomas "officially recognized by the state." In subjects pertaining to religion they grant degrees on the authority of their ecclesiastical charters, it being irrelevant that these are not recognized by the state. The Catholic universities still prepare some of their students for national degrees, and this procedure has been facilitated by the reorganization of the state university system since 1968. The Orientation Law of that year authorized state universities to sign conventions with private institutions covering programs and inscriptions of candidates for national degrees. Many such agreements were subsequently negotiated in a manner to assure private students an equitable chance on their examinations while also guaranteeing the Catholic universities control over their programs.[26] These institutions have some other limited connections with the state. A few units, for example, cooperate in research efforts funded by the Centre National de Recherche Scientifique. Their students, like those in most other private institutions, are eligible for official student status, which confers social security benefits and a variety of student discounts for meals, transportation, and entertainment. Thus, the Catholic universities recently passed their centennials operating without great disadvantage on the periphery of the state system of higher education. Lacking the resources, the public backing, and probably the desire to provide mass higher education, they have been thriving in their own particular niche by fulfilling a broad variety of specialized tasks.

Short-cycle technical higher education is organized in two separate systems with quite different origins. The *sections de techniciens supérieurs* (STSs) are a creation of technical secondary education that graduated into the postsecondary realm. First established in 1952, they provide two years of practical technical postsecondary education within existing secondary schools, both public and private. Then in 1966, in a major centrally inspired innovation, the Ministry of Education created *instituts universitaires de technologie* (IUTs), which offered similar—though somewhat more theoretical—two-year programs within a university context. It was widely expected that IUTs would eventually supplant STSs, but this has not been the case. In fact, during the 1970s the IUTs have responded to the increasing demand for short-cycle education by becoming more selective. The STSs have consequently expanded more rapidly, and now count the majority of short-cycle enrollments. The role of private institutions has been one of the factors contributing to the vitality of this sector, and the private presence there has been strengthened by its links with the secondary system.

The STS programs lead to a *brevêt de technicien supérieur* (BTS), which is somewhat different from other degrees in higher education. The BTS is awarded on the basis of nationally conducted examinations organized by the Ministry of Education, much like the baccalaureate exams. At last count the ministry had authorized some eighty different specialities for the BTS. Preparation for an exam of this type can be done within state or Catholic technical *lycées,* in a large number of private schools specializing in preparation for the BTS, or even through self-study. Thus, this is an area in which the private sector can assume a significant role. As table 5 has shown, their fifteen thousand students in 1976 represented nearly a third of these enrollments. However, this figure actually represents two different forms of independently organized programs.

The seventy Catholic technical *lycées* that prepare the BTS are little different from their public counterparts. Essentially they offer postsecondary instruction in those subjects already taught in the *lycée*. Nor is their tuition much different. These institutions are unique in the French private sector in that they qualify for direct government subsidies under the terms of the Debré Law (1959), which provides for government support for Catholic schools. This legislation expressly forbids the subsidization of higher education, but the Catholic *lycées,* as part of technical secondary education, nevertheless qualify. The other types of private short-cycle programs are those organized in small specialized schools. Some of these schools have been organized by local chambers of commerce and industry to satisfy local needs, but others are private proprietary institutions. This last category is primarily devoted to business-related skills, preparing for the BTS in secretarial skills, accounting, or commerce. The first two of these programs together account for almost half of the students aspiring to a BTS, meaning that they also include large enrollments in the public sector. The programs in which the private sector has a larger than average proportion of enrollments are (in order of size), secretarial training (41 percent), commerce (47 percent), laboratory technicians (45 percent), home economics (58 percent), electronics (35 percent), and tourism/public relations (71 percent).[27]

One of every ten French *bacheliers* chooses to enter higher education in a *classe préparatoire des grandes écoles*. In this unique French institution many of the most capable secondary school graduates remain in a *lycée* for an additional two years of intensive schooling in preparation for entrance examinations to the *grandes écoles*. Almost two-thirds of these students study one of the mathematics curricula, nearly 20 percent are in letters, and better than 10 percent prepare for the elite commercial schools (a one-year preparation, often repeated).[28] This is a highly competitive sector where the ability to get students admitted to prestigious *grandes écoles* is the mark of institutional success, which in turn is necessary to attract enough students to operate this specialized and intensive form of instruction on an adequate scale. The private share of this market, although increasing, was only about 11 percent in 1978. With these classes concentrated in the Paris area and in the most prominent state *lycées,* Catholic secondary schools have had difficulty competing. Where they have been able to establish *classes préparatoires* it has usually been in only one or two carefully chosen programs. A few private institutions devoted exclusively to this form of instruction have flourished. Each of them tends to employ its own formula for success. The Jesuit Ecole Saint-Geneviève in Versailles has one of the largest offerings of classes, and boasts the third best record in all of France on the major *concours*. The Institut de préparation aux études supérieures organizes only a single class for the commercial *concours*, but almost all of its students are successful. The Institution Frilley pursues the opposite strategy, allowing large numbers to prepare the commercial *concours*, but their rate of success is consequently rather low.[29] A portion of the private enrollments are supplied by some of the commercial schools themselves, which have organized their own preparatory classes.

The French *grandes écoles* are essentially specialized schools that offer advanced and highly specific professional training. They are thus a heterogeneous collection of institutions for which no single definition suffices. Almost any generalization about them requires qualification. On the other hand, there is no doubt about the ideal type of a *grande école*. It would select its students after the second year of the *classes préparatoires* through a severely competitive examination; give those talented enough to be admitted three years of specialized instruction, including apprenticeships (*stages*); and then send them off to receive premier starting salaries in their professions, clearly marked for the highest leadership positions. The status of any particular school depends upon the selectivity of its entrants and the starting salaries of its graduates. Since these criteria are mutually reinforcing, they accentuate the hierarchical character of this sector, although this feature is counteracted somewhat by the sheer diversity of preparations involved. As one moves down the hierarchy the departures from the ideal type increase. Recruitment becomes less competitive and more varied; the level of study is lower, sometimes only three years of postsecondary work; and the likely occupation of graduates becomes more narrowly technical and less managerial. Still, given the abysmal job market for university graduates during the 1970s, credentials from the *grandes écoles* have been the most valued currency among employers. The extreme diversity of this sector, its diffuse forms of regulation, and the crucial role of status have all made this sector congenial for private institutions. Reputations once made become self-perpetuating within this kind of setting. In some cases this has given established private schools a competitive advantage over more recent state-sponsored rivals. The role of competition, however, is limited here. Far more important is respect for acquired positions, so that established schools become virtual monopolies. This condition too has facilitated independent institutions in securing a limited, but prominent place among France's *grandes écoles*.

The most clearly organized group of *grandes écoles* are those training various types of engineers. Since 1934 an official Commission des titres d'ingénieurs has served as an accrediting agency authorizing approved schools to grant the *diplôme d'ingénieur*. As of this writing some 153 schools had received its benediction, while another 10 engineering schools (9 private) were functioning beyond the pale. The 50 private engineering schools granted one-quarter of the engineering degrees in 1979. Only 2 of these schools could be rated near the top of the hierarchy—the Ecole supérieure d'electricité and the much smaller Ecole supérieure d'optique, both of which are located on the outskirts of Paris. Seven Catholic engineering schools fall roughly into the middle ranks of *grandes écoles*. They all contain their own *classes préparatoires* (for which entry is competitive), and the classes entering the actual *écoles* are then selected from both internal and external candidates. Near the bottom of the scale are some small and highly specialized private schools training engineers for such industries as textiles, tanning, welding, reinforced concrete, and perfume.

The *grandes écoles* of commerce and management—France's business schools—demonstrate once again the affinity between private enterprise and private higher education. Most are associated with local chambers of commerce, and others are private enterprises in their own right. Their students are largely destined for the private business sector, despite the fact that France's extensive bureaucracy and nationalized industries might also utilize their skills. Of the alumni of the most prestigious school, the Ecole des hautes études commerciales, for example, 87 percent work in the private sector.[30] As with other types of *grandes écoles,* the pecking order at the summit of the business school hierarchy is clear and widely known. After HEC comes the Ecole supérieure des sciences economiques et commerciales, originally founded by the Institut Catholique de Paris,[31] and then the Ecole supérieure de commerce de Paris which, like the HEC, is associated with the Paris Chamber of Commerce and Industry. Each of these schools accepts only one of ten candidates taking the *concours*. Graduates of the first two command starting salaries that are inferior to only the top five engineering schools.[32]

Outside of Paris there are nineteen Ecoles supérieures de commerce et d'administration des entreprises sponsored by local chambers of commerce and industry. All but one include preparatory classes, and all offer three years of business studies leading to a diploma recognized by the state. These schools and their Parisian analogues occupy the borderland between public and private higher education. The CCIs are public elected bodies that have a share in the taxing power of the state. Part of their funds are allocated to cover the operating costs of the business schools they administer. As legal entities, these schools are subject to a complex array of regulations deriving from multiple jurisdictions. In fact, however, they are quite autonomous, and tend to be responsive to personal interactions with local businessmen.[33] Even this pattern has its complications: in Nancy, Grenoble, and Strasbourg the CCIs have sponsored business schools that have been integrated into state universities, while the business schools of the Catholic universities of Lille and Angers have received the patronage of several local CCIs. All together these provincial business schools, plus another three Parisian schools offering a diploma recognized by the state, constitute the middle of the business school hierarchy. They vary from being highly selective to admitting 50 percent of those taking the *concours*. At the base of this pyramid are sixteen private schools that admit directly after the baccalaureate for a three-year course.

It would be misleading to leave the impression that the private sector has been able to monopolize business education. The figures given in table 5 fail to distinguish many students pursuing similar programs in the universities, although this is only a development of the 1970s. The pre-1968 faculties had no interest in so mundane a subject. In fact, when the Ministry of Education first took initiatives in this area it did so without disturbing either the faculties or the acknowledged monopoly of the private business schools. In 1955 it began creating Instituts d'administration des entreprises associated with existing universities. Their role was to teach the rudiments of management to those who had already been trained, usually in law or engineering.[34] The creation of IUTs in 1966 followed a similar logic: they would fill a gap in short-cycle managerial education at the university level without affecting the faculties or the schools. It was only after 1968 that the state began to offer programs in administration and management that were comparable to those of the commercial *grandes écoles*. In the decentralization of the University of Paris, which was part of the 1968 reform, Paris IX (at Dauphine) established programs in management and related fields. Another consequence of these reforms was the creation of several new university master's degree programs in this area. Only one of these, the program in data processing applied to management (MIAGE), can be said to have broken new ground. The master's in management (MSG) and the master's in accounting and finance (MST) largely overlap with the offerings of the independent *grandes écoles*. These degrees were offered by the economics departments (*unités d'enseignment et de recherche*), but, in 1975, legal departments entered this field with an interdisciplinary program in "Economic and Social Administration" that included options for both private and public administration. In addition, students at the various *instituts d'études politiques* have, during the last decade, increasingly opted for studies oriented toward private enterprise.[35]

The movement of state higher education into the domain of the business schools forms part of a larger pattern. During the 1970s the universities began to compete with the engineering *grandes écoles,* public and private. The IUTs attracted their largest enrollments in management programs, and these programs became the most competitive in the STSs as well. In fact, some underlying trends of the 1970s favored the independent institutions. The traditional faculties of the unreformed universities were largely cloistered behind the high walls of their own academic concerns. If they at all considered the likely destinations of their students, they took for granted the customary careers in teaching, research, and the civil service. It was evident by 1968, however, that the enormous enrollment growth of the preceding years was swamping these traditional career paths. The Orientation Law that followed the student rebellion of that year was just the first step toward reform. A complete restructuring of the universities was only implemented in 1971, and the years since have witnessed halting, piecemeal progress toward the goal of greater differentiation. Meanwhile, the dearth of suitable jobs for university graduates became an increasingly gloomy preoccupation.

Current and Future Trends

During the 1970s independent schools flourished as never before. Their survival on the periphery of the state system has always depended upon their close nexus with certain occupations, particularly in the private sector. Now the saturation of traditional graduate careers made this necessity into a virtue of considerable value. In the deepening competition for jobs the standing of the private schools vis-à-vis the universities has been enhanced by their selectivity. In France preselection exercised through competitive examinations has always been held in higher regard than the postselection, through failure and attrition, that takes place in the universities.[36] Given this dichotomy between public and private sectors, then, it is clear why the reform effort caused the universities to expand toward the periphery.

It now appears likely that the struggles of the spring of 1976 will prove to be a decisive watershed in the entire reform process. The government's reform of the second-cycle (the third and fourth years of university study), promulgated early that year, sought to remedy just those problems mentioned above. University degree programs were to be formulated with a definite occupation in view; responsiveness to occupational conditions was to be guaranteed by the participation of technical study groups containing representatives from the profession in question; and, entry to these programs was to be selective rather than open. Some considerable overstatement in the original government proposals aggravated the negative reactions of students and teachers, but the eventual resolution of this conflict appears in hindsight to have been a victory for the government.[37] The new degree structure is now largely in place, and preselection has become inescapable for an increasing number of sought-after programs. Paris Dauphine, for example, has been forced to become a selective university. After experimenting with lotteries and other mechanisms of handling the excess demand for its places, it has recently resolved to accept the most qualified candidates. Now, with four applicants for every opening, it is more selective for management studies than some of the commercial *grandes écoles*.[38]

Although the current direction of change is likely to affect French universities significantly over the next decade, there is less reason to expect it to alter the existing balance between the public and private sectors. The nature of France's peripheral private sector imparts a considerable degree of stability. Its evolution has forced it to assume specialized tasks that the state disdained to fill. Now that competition has emerged in some areas of this market the position of private institutions is largely assured by their established reputations. Those schools that have achieved high prestige have little to fear. The reverence for preselection, and its self-fulfilling character, virtually guarantee that the hierarchy will not be greatly disturbed, even if some public units like Paris Dauphine succeed in joining these favored ranks. At the bottom of the hierarchy a variety of private schools continue to prepare the BTS. This is clearly an area of fluidity and diversity, where private initiatives will always be able to find a niche. Perhaps only in the middle range, at the level of the *petites grandes écoles,* could a great success on the part of the university reform effort prove detrimental to private institutions. But this strata represents only a small part of private enrollments, not all of which would be lost in any case. It seems most plausible, then, that the private sector in France will retain something like its present share of the nation's postsecondary enrollments.

Perhaps it is more interesting to ponder whether the state universities can be as effective as the private sector in offering courses closely tied to labor-market opportunities. Compared with the dismal record of the unreformed university, the recently created second-cycle programs have shown a surprising capacity for producing innovation and diversity. The quality of these programs is less easily judged. The government has never chosen to lavish resources upon its universities. Relative French expenditures on higher education are among the lowest in western Europe, and per-student spending declined steadily through the 1970s.[39] Most important will be how these new programs fare over the long run. In the highly centralized French system it has always been easiest to innovate by supplementing existing programs without tampering with the vested interests already established. If the second-cycle innovations of today become tomorrow's entrenched interests, the public sector will prove less capable than the private of staying in touch with an ever-changing job market.

On balance, an evaluation of France's private sector must begin from the limited scope it is allowed by the dominant state system. Services available in the public sector are only duplicated in two types of private institution, the preparatory classes for *grandes écoles* and the STSs, and these are both outgrowths of secondary education. In higher education *per se* the most notable private undertakings have been the Catholic universities and the various schools oriented toward the private sector of the economy. The plethora of programs now offered by the Catholic universities suggests an admirable record of innovation and diversification within their particular domain. Their chief incentives for this course of development have been service to the Catholic community and institutional survival. These activities have helped to sustain the academic cores despite their disadvantages vis-à-vis state universities. This situation contrasts rather sharply with the Catholic universities of Belgium and the Netherlands where the state-supported academic core sets the tone for the institution. The commercial schools and other independent technical schools have traditionally been the source of much highly trained manpower for private indus-

try. Their independence combined with their close ties with industry have accentuated a practical orientation much appreciated in
the business community. They are thus less susceptible to "academic drift" than the professional schools under government control.
This constitutes yet another factor why the private *grandes écoles*
have little to fear from the encroachment of the public sector.

The private mode of organization in these cases is not without
its drawbacks. There is a decided element of privilege surrounding
the most prestigious of these schools, although the situation is no
different in the highly selective state schools. It is chiefly the uncertainties of a prolonged recruitment process that discourage students
from modest social backgrounds. Among less well established
schools, suspicions linger about the quality of the programs offered.
The handbook for French students, *L'Etudiant,* explicitly warns
against the exaggerated claims made by some of these schools.[40]

The small French private sector in the final analysis has quite
effectively filled the lacunae left by the dominant state system of
higher education, and it has remained rather feeble in those areas
where the state universities possessed the advantage. Its strengths
have been fulfilling the needs of special constituencies and cultivating close ties with the private sector of the economy. Its weaknesses
have been in the academic disciplines and scholarly research. This
configuration might even be regarded as the typical pattern for a
peripheral private sector. However, the next two cases will show
that such a general pattern does not necessarily hold for singular
institutions located on the periphery of dominant public sectors.

Sweden: The Stockholm School of Economics

Until late in the nineteenth century the higher educational needs of
Sweden were largely met by state universities. The most venerable,
the University of Uppsala, was founded by a Papal Bull in 1477, but
did not attain a secure existence until early in the seventeenth
century under the tutelage of the by-then Lutheran monarchy. A
second university was added that same century in Lund (1668) after
the territories of southern Sweden were added to the kingdom.[41] On
an implicitly regional basis these institutions fulfilled the public
need for doctors, lawyers, churchmen, secondary school teachers,
and civil servants. Instrumental training at a lower level of schooling was available in several technical institutes. The creation of
new knowledge, whether in the sciences, humanities, or arts, was
more closely associated with the various Royal Academies than with

the university faculties. Structured according to the prevailing German pattern, the universities were basically self-governing; they were largely self-financing as well with the help of endowments established by past Royal gifts. Thus, with essential educational tasks fulfilled at small cost to the public purse, the state had little need to concern itself about higher education. It was natural, then, that groups desiring more higher education than was then available had to resort to private voluntary initiatives.

The creation of private institutions of higher education in Sweden occurred in two rather different waves. Considering the small numbers involved they can only be called "waves" because similar conditions at similar stages of educational development were producing like results elsewhere in Europe. The impetus behind the first wave was "civic boosterism," that is, the wish of local patricians to enhance the intellectual level and cultural standing of their city by making it a seat of higher learning. The civic universities of England are probably the best-known exemplars of this type.[42] In Sweden civic leaders founded such universities in Stockholm (1877) and Gothenburg (1891). Although these undertakings required a good deal of voluntary effort, one or more sizable donations to get off the ground, and often a subsidy from the municipality as well, it is difficult to state precisely what expectations lay behind their creation. In a general sense these universities emanated from a prosperous and confident middle class that was optimistic about both the pecuniary and nonpecuniary value of knowledge. But, in fact, such impulses could produce different emphases. Stockholm College aspired to academic legitimacy from the outset, and consequently sought distinguished scholars for a faculty concentrated in mathematics and natural science. As a result only a limited number of students were qualified to study at so advanced a level. The founders of Gothenburg, however, wanted knowledge that was accessible to the general public in order to raise the cultural level of the city. The school began as a "free academy" that stressed the humanities, languages, and social science. Over time both institutions gradually conformed to the academic patterns and degree requirements of the ancient universities. Thus, the independent colleges in Sweden's two largest cities came to provide a regional alternative for students who did not wish to leave their cities for the small university towns of Lund or Uppsala.

The voluntary efforts that were channeled into the second wave of foundings had a more specific focus. The benefactors behind the "schools of economics" that were established across northern

Europe wanted to create courses of study that would be directly applicable to the commercial and financial realm, while at the same time enhancing the prestige of those professions. In other words, they sought to supplement existing university systems that were wholly oriented toward established disciplines and traditional professions.[43] The London School of Economics (f. 1895), despite its idiosyncratic connection with Fabian socialism, was probably more of a prototype for these schools than either the French schools of commerce or the American business schools, both of which antedated them. Their goal from the beginning was to achieve equivalence with university training, including the right to grant the doctorate. The Stockholm School of Economics (f. 1909) and the Gothenburg School of Economics (f. 1923) consequently aspired from their foundings to produce graduates of university-level quality, while also contributing to the advancement of economic knowledge. They envisioned their programs as a private-sector equivalent to the training received by aspiring civil servants in the universities. This clearly defined mission helped to buttress their independence when the environment of higher education in Sweden changed.

The unbroken governance of the Swedish Social Democrats from 1932 to 1976 is testimony, among other things, to the high degree of consensus present in Swedish society. An element of that consensus, and of the social-democratic commitment to reducing social inequality, has been the expansion of educational opportunity. In higher education this has produced a government commitment both to encourage growth in private demand and to supply additional university places. University enrollments began to increase shortly after World War II, and continued to accelerate for the next two decades.[44] From the outset, growth presented problems for Sweden's two private colleges.

Neither institution was ever in a position to cover its operating costs from tuition revenue. In effect, the marginal cost of each additional student was greater than the additional revenue brought in: more students meant that more funds had to be generated externally to cover the increase in operating costs. In their earliest years the necessary sums were provided by private philanthropy, but after the turn of the century both colleges came to depend upon subsidies from their respective municipalities. Such support constituted recognition that they were providing a public service to the region. In the centralized Swedish state, however, it was the national government that controlled the bulk of public resources; and under the Social Democrats that government was increasingly willing to assume full responsibility for higher education as a part of its social policy. The colleges in Stockholm and Gothenburg began receiving government subsidies in the 1930s as their offerings were expanded and brought into line with the old universities. In 1948 a further step was taken when the state eliminated tuition in private institutions, replacing this source of funds with further state subsidies. These steps were, at least in part, *quid pro quo* arrangements that allowed uniform degree requirements and conditions of attendance to be extended throughout Swedish higher education. At this point the two colleges were financed by the return on their endowments, a fixed municipal subsidy, and a state grant to cover the bulk of their operating expenditures. The state's obligation was thus an open-ended one: soon it became total. Gothenburg was reorganized into a state university in 1954, and Stockholm followed in 1960.

There was nothing doctrinaire about these actions. Rather, the circumstances of nationalization made it quite apparent why Gothenburg and Stockholm could not continue as independent entities. The structure of national degrees assured that all university-level instruction had to bear the high overhead costs associated with research and personalized teaching. The cost-cutting techniques common in mass private sectors, for example, were out of the question. The expense of augmenting a research-oriented faculty was great; that of conducting up-to-date research in the natural sciences was greater still; and the capital expenditures necessary for new buildings, absolutely crushing. In 1945 the Gothenburg academy was still able to accommodate its five hundred students in its single original building. To expand further, however, it was forced to begin renting space throughout the city. With nationalization, the responsibility for all these diverse properties was taken over by the National Board for Public Buildings.[45] Stockholm College was similarly confronted during the 1950s with the need for a new campus to house its burgeoning population. The site it preferred in central Stockholm had to be ceded by the city and accompanied by an immense grant for construction. Negotiations eventually broke down as it became apparent that the city, far from wanting to make such commitments, wished to dismiss its financial obligations to the college altogether. Stockholm College had little choice, then, but to accept the state's offer to create a new suburban campus at the price of becoming a state university.[46] For both colleges, then, the capital requirements of expansion could only be met by the national government. Yet, this does not entirely explain why Sweden chose to take over its independent colleges.

After 1948 the two private colleges had a status not unlike the independent, but state-financed universities of Belgium and the Netherlands discussed in chapter 3. However, in both those countries the groups backing the private universities correspond with major cleavages within pluralistic societies; cleavages, moreover, that had become institutionalized in the political life of the nation. In the homogeneous and egalitarian society of Sweden these private colleges no longer related to, nor solicited support from, any particular segment of the population. Nor were their regional roles relevant given the state's assumption of responsibility for the uniform provision of higher education across the country.[47] True, the faculty and administration lamented the loss of independence entailed in becoming a government institution, but this in retrospect seemed a small price to pay. Between 1954 and 1969 the University of Gothenburg grew from 1,500 to 21,000 students. The University of Stockholm went from 7,000 in 1960 to 32,000 a decade later. There did not appear to be any compelling reason for preserving independent control within the context of an overriding national policy of increasing access to higher education. Their altered status was thus fully appropriate for the role they had already assumed—components in the state provision of higher education.

The Gothenburg School of Economics eventually met the same fate, if not for the same reasons. It remained a small and highly selective school during an age of expansion, but it eventually faced financial problems that were beyond its limited capacities. In 1971 it was absorbed by Gothenburg University. In a sense, perhaps, its distinctive position was crowded out of existence. Always overshadowed by its more vigorous and prestigious sister institution in Stockholm, the 1960s saw the economics curriculum become widely available in the state universities as well. Its demise left the Stockholm School of Economics virtually alone as an independent institution of higher education.[48]

Although the connection between the School of Economics and the Stockholm business community has been its principal source of strength since its inception, this has by no means been its only one.[49] After the first decade of its existence the demand for places at the school began to exceed the limited number of openings. As it began to choose the most qualified applicants for its students, the reputation of the school and its graduates rose. Today it is undoubtedly Sweden's most elite institution of higher education, selecting its students from among the country's top secondary school graduates. It also has managed to occupy the summit of the academic hierarchy. Since about 1960 graduate education and research have proliferated. During the same period the school's graduates have ceased to flow exclusively into private industry, as many have chosen to pursue careers in research or the public sector.

Maintaining an elite academic institution requires a distinguished, research-oriented faculty, ample library, and, in this day and age, computer facilities. Such necessities add considerable overhead to basic instructional costs. The Stockholm School of Economics has kept these expenditures under control in part because of the nature of the subjects, but mostly because it has avoided large capital costs by staying rather small. The school has only needed to make several additions to its original building. External voluntary support is continually raised by the school's Association of Alumni. Several Swedish corporations have also been consistent contributors. However, when special capital needs have arisen the school has benefited throughout its existence from the patronage of the Wallenberg family. External support together with endowment income and other revenues account for the bulk of the school's resources. In recent years the government payment in lieu of tuition, plus a subsidy for the library, have accounted for less than one-third of the operating budget.

Rather close interaction between the government and independent institutions, whether profit-making or otherwise, is a matter of accepted principle in Sweden. Thus, the government appoints the chairman of the school's Board of Governors, confirms its professors, and exercises a general oversight over its activities. Certainly the most important point of contact, however, is the contract that specifies the level of annual subsidization for the school. During the negotiations for this contract the government's leverage for influencing the activities of the school is obviously great. Prior to the agreement for a ten-year contract in 1969 the question of nationalizing the school was "in the air," even though it apparently never became part of the formal discussions. The school's association with the business community and its general support for a market economy place it at the conservative end of the Swedish consensus. These attributes in combination with its elite academic status have never sat well with those on the left of the political spectrum. In the late 1960s the Social Democrats of Stockholm went so far as to pass a resolution calling for nationalization, but this view never represented the policy of the national party. Still, the difference in outlook between the Stockholm school and the social-democratic governments has produced a certain kind of pressure.

Perhaps the most overt result of this was the expansion of entering classes from 150 to 275, in part to deflect charges of elitism. More intangibly, the need to remain above reproach encourages the school to be rigorously meritocratic in the selection of students and faculty. Too much emphasis should not be placed upon these potential tensions: accommodation rather than politicization has characterized relations between the government and the school.

In general the personnel of the school place a high value on its independent status. They cite their relative freedom to pursue academic and vocational goals without bureaucratic impediments, plus the freedom to experiment with new programs. Since the school's independence was called into question in the late 1960s an interesting trend has become evident. Without sacrificing any of its academic strength, the school has been extending and revitalizing its links with private industry. An apprenticeship program was recently established to allow students to spend a year in private industry before their final year at the school; and a number of seminars for business leaders are now given each year to discuss connections between research at the school and applications in industry. Many new links are being forged through associated organizations. In 1969 the association responsible for the school (Handelshögskoleföreningen) founded a parallel "Swedish Institute of Management," which offers a variety of programs of continuing education for businessmen at all levels. Since then this institute has jointly sponsored the Marketing Techniques Center (1975) and the Institute for Management of Innovation and Technology (1979), which provide more specific services. The school has also strongly emphasized international business, establishing ties with the European Institute for Advanced Studies in Management and the International Schools of Business Management, besides starting its own Institute of International Business (1975). The overall result has been to create an organizational network centering on the School of Economics, its faculty, and its facilities. Since most of these ancillary organizations generate their own revenue from the services they render directly to corporations, these developments have strengthened the financial base of the entire institution by absorbing a portion of the overhead costs. More importantly for the long run, these activities have solidified and activated support among the group that has always been the principal beneficiary of the school's activities.

In 1979 the Stockholm School of Economics negotiated and signed without controversy another contract with the state establishing the terms of its operations for the next fifteen years. Preeminent academically and closely integrated with industry, it has achieved enviable success in two paths that are not always easily reconciled. In this respect, the school has amply fulfilled the spirit of the U-68 Reform that has sought to promote greater industry-university integration in the public sector. The school certainly contributes to the prestige of Swedish letters, and particularly during the past decade, it has compiled a record of innovations as well. Negatively, it might be argued that its stature tends to leech talent from the state universities; but in fairness it should be added that the school cooperates fully with other economics faculties in matters relating to research. Today the school is in a strong position to continue its success. By cultivating an ethos that is understood and appreciated among its supporters in private enterprise, the Stockholm School of Economics has preserved its original *raison d'être,* and by doing so, maintained its independence as well.

The University of Buckingham: Starting Up

On February 6, 1976, a formal ceremony took place in the town of Buckingham, some twenty-five miles northeast of Oxford, opening what most people would regard as Britain's only private university.[50] If there is an element of doubt about that distinction, it would not concern the privateness of this new venture. Rather, the question would be about the precise nature of the other forty-four universities in the United Kingdom with which it would be competing: each exists as a legally independent entity, and together they are sometimes described as the "autonomous sector" of British higher education.[51]Yet, during the twentieth century these universities have become completely dependent upon government support. In the late 1960s concern that this trend was producing menacing consequences united a small group of people both inside and outside of academic life. British universities, in their view, had become a state monopoly with inherent tendencies toward politicization, complacency, inefficiency, and, ultimately, stagnation. It was their determined efforts to supply a private alternative that came to fruition in Buckingham on that February day. The story of the birth of the University of Buckingham, and of its subsequent struggle to survive, is particularly apropos to the consideration of peripheral private sectors. The college was, first of all, born from a perception of the importance of privateness for independence in higher education. Secondly, it illustrates the formidable entry problem posed by challenging the *de facto* hegemony of existing institutions. And finally, it raises again in another context the recurring issue of the coexistence of private institutions dependent upon private resources with equivalent state institutions funded from the public purse. The "University College at Buckingham" (UCB), as it was first known, is thus a far more interesting case than its numerically insignificant position on the periphery of the British university system might indicate.

It may appear somewhat curious that a group of eminent academics should have resolved with such conviction and tenacity that Britain had need of a private university. Compared to universities elsewhere in the world, those in Britain enjoy great autonomy, self-government, complete academic freedom, low student-teacher ratios, and one of the highest average per-student expenditures in the world.[52] Most of the universities derive their legal independence and their right to confer degrees from Royal Charters granted over a span of 750 years. For the three ancient Scottish universities, the same powers were granted by act of Parliament. All of these universities nevertheless form part of a state system of higher education. From the middle of the nineteenth century until the 1930s a succession of Parliamentary Reform Commissions investigated the organization, governance, and financing of different universities, and then proposed and enacted various legislative alterations. These episodes represented assertions of ultimate public responsibility over the universities, even while their independence was consistently respected.[53] This responsibility eventually became exercised in the matter of finance. In 1889 the government began making grants on a regular basis to eleven institutions. Over time both the number of recipients and the sums involved increased, but it was not until the conclusion of World War I that these arrangements received a further degree of institutionalization. The University Grants Committee was created in 1919 under the Treasury to determine the needs of the universities and to allocate the Parliamentary grant accordingly. When Oxford and Cambridge were included a few years later, Britain possessed a unified system for public support of university education.

The University Grants Committee (UGC) has been widely praised, and more recently eulogized, as the ideal means of reconciling external public financing of universities with the internal sovereignty of academics.[54] It has consistently interpreted its own role as providing public oversight of the universities, while serving as a protective buffer to shield them from intrusions of partisan politics or government bureaucracy. From its inception until 1964—the heyday of the UGC and the period for which the preceding description would be most apt—this role was made possible essentially by two conditions: the complete decentralization of financial control and the tacit relationships between the universities, the UGC, and the Treasury. The basis of decentralized control was the five-year block grant made by the UGC to each university, which then had the freedom to apportion the funds as it saw fit. Capital grants and comparatively minor earmarked sums had to be spent as specified, but the block grants came to be the chief source of operating income and the guarantee of university autonomy. How their magnitudes were determined was consequently of crucial importance.

The process began in the universities themselves with attempts to foresee budgetary needs for a five-year period (quinquennium). These estimates were then refined and finalized in discussions with representatives of the UGC. After receiving budget projections from each university the UGC then negotiated with the Treasury to establish a lump sum for all of them together. This sum would be turned over to the UGC to allocate among the universities in accordance with the understandings previously negotiated. That these delicate and, for the universities, quite fateful negotiations could proceed without generating conflicts or recriminations was undoubtedly assisted by the common social and academic backgrounds of the participants. More than half of the UGC were consistently drawn from the ranks of academics, and the other members were likely to have similar Oxford or Cambridge backgrounds. The same could be said for the Treasury officials with whom they dealt. Together, the twenty members of the UGC, some thirty (before 1960) university heads, and the relevant Treasury officials formed a circumscribed community of gentlemen who could trust one another to honor their informal understandings. Without this sense of community it would be difficult to account for the remarkable persistence of the intricate balance between the interests of the state and the prerogatives of the universities. Nevertheless, underlying the entire operation of the UGC was a more fundamental consensus about the proper nature of an English university.

The English university ideal was certainly inspired by Oxford and Cambridge, as A. H. Halsey and Martin Trow have written, but without ever necessarily being an accurate reflection of actual conditions or practices there.[55] Universities, and more particularly their constituent colleges, were expected to be relatively small and intimate residential communities; students were to be carefully selected from throughout the nation on a personal basis; once members, these students could count on close personal supervision from their dons. The goal was cultivation of the intellect through advanced academic specialization, but not specific training for a profession. To accomplish these ends the dons required powers of self-government and complete autonomy from the government.

This conception of the university has by no means been a mere pipe dream of dewy-eyed dons; rather, it has been an active force in shaping British universities in the twentieth century—in large measure through the UGC. The Victorian and Edwardian civic university foundations, for example, were originally a far cry from this ideal, but they were much less so after forty years of subsidization through the UGC. Even more to the point, these norms molded the great postwar expansion of British universities. New universities, excepting the technological universities, were placed in the smaller and older nonindustrial towns instead of the major population centers (which were invariably chosen as university seats in continental Europe). Such care was taken to provide students with residence halls and maintenance for living expenses that the percentage of resident students actually rose with the rise in enrollments.[56] At the same time a student-teacher ratio of about eight to one was maintained; in fact, during some of the most rapid growth it even improved slightly. As a result of this approach British universities were able to protect and preserve the considerable virtues that have already been mentioned.

But the price of excellence in this case was a university system that was both elitist and expensive. Even after the expansion of university places, only 6 percent of British youth could expect to gain the privilege of entrance. Those who did attend, of course, were far from being representative of British society,[57] but providing for their costly instruction consumed approximately 10 percent of the nation's entire educational expenditure. In short, by the middle of the 1960s there were clearly troubles brewing in this academic paradise: not, perhaps, of the severity of the problems that were shortly to convulse universities elsewhere in the world, but nevertheless large enough to cause disquiet among those who believed most fervently in the English ideal of a university.

Part of the problem was simply the cost of maintaining the universities in the style to which they were accustomed. In 1957, with 90,000 students, the universities required a recurrent grant of £25 million. A decade later, and already under considerable government pressure to economize, for 190,000 students (+111 percent) they were receiving a recurrent grant of £140 million (+460 percent).[58] Opinion was becoming widespread that such large and growing sums of public funds necessitated stronger measures of public accountability. As a direct result, in the space of a few years several important changes were made in the relationship between the universities and the state. In an organizational change of considerable significance the UGC was transferred in 1964 from the Treasury to the Department of Education and Science (DES) so that the claims of the universities could be evaluated in the context of the overall education and research needs of the country.

What the higher education needs of the country were at this juncture, according to the DES, was soon made evident in the enunciation of the "binary policy" in 1965. No additional universities were to be chartered, and most of the further expansion of higher education was to take place in a different sector, under direct public control, made up of "polytechnics." The polytechnics were to be everything that the universities were not: urban institutions for commuter students offering practical training on, it was then hoped, a less costly basis. Although the implementation of the binary policy was undoubtedly the most important development of the 1960s in British higher education, its relevance here is chiefly to illustrate how the tide had turned against the unchallenged ascendency of the university ideal, protected by a closed community of like-thinking gentlemen. Henceforth the UGC would take a much more active role in molding university policy to national needs—and restraining it within national means.[59]

Although direct interventions by the UGC to cause the termination of underutilized programs were few and minor, more pervasive changes in this relationship were of greater significance. In 1967 the UGC issued a "memorandum of guidance" to the universities, specifying criteria on which allocations would be made for the coming quinquennium. This placed pressures of the most direct sort on universities to conform to an overall policy set by the DES. This was followed by the decision to open UGC and university accounts to inspection by the Comptroller and Auditor General. The drift of events from university autonomy toward accountability and some measure of central direction was by this time unmistakable. Moreover, although conditions would certainly get worse, especially when the inflation of the early 1970s destroyed the security of the quinquennial grant, the darkest forebodings were provoked by uncertainty about the ultimate extent of this trend.[60] These fears were felt most acutely by conservative defenders of the university ideal. The reaction of some of them was a critique of current practices that became part of the birthright of the University of Buckingham.

Origins and Development

That the idea of an independent university should become the focus of this growing discontent may well have been precipitated by a letter to the *Times*. Dr. John Paulley wrote in May of 1967 that the undue dependence of British universities upon the state might be partially counteracted by creating an independent university based on voluntary support—something like the great American private universities.[61] The author was contacted by Professor Harry Ferns of the University of Birmingham, who had himself just written that the detrimental effects of university dependence might be overcome by channeling public funds through students instead of directly to institutions. Paulley and Ferns together then met with Professor Max Beloff of Oxford, whose indictment of the current situation had also just appeared. While not intended for this purpose, Beloff's argument had expressed the kernel of the case for an independent university. Dismissing an existing controversy over auditing university accounts, he stated that the basic faults were inherent to the system: "It is not possible to depend upon the public purse—least of all in a democracy—and expect autonomy." The "dead hand of uniformity" was being imposed on British universities by the UGC and the DES, in part because Britain lacked, "as compared to America . . . great private institutions, alongside state-supported ones, which by example and emulation and through mutual support can assist each other's development in freedom."[62]

A movement to launch an independent university in Britain gradually blossomed under the aegis of the Institute of Economic Affairs, a small research organization specializing in the study of free-market economics. It convened two conferences on the topic in 1968, and also commissioned Harry Ferns to undertake a further analysis of the subject.[63] By the end of that year the institute began circulating a "Declaration on the Urgency of an Independent University" which eventually was endorsed by over one hundred signatories, most of whom were senior academics.[64] These efforts led early in 1969 to the formation of the Planning Board for an Independent University chaired by Sir Sydney Caine, former director of the London School of Economics. From that point another four years of work were required before the college could become formally incorporated as an educational charity. Three years of additional organizational efforts transpired before it admitted its first class of students. The interesting details of this process have been recorded in a semiofficial history of the foundation and early years.[65] More fundamental to understanding this development is the nature of the movement that brought it about.

It was inescapable that the attempt to found an independent university should acquire a political coloration. Although the general drift of university policy in Britain largely transcended party lines, the most ominous developments occurred during a period of Labour Party rule (1966–70). The movement attracted adherents on the basis of several intertwined conservative themes. Academic traditionalists were most concerned about the matter of university autonomy; others stressed the debilitating moral effects of complete reliance on the state; and a few, like Harry Ferns, were dazzled by the idea of unleashing free-market forces in the field of education. Such enthusiasms occasionally gave rise to rather extreme statements, but the actual position of the leading figures were for the most part realistic and moderate. Sir Sydney Caine, for example, fully recognized the necessity of greater state control over the state-funded universities, and even testified to this effect before parliamentary committees.[66] Yet he also felt that considerable benefit would result from the existence of an independent competitor. But, if most of the support for an independent university came from right of center, the movement was anathema to those on the other side of the political spectrum, including most of the higher education establishment. They naturally found the critique of state-funded universities that lay behind this movement to be highly contentious in itself. In addition, the British Left had long opposed private education in the primary and secondary grades as a source of privilege, helping to perpetuate class divisions in British society. An independent university funded by tuition fees seemed to them yet another means for wealth to be used to sustain social status. For these reasons, then, an independent university has been an issue of considerably greater symbolic importance than its actual role in the provision of higher education would alone justify.

During the early years of the movement there were numerous conceptions of what an independent university ought to be. Some of them, particularly visions of a large institution that would partly compensate for the inadequate supply of university places in Britain, proved to be far off the mark. Max Beloff, the first principal of the college, later admitted that its proponents were determined to bring an independent university into existence, even though they "had no idea of . . . what it was going to be like at all."[67] In short, it became a matter of principle for them, and as such transcended any specific arguments that might be raised to support or oppose it. A consensus of sorts did exist that the new college would compete directly with existing universities in offering degree-level programs, but it was felt that they would somehow do so differently and better. In any event, the potentialities of the UCB were strongly shaped by the circumstances of its creation.

The barriers to entry in a mature system of higher education are considerable. Besides concrete problems of locating and financing a campus, there is also the intangible challenge of gaining legitimacy in the context of the surrounding academic system. Raising capital was from the outset a serious and continuing problem for the UCB. Small contributions from sympathizers were sufficient to start and sustain the Planning Board, but major gifts were necessary to get the college off the ground. It took a certain amount of good fortune, then, to secure both a site and the necessary financial backing. The town of Buckingham was chosen when it became clear that the enthusiasm of local officials for a university would make it possible to acquire a suitable site on reasonable terms. The land was then purchased with a grant from a British businessman, Ralph Yablon. Finally, an anonymous (at the time) gift of £1 million from a Liberal peer, Lord Tanlaw, made it possible to reconstruct the dilapidated buildings, and to begin the hiring of a permanent staff. This gift allowed the University College to be actually brought into existence, but the great difficulty of fund raising also assured that the new institution would be a small one.

Acquiring legitimacy for the new college was a more protracted process, which has yet to be fully completed. The project began with one immense advantage by having the backing of many senior academics. When Max Beloff, a distinguished Oxford professor of government, agreed to become the first principal, he brought to the college the kind of credibility that was indispensible in the British academic world. Enough other supporters followed their convictions with commitments to the new institution to provide a solid nucleus of senior staff. The mid-seventies happened to be a buyer's market for junior faculty, and the school's location near Oxford made it relatively easy to attract visiting teachers. As a result, the college was able to open with a staff that was comparable in quality to at least the other new British universities.[68] An important barrier was crossed when the college was accepted in the British system of external examiners, whereby professors visit other institutions and scrutinize examinations. This system guarantees that all British university degrees meet acceptable standards. By obtaining membership in the system Buckingham could reasonably claim that its graduates were of the same quality as those from state-funded universities. This was of crucial importance because Buckingham, as it was originally constituted, could not award degrees at all.

It became apparent quite early that the new school could not expect a Royal Charter to grant degrees until it had proved its worth as a permanent, functioning institution. (Hence, the original name, "university college," rather than "university.") This, of course, posed the serious problem of assuring Buckingham students that they would receive appropriate recognition for their work. One possibility that was actively pursued was to offer degrees through the Council for National Academic Awards (CNAA)—a body established to validate degrees from the polytechnics and institutions of further education. After time-consuming negotiations that delayed the opening of the college, it turned out that the CNAA could not accept the two-year intensive degree program (in place of the customary three years) that Buckingham intended to offer. As discouraging as this episode was at the time, it belied the rigidity of the British higher education bureaucracy, and thus underscored the *raison d'être* for a private university. It also forced the college to certify its graduates in its own name. The result was the UCB license, which stood for the same academic attainments as a university bachelor's degree. The difficulty was getting others to recognize it as such. Private employers posed little problem, since many were sympathetic with the entire undertaking. The most important breakthrough occurred when the professional bodies that controlled certification for the legal profession accepted the law license of Buckingham as equivalent to a university law degree. Somewhat later the accountancy profession made similar adjustments. The college was thus able to prepare students for these professions on an equal footing with chartered universities. It soon became apparent that a *de facto* equality reigned for graduate study as well. Largely because of the academic standing of the Buckingham senior faculty the school's graduates were able to secure admission to graduate programs on their own merits. The most significant area where the license was not recognized was the civil service, but in 1981 the Civil Service Commission, after a thorough investigation of the college, granted the license parity with a university honors degree.

Buckingham passed another milestone on the route to becoming a full-fledged university in the summer of 1980 when the Conservative government of Margaret Thatcher changed the status of student maintenance grants from discretionary to mandatory. This step reduced by about one-third the cost of attending Buckingham for British students, thereby possibly expanding the college's potential clientele. Finally, in February, 1983, the Thatcher government permitted Buckingham to attain the status of a full-fledged university, awarding it the first Royal Charter for a nongovernmental institution of higher education in the twentieth century.[69] It thereby gained the power to grant degrees on its own authority, and was able to change its title to the University of Buckingham.

There is considerable irony in the fact that a movement that began by decrying excessive government influence in higher education should owe a key element of its success to having friends in high places. For, it was the same Margaret Thatcher, then in opposition, that extolled the virtues of private initiative at the college's opening ceremonies in 1976. Such friendships, of course, carry with them reciprocal enmities as well. The Labour party has threatened to review both the charter and mandatory grant status if it should return to power. Of more immediate concern might be the widespread resentment that the ready granting of a charter rekindled throughout British higher education. Since there are no clear precedents for a university charter it is difficult to argue that Buckingham is too small or too narrowly focused to qualify. Its educational resources are nevertheless paltry, as the *Times Higher Education Supplement* was quick to point out, when compared to many of the polytechnics.[70] Thus, the formal legitimacy that Buckingham achieved was accompanied by considerable informal disapproval in the academic community. In the long run, however, Buckingham's Royal Charter could provide it with the insulation from politics that is essential to its development as an educational institution. One thing seems certain, though: the charter virtually guarantees that the University of Buckingham is here to stay. But how close is this creation to the hopes and aspirations that motivated its original founders?

The Predicament of Britain's Peripheral Private University

In its eighth year of operations (1983) the University of Buckingham (UB) had over 470 students, more than 40 academic staff, and a decided air of permanence. Since opening, it added an eight-acre campus to its original site, and it has slowly developed its facilities to accommodate an optimal future student body of 600. Compared to other universities its offerings would have to be considered minimal, or even truncated. There are three rather conventional schools of study—law, economics, and accounting—and three interdisciplinary schools—politics, economics, and law; history, politics, and English literature; and the most recent addition, biology and society. There is also a School of European Studies that operates in conjunction with the other schools. To develop all this required some compromises with the original goals of an independent university. In particular, the college has been constrained by its financial situation and by the conditions for student recruitment. More generally, the circumstances of competition with the state-funded university system have tended to push UB toward the periphery, away from the mainstream of British academic life where it would undoubtedly have preferred to be.

One of the major misperceptions of the original project concerned the likely economics of an independent university. Max Beloff has observed in retrospect that, as good market economists, "the founders should have known how hard it is to sell something which one can get elsewhere for free or, at any rate, for much less."[71] In fact, at this stage of its development Buckingham has largely accomplished this feat, although not without difficulty. Revenues from student tuition are now sufficient to meet the university's operating budget, but attaining this balance has meant keeping expenditures low and tuition rather high. UB has had little choice but to fulfill its promise to operate more efficiently than other British universities. This has been done by staying in session throughout the calendar year, which of course makes their chief organizational innovation a financial necessity, and by keeping overhead expenses to a minimum. Part-time and temporary academic staff, for example, were more numerous in 1980 than regular faculty, and the university leases certain facilities, like athletic fields, that it would ideally prefer to own. The college has also had to concentrate from the outset on cheap subjects like law and accounting. The School of Life Sciences (biology and society) brought the first natural science offerings only in 1980, and a capacity to teach the physical sciences is still absent. On the income side of the ledger their situation dictates that tuition must be increased with inflation to cover the rising costs of operations. In 1981 a 23 percent tuition hike to £3,200 per year was required, and 1982 brought another rise to £3,600. Taking living costs into account, a Buckingham degree now costs more than

£10,000. Grants from Local Educational Authorities for British students only cover up to a third of this. The small amounts of financial aid currently assist just 10 percent of the students, so that the high cost obviously diminishes the pool of students who might attend Buckingham.

If the situation created by tuition dependence currently seems to be under control, a far more serious problem is presented by the lack of sufficient capital. This lack has been a continual drag upon the development of the school, and probably represents the gravest threat to its survival. Capital limitations are the chief factor holding Buckingham to its current size of under five hundred. Even to accommodate these students adequately there is need to install a new refectory, a student commons area, and to expand the libraries. Looking ahead, it will soon become necessary to transfer most of the students from their current lodgings in the town of Buckingham to campus residences. In addition, there is an outstanding bank loan of over £1 million at a substantial rate of interest.[72] Clearly the university's future depends, just as its past existence has depended, upon finding sufficient voluntary support.

UB benefited from numerous gifts during its short history, but with the exceptions of the benefactions of Lord Tanlaw and Ralph Yablon, which originally put the institution afloat, this voluntary support has tended to come in small parcels. Several aspects of the charitable environment in Britain may be responsible for the difficulty of raising funds. British tax laws have allowed only limited concessions for charitable giving, and have made it rather cumbersome to claim even these.[73] In addition, the high inflation and low economic growth of recent years have not been conducive to individual or corporate giving. The large foundations that might have given Buckingham some needed assistance have chosen not to become involved.[74] It should also be borne in mind that the state-supported universities actively pursue potential higher-education donors as well. Whether for these reasons or others, a fund-raising drive launched in 1980 fell well short of its target. In reaction, the Appeals Office was reorganized along lines similar to those of American private universities. In a somewhat un-English manner, this has meant more systematic combing of foundations and trusts for possible gifts, identifying and regularly communicating with likely "friends" of the university, and the forthright presentation of the appeal in widely circulated brochures. Their original goal was to meet the needs described above by bringing in at least £1 million annually from 1983 through 1987. Unless they succeed Buckingham will not have the means to evolve from its current provisional status.

A second major way in which Buckingham undoubtedly differs from its founders' preconceptions would be in the nature of the student body. Since its inception more than half of the students have enrolled in the School of Law: in the fall term, 1981, 256 of the 410 students in residence could be found there.[75] If one includes the next largest schools of accounting (44 students) and economics (29), fully 80 percent of the Buckingham students are taking preprofessional curricula that are nearly identical across all British universities. Another imbalance exists in the nationalities of the students: as of 1981 the largest contingent was Malaysian (130), with British students in second place (101), followed by a substantial number of Nigerian students (75). The remaining quarter of the student body consisted of occasional students from the United States (18), and small groups from western Europe and several former colonies of the British Empire. Buckingham had originally intended to be cosmopolitan, but hardly to such an extent, or with such a degree of dependence on just two foreign countries. To understand these skewed patterns it is necessary not only to consider Buckingham's distinctive offerings, but also their relationship to the rest of British higher education.

Buckingham was compelled by its birthright to be different both to justify its existence and to find its niche within the system. Its most startling departure from convention was the introduction of a two-year degree course. Buckingham students study for eight consecutive ten-week terms, compared with courses totaling seventy-two to eighty-four weeks over three years at other universities. Buckingham's system obviously represents a significant reduction of the opportunity and maintenance costs involved in a university education. A second major innovation has been the program for education in a European framework. The different combinations of study in the School of European Studies (a three-year program, including one year of foreign study) are intended to produce lawyers, administrators, and economists with the background, training, and linguistic capacity to function in the European Economic Community. Included in this school are single-year courses that allow foreigners to learn the essentials of English law, or permit Buckingham students to attain a diploma in French law. A third distinguishing characteristic has been the commitment to provide a teaching-intensive environment by virtue of its intimate scale and emphasis upon tutorials. Finally, three interdisciplinary schools offer students the opportunity to specialize in more than one major subject area. These curricula, and to a lesser extent the supporting courses that are required in all the schools, aim for a broad intellectual preparation of high academic standard that Buckingham would like to make the hallmark of all its graduates.

The organizers of the UB were undoubtedly correct in their perception that some, particularly more mature students, would welcome the chance to attain a university degree in just two years. Indeed, fully half of the UB students are beyond the eighteen- to twenty-two-year-old age range of most university students. Students in a hurry, however, tend to be those with the strongest vocational motivations. This in part explains why the preprofessional schools have so strikingly overshadowed the liberal arts components, even though the mission of providing a superior liberal arts education was originally fundamental to Buckingham's identity. No one seems to have anticipated the great appeal that a two-year degree course would have for students from third-world countries. Yet, the typical Malaysian at Buckingham turns out to be a mature civil servant studying law in order to advance his career in his homeland. For such a student the opportunity costs of higher education are likely to be paramount, so that saving a year by attending Buckingham would have considerable attraction. The UB is naturally appreciative of its third-world clientele, without whom its survival would certainly be in doubt, but it is also aware that acceptance as a British university requires having more than one-quarter British students.

Buckingham admits only British students who otherwise qualify for university entrance (i.e., who pass two A-level examinations), but it is less clear why the one hundred or so British students chose to attend Buckingham. Only a few are mature students attracted by the two-year course of study. The majority tend to be young people who have either deviated in some way from the traditional schooling sequence, or come directly from secondary schools after failing to be accepted in the universities they had originally chosen. In most cases these students came to the UB for reasons that had little to do with the particular strengths and distinctive programs that the university has cultivated. The department of European studies, which is largely made up of British students, comes closest to being a positive draw, but as of 1981 it had only twenty-three majors. Almost no British students study economics, even though this is unquestionably the university's strongest field academically. This is no doubt because there are many open places in economics in the state-funded universities. Conversely, most of the British students at Buckingham study law, places for which have been tight in the university system.

Furthermore, the UB has not yet received any recognition for its commitment to teaching. For that matter, Buckingham is actually little known, and still less understood within the United Kingdom. This situation clearly indicates that the UB has yet to develop a powerful magnet of attraction—some particularly successful course or program that would make it the first choice of potential students and that would project a positive image of the university throughout the country. The two other singular institutions discussed in this chapter, the Ecole Libre des Sciences Politiques and the Stockholm School of Economics, both succeeded by establishing such magnets, and thereby assured themselves of both top quality students and external supporters. In other words, they found a niche within the higher education system, a set of tasks that they were able to perform better than rival institutions. Once established, such a niche can provide a considerable degree of security against competitors. Lacking such a niche, however, as is now the case with Buckingham in the United Kingdom, a peripheral institution will be strongly affected by conditions within the dominant public sector.

It would, of course, be presumptuous to expect the UB to have created a niche for itself in less than a decade of existence, but several developments indicate that the potential could be there. For one thing, the financial agonies of the state-supported universities seem to have assisted student recruitment at Buckingham. The imposition in 1980 of full-cost fees on all foreign students in the universities placed Buckingham on the same footing as other institutions in terms of cost. In fact, since it has lower unit costs than state-supported universities, the UB should be able to underprice them for foreign students. More importantly, applications from British students were up 100 percent for the 1982 academic year, and by 1983 the proportion of British students was approaching 40 percent.[76]

Any positive scenario concerning Buckingham's future would have to be predicated on a solution to its current problems of undercapitalization, but there is optimism at the university that this can be managed. The systematization of fund raising promises to bring some improvement, and the bestowal of a Royal Charter should provide an additional impetus to these efforts. However, should the

UB succeed in developing the needed facilities and a sound financial foundation, what would the future be likely to hold for Britain's single independent university?

The paramount institutional goal of the UB is clearly to excel rather than to expand; yet, the logic of its position on the periphery of a dominant public university system might very well dictate that it will be necessary to expand in order to excel. As presently constituted, or even increased to its projected optimum population of six hundred students, it would seem difficult for the UB to transcend its current role as primarily an institution of convenience for career-oriented British students. The resources of the state-supported universities, even in a period of serious retrenchment, are likely to remain considerably more bountiful than anything Buckingham can generate. Under such circumstances the UB might be competitive with the lower half of the university list, but it would have to content itself, as it largely does now, with the overflow from that system. Such a role could easily supply enough capable students to keep the college comfortably functioning, but such an existence would not be a very powerful vindication of an independent university. For this the UB will most likely have to make further adaptations to its unique situation. The most plausible direction that this might take would involve embracing the affinity between business and private higher education seen elsewhere in this chapter.[77] Advanced education for business careers is not well developed in Britain today, although two small business schools are funded through the UGC as part of the university system. In 1981 a new entry to this expanding field was launched in London with the intention of offering MBAs under the auspices of two American universities.[78] Buckingham is rather well suited to enter the business administration field. It would fit quite well with the strengths that the university has already developed in economics, law, and accounting. The European studies program could also provide a valuable complement. And, the academic credibility that the UB has established would be a guarantee against the shoddiness of some programs that attempt to capitalize on the high current demand for these credentials. Moreover, the logic of Buckingham's peripheral situation indicates that a secure niche might best be found in a relatively open and growing field like business education. Success in such a program could bring the institution considerable rewards in terms of superior students, national reputation, and outside financial support.

Whether Buckingham chooses to introduce a program in business administration, or finds other more attractive options, of course remains to be seen. What is clear at this juncture is that its founders have been successful in creating an independent university, and in adding some new alternatives to the state-dominated British system of higher education. Buckingham is in important ways different from the other universities, and it has been struggling against an adverse financial tide to improve itself as well. It has been handicapped in this quest by not being able to appeal to a clearly defined external constituency that might identify with the college, underwrite its financial needs, and assure its supply of students. Such groups, it has been seen, have provided the mainstay of singular institutions in other countries. Instead, Buckingham owes its continued existence to a stubborn British conviction about the stultifying effects of monopoly and the beneficial consequences, for both the individual and society, of independence and self-reliance. While many British men and women endorse these principles when, say, voting for members of Parliament, they have been reluctant to stake the educational destiny of their children on such premises.[79] The University of Buckingham consequently faces continued uncertainty over the role that it should fulfill. If it utilizes its hard-won independence to adapt to the changing circumstances of British higher education, however, it may yet develop its own distinctive role, just as singular institutions in other peripheral private sectors have done.

Peripheral Private Sectors: Paradigm and Actuality

Of the three basic types of private sectors that have been considered, peripheral private sectors undoubtedly share the fewest general characteristics with one another. Each case supplements its corresponding dominant public sector in a different way, so that the resulting configurations would seem to have little in common. Beneath the surface, however, there are several tendencies that can be detected in each system.

First, here, as in other developed countries, it is exceedingly difficult to support an academically competitive institution solely on the basis of tuition revenues. As a consequence, institutional finances under contemporary conditions tend to be problematic in all these cases. The institutions have variously met this problem through public subsidies, voluntary support, or internal efficiency in their operations. The Stockholm School of Economics, besides receiving external support from the business community, relies upon a government payment in lieu of student tuition. The French schools of commerce are also sustained by semipublic funds through local chambers of commerce and industry. Where public funds are lacking, economical operation and some voluntary support seem necessary for survival. The Roman Catholic Church has demonstrated its capacity to operate educational institutions at minimal cost throughout the world, and the five Catholic universities of France would be no exception. In addition, they have broadened their sources of income by supplying a variety of services to the Catholic community. Finally, Buckingham would be the most tuition-dependent of the major peripheral institutions considered here, and this situation necessitates a host of cost-limiting measures, including year-round operations. The UB nevertheless must still rely upon external fund raising to meet its capital needs. These inherent financial limitations generally preclude peripheral private institutions from some of the more costly tasks of higher education. Thus, research in the natural sciences is almost exclusively confined to the dominant sectors, and in only one exceptional case (the Catholic university at Lille) can a faculty of medicine be found in these private sectors. When it can be afforded at all, the scholarship that emerges from peripheral private institutions is likely to be in the social sciences or humanities.

A second general characteristic of this structure is a tendency toward market segmentation rather than open competition with the dominant public sector. A certain amount of duplication of function is of course inescapable, but private schools tend to develop a special niche for themselves where they are shielded from direct competition with the publicly financed sector. The role of Catholic education is obvious here. Just as salient is the traditional affinity between private higher education and the preparation for careers in private industry. In Europe this type of instruction was previously (but no longer) eschewed by state universities, which principally prepared for the liberal professions and the civil service. But even today, when some public universities are eager to offer credentials for business, businessmen themselves still seem to feel more comfortable with institutions that are imbued with the culture of private enterprise. Perhaps the University of Buckingham provides the best corroboration of the tendency toward segmentation: founded with the intention of challenging the strength of the publicly supported universities by providing a well-rounded, liberal education, it has been forced by the circumstances of its existence into fulfilling several peripheral roles. When seen from the perspective of peripheral private sectors, the actual tasks of the UB seem more appropriate to its status than its original aspirations.

Since dominant public sectors generally concentrate upon the university component of higher education, the most fertile soil for peripheral private sectors is usually found among what are sometimes regarded as the nonuniversity functions. These rather explicitly vocational or service programs have grown considerably in recent decades, thereby expanding the scope for peripheral private sectors. In the French private sector, for example, the *sections de techniciens supérieurs* and most of the nonvocational service programs in the Catholic universities did not exist as higher education a generation ago. These kinds of programs tend to be short, practical, and specifically focused. Ideally, this area of higher education should be dynamic and market-sensitive. Having at least a part of these functions under private control helps to assure needed fluidity and responsiveness, thereby contributing to the diversity and adaptability of the system as a whole.

The singular institutions examined here make their contributions somewhat differently. They owe their original existences, above all, to the fulfillment of some indispensible function neglected by the public sector. Even in the specialized niches that they occupy, adjustments are still necessary to keep abreast of the times. The Ecole Libre des Sciences Politiques provides the negative example of this dictum. Its social relations, intellectual orientation, and educational purpose harmonized too perfectly, and it ossified within its original niche. Its opponents had good reason to replace it with state institutions that would be more open to students and to ideas. Conversely, the Stockholm School of Economics undoubtedly owes its continued independence to its capacity to adapt to changing conditions in the political milieu, the academic world, and the realm of business—the three constituencies with which it interacts. The University of Buckingham represents a third case, where the pressures of institutional survival will undoubtedly dictate some future adaptations before its inchoate niche is fully elaborated. When singular institutions fulfill vital roles, as in the first two cases, it would seem absolutely essential that they remain mindful of their public responsibilities.

Finally, it may at first appear adventitious that peripheral private sectors are associated with political conservatism in each of these countries, but closer consideration can relate this association with some inherent traits of these private institutions. Dominant public sectors are in themselves a manifestation of a bias toward publicness in these societies—a belief that democratically chosen governments should properly have the responsibility for meeting the higher education needs of the population. The specialized tasks assumed by peripheral institutions seem to lie somewhere near the borderline of this general domain. They are oriented above all toward the needs of specific, delimited constituencies. It is these private purposes more than their private control that puts peripheral private institutions at odds with the ideology of state responsibility. The identification with conservative interests, then, is virtually inescapable, but for the moment this does not seem to present insurmountable problems. Higher education as a whole constitutes a complex interpenetration of public and private interests. Peripheral private sectors provide a valuable supplement to dominant public sectors precisely because they serve the legitimate, collective, private ends of their sponsors. As long as those sponsors remain members in good standing of the national polity, that role constitutes the essence of public service for these private institutions.

Chapter 5

The American Private Sector in Comparative Perspective

The approximately 2.5 million students studying in privately controlled institutions of higher education in the United States nearly equal the entire enrollment of the seven private sectors discussed in the previous chapters. The American private sector is thus easily the world's largest, containing by itself a major share of all private enrollments in higher education. It is also arguably the most complex and least easy to characterize.

In part the complexity of the private sector in the United States is a direct product of its considerable size. For the past decade about 45 percent of college-age cohorts have been enrolling in higher education, and of course in certain areas the percentage has been even higher. This has meant that the American system of higher education as a whole has had to accommodate an unusually wide range of ability levels. Indeed, while some institutions expect their undergraduates to participate in faculty research projects, others must provide remedial courses just to give incoming students the basic skills needed for college work. The high rate of enrollment also requires considerable diversification in the tasks of higher education. Government bookkeeping, for example, officially recognizes 304 different bachelor's degrees spanning 24 fields.[1] But there are other complicating features of American higher education quite irrespective of its size.

In the American system the division between undergraduate and graduate study has been crucial in shaping institutional patterns.[2] With few exceptions, the elite places of study in the United States—those at which prestigious and lucrative career prospects are most assured—are located on the graduate level. Temporary high demand may cause the services of some fortunate bachelors to be bid up for a time, as was the case with petroleum engineers at the beginning of the 1980s; but in both engineering and business the most attractive entering positions are largely reserved for holders of master's degrees. More importantly, the traditional professions of medicine and law are only studied on the graduate level in the United States. For this reason the opportunity to matriculate at Harvard, say, is less of an automatic ticket to success than admission into the Ecole Polytechnique, the University of Tokyo, or the Stockholm School of Economics. The existence of these two educational tiers has a number of ramifications. For one thing, it permits an enormous degree of latitude in the undergraduate curriculum. The basic functions of the undergraduate tier can be to provide general intellectual development, especially in the liberal arts; to provide vocational instruction for certain careers; or to prepare for graduate/professional school. Historically, private colleges have favored a general, unfettered undergraduate curriculum, with professional training deferred to the postgraduate level, while public institutions have been pressured in the direction of offering terminal vocational bachelor's degrees.[3] (That distinction would be far less valid today.) Nevertheless, private colleges have been able to emphasize their individuality by capitalizing on the choice that is inherent in these alternatives, and also on the wide latitude permitted in approach and style. Graduate curricula are far more rigid, but many private universities in urban areas have taken advantage of a rapidly growing demand for these programs. Thus, the graduate tier has offered further possibilities for distinctive institutional specializations.

A third element of complexity results from the federal political structure of the United States and the fact that responsibility for education is lodged on the state level. This produces fifty public sectors, albeit with basic similarities, but also having important differences of size, scope, prestige, and priority. Each public sector, with the sole exception of sparsely populated Wyoming, is complemented by a different configuration of private institutions. In particular, the public-private patterns vary considerably across regions. Private higher education was long dominant in the Northeast, with public systems developing relatively recently in Massachusetts, Pennsylvania, and New York State (but not New York City). In the Far West, state institutions have led the growth of higher education, leaving the private sector with a comparatively small percentage of total enrollments. There is consequently an asymmetry in the American private sector. The oldest private universities, now among the most prestigious, are all found in the Northeast; liberal arts colleges can be found in almost every state, but they are most dense in the area stretching from New England into the Midwest;

and, nearly all the major cities in the eastern half of the country have been the seats of private universities bearing their names.

The many institutions of the American private sectors of course share numerous similarities. They have been shaped to a considerable extent by the same legal parameters surrounding degrees and accreditation. By virtue of being private, and with few exceptions nonprofit,[4] they also share certain organizational features. Finally, they possess a set of related interests concerning developments in the public sector and, in particular, aspects of federal policy toward higher education as a whole. Beyond these common features, however, it becomes difficult to make collective generalizations about private higher education in the United States. One issue that inevitably lumps these institutions together is the relative decline of the private sector over the last generation.

In 1951, for the last time, American private colleges and universities enrolled more students than their public counterparts. Thereafter for the remainder of the decade each additional student in the private sector was matched by more than two new students in public institutions. To a considerable extent during these years the two sectors were embarking on divergent courses.[5] After the years of overcrowding caused by the influx of veterans studying on the GI Bill, many private schools sought a period of consolidation in which to reassert their traditional roles. They willingly restricted their size despite an increasing pool of applicants, and as a result became more selective in choosing their students. Public institutions meanwhile were gradually expanding to accommodate a burgeoning popular demand for higher education. When the baby-boom cohorts reached college age in the early 1960s they produced an avalanche of enrollments that affected both sectors. American higher education added three million additional places from 1960 to 1967, but only six hundred thousand of them were in the private sector. After this date the different strategies of the two sectors are even more evident: enrollments in the private sector remained almost static for the next seven years at just over two million, while the public sector added another two and one-half million students. The 1975–76 academic year brought the final spasm of growth in this cycle, and it left the private sector in its current position of claiming less than one-quarter of the enrollments in American higher education. In the past generation, then, the private sector more than doubled in size, yet lost half of its share of the American student market. While these figures might be analyzed in numerous ways,[6] several unambiguous aspects of this development are pertinent to the relative position of the private sector.

The relationship between public and private sectors in the expansion of American higher education is very nearly the inverse of that experienced by the mass private sector of Japan. In the United States the public sector created places for a broader socioeconomic participation in higher education, while a major portion of the private sector concentrated on the traditional clientele with stronger academic preparation. Moreover, public-sector growth took place in two stages. From the end of the 1950s through the 1960s this expansion was due chiefly to the creation and enlargement of state colleges and universities. The second stage, which overlapped the first by only a few years and extended to 1975, saw enrollment growth concentrated in two-year community colleges. Each of these stages had little direct effect upon the private sector. The elaboration of the state systems of colleges and universities affected few of the markets for private-college students, except when they penetrated urban areas (where students were relatively abundant in any case). The community-college movement was pitched at a clientele that, at this time, was largely lacking in income, aptitude, and motivation compared to private-sector students. If anything, the community colleges were competing at the margins with state institutions. Indeed, during the years of most explosive community-college growth (1970–75), they added more than two and one-half times as many students as the state colleges and universities. By mid-decade it would seem that the sources that had fed the expansion of both types of institutions were fully served. For the remainder of the 1970s the private sector actually added more new students than community colleges and state institutions combined.[7]

The shrinkage of private-sector enrollment share to less than one-quarter of the total, then, no more represented a "decline" than did a similar reduction registered by the public universities in Japan. Like them, private institutions in the United States have, with few exceptions, been reluctant to grow. Of the sixty largest universities in the United States, only six are privately controlled: five of these are in large cities where they find a considerable part-time clientele, and one—Brigham Young University—aspires to fulfill the entire higher education needs of a uniquely delimited population. Furthermore, the importance of the private sector looms larger when more discriminating measures are employed. In 1980 the private sector enrolled a third of the nation's full-time students, and awarded a third of all bachelor's degrees. It granted 37 percent of the master's and Ph.D. degrees given that year, 39 percent of the medical degrees, and 63 percent of all legal degrees.[8] Ultimately, however, the significance of the private sector cannot be expressed very well in quantitative terms. It lies, above all, in the diverse and crucial roles that are fulfilled by different kinds of private institutions. Many of these roles are identical to those found in other private sectors, but the multifarious American private sector fills other roles as well.

Compared to the United States, the private sectors of the other seven countries considered here can largely be explained in terms of a single overriding purpose. The mass private sectors of Japan and the Philippines chiefly owe their existence to the limited quantities of state higher education provided at public expense. The role of private universities, in a sense, has been to supply *more* higher education to meet the popular demand. In Belgium and the Netherlands parallel public and private sectors have resulted from conscious political decisions that both types of institutions should coexist on an equal footing. The state accepts financial responsibility for this public service in order to allow private universities to express the cultural *differences* inherent in these pluralistic societies. In the state-dominated higher education systems of France and Sweden peripheral private sectors accommodate *differences* of another kind. The interests of special constituencies, which are for various reasons left out of the dominant public sectors, have found outlets there in private institutions. These schools, however, tend to be limited in scope, either because of their specific focus, or due to the practical impossibility of emulating comprehensive state universities.

In the abstract these examples suggest two "pure" functions of private sectors: supplying *more* and supplying *different* higher education.[9] A third pure function that might justify private institutions figures only exceptionally in these systems. That would be providing education that is in some sense *better* than that available from the state. "Better" can, of course, have numerous meanings in this context. The subjective side of this issue involves the suitability of certain schools for particular individuals, but is difficult to deal with systematically or comparatively.[10] There are more tangible aspects of quality, however—those by which an institution may be said to have attained some recognized form of excellence. The Stockholm School of Economics, for example, has achieved undisputed eminence in those few academic fields within its purview. The leading private universities of Japan, together with the commercial *grandes écoles* of France, exhibit an excellence derived from the selectivity of their student bodies—their attractiveness in both cases mirroring exactly the attractiveness of the career prospects for their graduates. The old Ecole Libre des Sciences Politiques perfectly exemplified stature that is associated with the patronage of a social elite, and the leading colleges of Manila today fulfill a similar role. In each of these cases the private institutions offer alternatives that are in some sense qualitatively superior to what is available in some or all of the public sector. In the American private sector this quality dimension is particularly prominent in the justification of certain institutions.

The great American private research universities in particular are unique in the extent to which they offer superior educational quality. Ratings of overall faculty quality consistently show the majority of the top research universities to be private,[11] but in several other factors affecting quality public universities cannot rival the best privates at all. Specifically, the private research universities have much more select student bodies; the sheer quantity of educational resources available on a per-student basis is extraordinary; and the richness of the admixture of research in the education-research matrix is unmatched in the public sector. True, these are largely measures of excellence for one kind of higher education, but it is precisely this type of exceedingly expensive instruction that is overwhelmingly the province of the state in most other national systems. The development of these private research universities is certainly one of the unique features of the American private sector—and a feature that will be examined in greater detail below. Nevertheless being *better*—the function of supplying superior quality—is actually only one facet of the American private sector.

In the analysis that follows all three rationales for the private provision of this necessary service—*more, different,* and *better*—will be employed as organizing principles for examining the American private sector. Large urban and suburban private universities coexist with nearby public counterparts in the nation's population centers, thereby providing *more* higher education to meet local demand. The myriad liberal arts colleges, with their intimate atmosphere, dedication to teaching, and diverse cultural orientations, above all provide *different* alternatives. And private research universities offer education that is in varying degrees *better* than that found in the bulk of the public sector. The common traits and significant variations within each of these groups of institutions will be analyzed separately later in this chapter. Before proceeding, however, several caveats are in order. These roles are by no means mutually exclusive: most private institutions would consider themselves in some ways *different* and *better*. Nor can every institution be fitted into these categories and their subdivisions. Besides the problem of borderlines, some private colleges are simply *sui generis*. This categorization is chiefly intended as an heuristic device, first, to break down the complexity of the American private sector and, secondly, to isolate the dynamic factors affecting each part. The focus will consequently be placed on those institutions that best exemplify these different divisions. The groups of institutions that will be analyzed here, then, are presented as archetypes of the principal varieties of American private colleges and universities.[12] First, however, it is necessary to examine an important underlying cause of this variety: the different sources of support for private higher education.

Sources of Support for the Private Sector

In table 6 the revenue sources of public and private higher education are given in a somewhat simplified form that corresponds roughly with actual education-related expenditures.[13] These few figures point toward some of the most distinctive features of the American private sector.

Viewed comparatively, the most remarkable aspect of the American private sector is the high level of per-student income (and hence expenditure) relative to the public sector. Even if public community colleges with their low per-student costs were eliminated

TABLE 6. Selected Per-Student Revenues, United States, 1978–79

	Public Institutions		Private Institutions	
	($)	(%)	($)	(%)
Tuition and fees from students	698	17	3,056	57
Private gifts	133	3	799	15
Endowment income	24	1	402	8
Federal restricted grants and contracts (research)	487	12	856	16
State and local governments	2,784	67	221	4
Total	4,126	100	5,334	100

Source: Adapted from National Center for Educational Statistics, *Digest of Education Statistics, 1981* (Washington, D.C.: Government Printing Office, 1981), p. 149.

from this comparison, a higher bottom-line figure for the public sector would do nothing to diminish the importance of this point. Its significance derives from the fact that while 80 percent of public-sector revenues are from public sources, 80 percent of private-sector revenues, ignoring student aid for the moment, are generated privately. Obviously the key to the welfare of the American private sector lies in its ability to tap private sources of revenue. The federal government is also inextricably involved in the financing of private institutions. In fact, to understand the significant divisions within the private sector it is necessary to understand the differential impact of each of these sources of income.

Tuition is the largest source of revenue for private schools, and it is also the cause of the single greatest disparity between public and private institutions. In 1984, for example, the average annual tuition was almost $3,900 more at a private than at a public university.[14] This pricing "gap" between public and private institutions has long been worrisome for the private sector. The uncomfortable truth is that the cost of private higher education is now higher than most private-sector students can be expected to pay. As a result some 63 percent of undergraduates in the private sector have been receiving need-based financial aid of some type or other.[15] The great bulk of these funds comes through a combination of different federal programs that have been put in place over the past two decades. These are supplemented by state programs, where they exist, and by varying amounts of institutionally supplied aid at most private schools.[16] The typical aid recipient might be given a financial package consisting of federal and institutional grants, subsidized loans, and obligations for part-time work. These federal programs and some of their implications will be considered more specifically in the following chapter. Nevertheless, there are some features of these arrangements that are germane to the role of tuition in the pricing of American higher education.

Student aid basically serves to make the price of higher education vary according to the student's ability to pay for it. This effect is consistent with its underlying purpose of equalizing educational opportunity. A significant portion of federal student aid is intended not to support students, but to permit them to support themselves. Thus, in fiscal year 1979, 47 percent of the Department of Education student-aid expenditures went for subsidizing student loans and work-study—programs designed essentially to use public subsidies to bring more private resources into the support of higher education.[17] Federal student-aid programs taken together constitute a marginal addition to the private funds that provide the income for private colleges and universities; but it is an indispensible margin all the same, because it goes to subsidize a large number of students who presumably would not otherwise be able to bear the full cost. In this respect, student aid has allowed private schools to raise their prices without fully facing the normal economic consequence of reduced demand. The private sector as a whole has consequently become dependent upon the perpetuation of these federal programs for its continued well-being. The crucial importance of financial aid could well be the most common element in the financial equations of different types of private institution. It is certainly more constant than the role of tuition itself.

As a broad generalization it would undoubtedly be safe to say that the higher the tuition a private college or university charges, the less tuition-dependent the institution is likely to be; and conversely, the lower the tuition, the greater the probable dependence on tuition revenue. The reason for this apparent paradox will become evident when the discussion turns to the subject of voluntary support. Basically, the highest tuition is charged by research universities and highly selective liberal arts colleges that have other substantial sources of income. Their students consequently receive a subsidy for their education from endowment income, alumni support, and other private gifts.[18] The less selective private colleges and universities, more often than not, have little of such supplemental income. Not only are they dependent upon tuition revenues, but they are also constrained by the capacity of their clientele to pay, even taking student aid into account. The profile of private-sector revenues given in table 6, then, can be rather misleading, because a considerable number of private institutions do not have appreciable revenues outside of tuition. For that reason, nontuition income is most indicative of the different roles fulfilled by different types of private colleges and universities.

The amount of federal support for academic science that a university receives best indicates its involvement in research in the natural sciences, and hence the degree of institutional commitment to advancing such knowledge. The distribution of these funds is powerfully skewed toward the leading research universities. The twenty largest recipients of these funds take in almost as much (42 percent) of the total as the next eighty (43 percent). And that leaves little for the remaining eighteen hundred four-year colleges and universities.[19] Although there is some fluctuation from year to year, public and private institutions are about evenly represented in the top twenty places of this hierarchy, but the relatively numerous large state universities outnumber privates by about three to one in the next eighty places. The weight of research-intensive medical education strongly influences the allocation of research funds. More than half of federal research and development funds are consistently allocated to biological science, and the majority of that total is earmarked specifically for medical research. Those universities with medical schools consequently compete for a much larger portion of the federal research budget.

The private universities that are large recipients of federal research funds also benefit from significant amounts of voluntary support. In this respect the distribution of federal research funds shows evidence of a "Matthew effect" at work in higher education: "unto him who hath shall be given. . . ."[20] Put more prosaically, the private universities seem to use their wealth in such ways as to guarantee the continuing flow of research contracts. But not all affluent institutions follow this course. The relative importance of tuition, federal research funds, and voluntary support in fact differs for private research universities, liberal arts colleges, and urban universities. These different patterns are depicted in figure 4.

Each axis of the triangle in figure 4 represents the percentage of income coming from one of three sources. The three coordinates of any given point thus add up to 100 percent. As one moves perpendicularly away from the left-hand side of the triangle the percentage of voluntary support in the total of general and educational expenditures increases; distance from the right-hand side indicates increasing percentages of federal support for academic science. The vertical axis of the triangle, then, is a residual, which for most institutions is largely covered by tuition. The closer to the peak of the triangle that an institution is located, then, the more completely it depends upon student tuition to meet its expenditures.

Area "C," which encloses the coordinates of eighteen large urban universities, extends from this point of full tuition dependence down the right side to the line of about 10 percent voluntary support. The area then extends leftward toward the federal research side of the triangle. This extension in fact represents the influence of those universities with medical schools, all of which derived 10 percent or more of their budgets from federal research funds. The liberal arts colleges (area "B") lie tight against the right-hand side of the triangle, indicating a variable amount of voluntary support, but virtually no federal research funds. Even among the elite of the selective liberal arts colleges (called Liberal Arts 1 in the

Carnegie Classification of Institutions of Higher Education), less than 2 percent of their budget would be so covered, and the less selective colleges (Liberal Arts 2) receive no funds at all from this source. The research universities in area "A" occupy the center of the triangle, indicating that they combine significant amounts of both research funding and voluntary support. Together these sources account for at least one-quarter of the budget, and in several cases more than one-half. Figure 4 provides a first cut into the

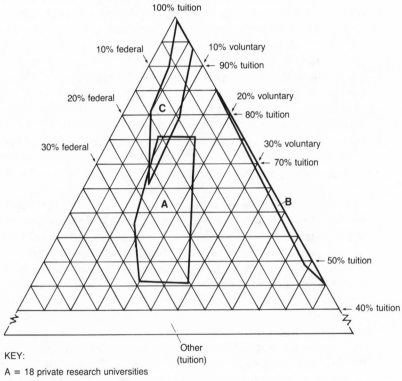

KEY:
A = 18 private research universities
B = 18 private liberal arts colleges
C = 18 large urban private universities

Fig. 4. Percentage of income derived from major sources, by type of American private institution. *Sources*: Compiled from CFAE, *Voluntary Support of Education, 1979-80; Federal Support to Universities and Colleges, Fiscal Year 1979* (Washington, D.C.: National Science Foundation, 1981). Representative institutions selected from sample described in note 12 to chapter 5.

American private sector, but to break down these three basic types of private institutions into more meaningful subdivisions it is necessary to delve more deeply into the matter of voluntary support.

Philanthropy has been instrumental in the shaping of the American private sector since the day that John Harvard achieved immortality by giving £799 to the newly founded college in the Massachusetts Bay Colony.[21] Voluntary support for private institutions has been encountered elsewhere in this study at Waseda, Buckingham, and the Stockholm School of Economics, but no other private sector can match the United States in the magnitude, the regularity, and hence the institutionalization of these gifts. In addition to the income from current giving, table 6 shows an average of half as much again received as income from endowment, largely created through past giving.[22] In 1979–80 private four-year colleges and universities received almost $2 billion in voluntary support, most of which can be attributed to four types of donors. Alumni supplied the largest component of private-sector gifts (27 percent), followed by nonalumni individuals (25 percent), foundations (23 percent), and business corporations (16 percent).[23] The last three of these categories represent rather heterogeneous kinds of giving, while alumni support plays an especially important role for certain kinds of institutions.

Foundations have played a crucial role in the development of the American private sector. The Carnegie Foundation induced many private colleges to drop their sectarian affiliations when it established the first pension system for college teachers. Subsequently, foundations took the leadership in stimulating scientific research on campus, in reforming medical education, and in developing the social sciences as disciplines. Their gifts have also helped to build the endowments of numerous private colleges and universities.[24] Since World War II, foundations have proliferated, but their influence has in many respects been overshadowed by that of the federal government. Grants in support of academic research are generally made by the largest foundations having professional staffs competent to evaluate research proposals. Besides research, foundation giving to higher education has been especially important for providing capital and for facilitating the development of new programs. Most important in this context is the natural affinity between private foundations and private colleges and universities. Many foundations consider sustaining the private sector to be their special responsibility; and this mission is reflected in the fact that about two-thirds of foundation higher-education dollars go to the private sector.[25]

Corporate contributions to higher education have increased markedly since the mid-seventies, and this is a source of support for which educators have high hopes for the future.[26] While some of these gifts can be construed as essentially disinterested, much of this giving can be associated with the broad interests of the corporation in two general ways. Many corporations specifically restrict their gifts to educational programs or research that is related to their industry. Companies also seek to build goodwill through their giving programs. This last consideration creates an important nexus between corporations and the colleges in their immediate community. In 1980, for the first time, research and related academic activities received the largest share of corporate gifts; support for local colleges undoubtedly comprised another significant share; and a minor portion was scattered widely as matching gifts for employee contributions.

The second largest category of voluntary support, nonalumni individuals, chiefly represents higher education's share of the general philanthropic giving of the country's wealthier citizens. Each private institution goes to considerable lengths to cultivate its own particular "friends of the college," for whom its locality, its special competence, or some personal connection might someday evoke a significant gift. As with corporations, the influence of proximity is especially important for this type of giving.

The continued devotion of graduates to the colleges they attended is certainly one of the distinctive features of American higher education. It is also the reason why alumni gifts are consistently the single largest source of voluntary support for the private sector. This did not come about by accident. Almost all colleges and universities maintain alumni offices for the purpose of staying in communication with and soliciting contributions from former students. But not all alumni feel the same degree of obligation to their alma mater. Alumni support is related rather closely to the undergraduate, residential educational experience. Few commuter students develop deep attachments for the institution whose classes they attend. For graduate or professional students, loyalties tend to be with particular professors (who may or may not remain with the university), with departments, and ultimately with the disciplines or professions they join. Undergraduates living on campus develop ties, above all, to classmates and college. These sentiments are clearly the most powerful in evoking future generosity.

Colleges that depend upon their alumni go to considerable effort to make the collegiate experience an intense and pleasant one. Great care is placed upon accommodations and other physical facilities, and the social life of the college is regarded as an integral part of the total campus activities.[27] An explicit attempt is made to establish a student's entering class as a perpetual reference group through five-year class reunions, as well as the regular alumni communications.

Alumni giving is an especially beneficial form of income for a private institution, since it is fairly reliable and largely unrestricted in nature. Perhaps most importantly, it comes from those who identify with and strongly support the mission of the school. For old grads the alma mater becomes virtually an end in itself, whose goal is to win football games or achieve other such distinctions, and also to educate more future alumni. These gifts require no accountability to parties outside the college. This income consequently, more than any other that a private college or university receives, allows the school to pursue its own internally generated objectives.[28]

Only certain kinds of private colleges and universities can manage to inspire a high degree of alumni loyalty. For that reason the extent to which an institution depends upon its alumni for voluntary support turns out to be a significant indicator of the nature of the school. In figure 5 the ratio of alumni support to total voluntary support has been graphed against the tuition value (see below) of voluntary support in order to further differentiate the three institutional types of figure 4. Each of the eleven areas of figure 5 (A1 through C5) represents the loci of three or more institutions identified by type in the key. The tuition equivalent, or "tuition value," of the 1979–80 voluntary support for each school has been calculated as follows:

$$\text{Tuition value} = \frac{\text{voluntary support used for current operations} + 5\% \text{ of endowment}}{\text{full-time students} + \frac{1}{2} \text{ part-time students}}$$

Thus, tuition value approximates the additional tuition each full-time student would have to pay in order to match the equivalent annual amount that past and present voluntary support is subsidizing his or her education. Discrepancies in tuition value are enormous: many of the urban service universities have less than thirty dollars, while the wealthiest of the Ivy League universities can count on near seven thousand dollars. The horizontal axis measures the proportion of alumni support to total current voluntary support. This ratio turns out to discriminate quite well between different types of both research universities and liberal arts colleges. For

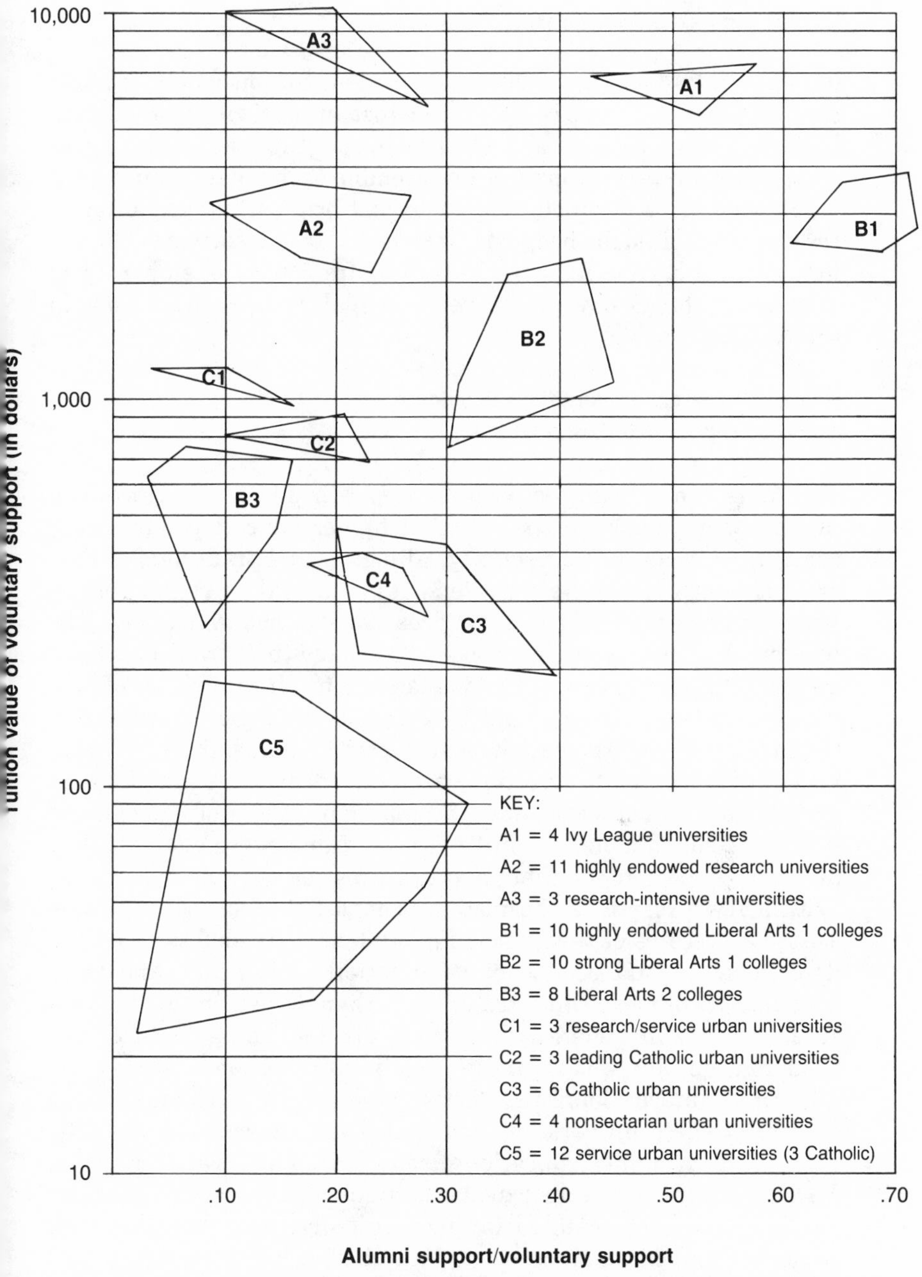

Tuition value of voluntary support (in dollars) (vertical axis)

Axis values: 10,000 · 1,000 · 100 · 10

Horizontal axis values: .10 · .20 · .30 · .40 · .50 · .60 · .70

Labels on plot: A3, A1, A2, B1, B2, C1, C2, B3, C4, C3, C5

KEY:
A1 = 4 Ivy League universities
A2 = 11 highly endowed research universities
A3 = 3 research-intensive universities
B1 = 10 highly endowed Liberal Arts 1 colleges
B2 = 10 strong Liberal Arts 1 colleges
B3 = 8 Liberal Arts 2 colleges
C1 = 3 research/service urban universities
C2 = 3 leading Catholic urban universities
C3 = 6 Catholic urban universities
C4 = 4 nonsectarian urban universities
C5 = 12 service urban universities (3 Catholic)

Alumni support/voluntary support

Fig. 5. Amount and type of voluntary support in American private colleges and universities. *Sources*: Compiled from CFAE, *Voluntary Support of Education, 1979-80; Federal Support to Universities and Colleges, Fiscal Year 1979* (Washington, D.C.: National Science Foundation, 1981). Representative institutions selected from sample described in note 12 to chapter 5.

urban universities the interaction between tuition value and this ratio is somewhat more complex. The institutions within the groupings that have been produced here by plotting the amount and nature of voluntary support often resemble each other in numerous other ways as well, including historical origins, participation in research, and student-body characteristics. In the sections that follow, then, the groupings created by figure 5 will be employed to analyze and break down the three principal types of institutions in the American private sector.

Private Research Universities: Providing
Superior Higher Education

The American private research university has been described as a unique phenomenon in the world of higher education due to the combined effects of "sovereignty, affluence and tradition."[29] Sovereignty has allowed these universities to have their centers of initiative within themselves; their great wealth has given them the wherewithal to pursue their chosen goals; and their traditions have guided each institution in its own fashion toward its vision of academic excellence. The criteria used in the Carnegie Classification identified thirty-six private Research 1 and 2 universities.[30] Twenty-four of those institutions have been included in this sample: each had tuition values for voluntary support in excess of $2,000, and voluntary support plus federal research grants were equivalent to at least 25 percent of their expenditures for current operations. With a few exceptions the median composite Scholastic Aptitude Test (SAT) scores of their incoming students exceeded twelve hundred (which would be above the ninetieth percentile), and their graduate enrollment consisted of more than 20 percent of the total student body. In general, their most distinguishing features are their considerable wealth and the willing restriction of size.

In an international perspective perhaps the most remarkable feature of these universities has been their capacity to meet the rising costs of higher education largely through private resources. Throughout the world the expense of higher education in a research environment has escalated far more rapidly than that of higher education in general since World War II. This has been due in part to the proliferation of new specialties, the increase in graduate study, and advances in the technology supporting research. Everywhere this trend has resulted in an overwhelming reliance upon national governments to meet these soaring costs. This has, of course, occurred in the United States as well. The American private research universities were in a position to become beneficiaries of the growing postwar federal support for science because of their efficient prior utilization of their own resources. They had gradually restricted their enrollments to students with high academic abilities, sought out top scholars, and improved the environment for scholarship.[31] Thus, when ever-greater federal support for science became available, and was allocated through the peer-review process to the most capable scholars, a considerable portion of these funds found their way to private research universities. What distinguishes these twenty-four institutions from other large recipients, public and private, is the large volume of research funding relative to the number of students.

Only four of these twenty-four universities exceed fifteen thousand students, and even this size, which is well under the average public university enrollment of about twenty-two thousand, is in these cases the cumulative result of numerous units that themselves tend to be of moderate size. Another four institutions have fewer than five thousand students, including Caltech, the nation's most selective institution, and Rice University, which was so wealthy that it charged no tuition until the 1960s. For all twenty-four, the median value of federal research funds per student was about $4,500—well above the level of the leading state universities.

Above all, the private research universities are characterized by a dominant commitment to the academic values underlying the disinterested pursuit of knowledge. These values are, of course, no different in the leading public universities. They are in fact common to the communities engaged in disciplinary research. The private research universities, however, have been able to concentrate single-mindedly upon expanding the frontiers of knowledge while also producing superior bachelors and Ph.D.s. Regarding undergraduates, it can scarcely be an accident that the ten schools with the highest tuition value of voluntary support also had the most select student bodies in terms of SATs.[32] The nation's most academically able students, it would seem, seek out the most highly subsidized undergraduate programs. These universities are similarly attractive to graduate students. In the most recent and most thorough reputational survey of graduate departments, private research universities claimed six of the top seven places, and ten of the first fifteen.[33] These results are consistent with previous surveys.[34] Even given the predominant emphasis upon academic values, there is considerable latitude in the manner in which each university can pursue its own style of excellence.

In figure 5, eighteen of the research universities are represented by three distinct clusters of institutions. The area "A1" is defined by those Ivy League schools with the greatest per-student wealth—Harvard, Yale, Princeton, and partly by virtue of its small enrollment, Dartmouth. These institutions were among the first to systematically exploit their alumni for support, and still depend upon them for approximately half of their voluntary support. Brown and Cornell also share this latter trait, but with less than half as much tuition value in voluntary support. The "A1" universities, in particular, benefit from large numbers of alumni who are not only devoted, but quite affluent as well. Their graduates are now located throughout the country, and indeed the world, and their recruitment of current students fully reflects this dispersion. These universities are consequently national institutions, despite historic ties to particular regions. Their alumni-dependence has a powerful influence upon their priorities. Above all, they take great care to cultivate the residential undergraduate college within the research university setting. Their research commitments must therefore be kept in balance with this overriding goal. The two most urban representatives of the Ivy League (Columbia and Pennsylvania) would share most of these same values, but in their pattern of voluntary support they fall with the universities of "A2."

The eleven universities located in "A2" either owe their affluence to one principal source of philanthropy, or else have derived it over time from numerous sources within the cities or regions where they are located. Carnegie-Mellon, Tulane, Duke, and Case Western Reserve all bear the name of their chief benefactors; while Chicago, Rochester, and Emory owe their present status to, respectively, John D. Rockefeller, George Eastman and the company he founded, and the fortunes spawned by Coca-Cola.[35] In each case the city in which the university was located has been a crucial factor in this philanthropy. In the case of Northwestern, Washington University, Columbia, and Penn the special relationship with their cities has been the chief rationale for sustained voluntary support. The intended roles of these universities, then, has been to provide local centers of culture and intellectual excellence. Their fund raising consequently tends to be focused on their locale, where it encompasses indigenous alumni, corporations, and certain prominent nonalumni—the latter two sources being particularly important for these universities. Graduate and professional training has been an important function, with such students comprising more than 40 percent of enrollments in most cases. Chicago is an extreme in this regard with more than three-fourths of its students in graduate and professional schools. Collegiate traditions, including big-time athletics, are sustained to varying degrees at Tulane, Northwestern, and Duke, which are somewhat less urban than the rest. All these institutions are in some sense national universities, but, in addition, their special relationships with their regional communities are significant components in their identities and sense of institutional purpose.

Four other research universities bear an affinity to the "A2" group. Vanderbilt would seem to belong with them by origin, location, and level of affluence; but it differs in having significantly more alumni support (35 percent). This is indicative of strong collegiate traditions in its undergraduate college. Rice is considerably more wealthy than other "A2" schools by virtue of its small enrollment and very large endowment. As a result, the endowment is capable of generating more than $5,000 in income for each student. Interestingly, Rice has used its wealth to keep its tuition well below that charged by other research universities—less than half that of "A1" schools in 1980–81. Brandeis differs from other research universities by its recent origins (founded in 1948) and the nature of its support. It has depended upon the American Jewish community for contributions while waiting for its alumni to become older, richer, and more numerous. The fourth of these universities, Stanford, is distinctive in several ways. Although its philanthropic origins are similar to some of the other "A2" universities, a recently completed fund-raising campaign mobilizing alumni and other sources of support succeeded in raising its tuition value above $5,000. This places Stanford among the top ten private institutions. It also consistently ranks in the top ten of all universities in faculty quality, a distinction that only the University of Chicago among the "A2" universities can claim. Stanford clearly endeavors to excel on a number of dimensions, including intercollegiate athletics, so perhaps it is appropriate that its position on figure 5 would lie in the area between "A1," "A2," and "A3."

The three schools located in "A3"—Caltech, MIT, and Johns Hopkins—belong in a class by themselves that might be called research-intensive universities. Their research efforts are so massive as to dwarf the resources directed toward their distinguished undergraduate programs. The per-student value of federal research grants ranged from $13,500 at MIT to $21,900 at Johns Hopkins (not including the university-administered Advance Physics Lab). These schools are also rich in voluntary support, in part because corporations and foundations participate in the funding of scientific research. MIT possesses the fourth largest private endowment, and the tuition value of voluntary support in the two other schools exceeds $10,000. Above all, they represent an extreme in the orientation toward research that is shared by all private research universities.

These twenty-four universities thus vary considerably in the emphasis given research in the matrix of institutional purpose. The research-intensive schools stand at one pole, while Dartmouth, which resembles the leading liberal arts colleges in many respects, defines the other. However, the overriding commitment to the values of academic inquiry are a constant throughout the group. Indeed, this integrity is the most valuable asset for each institution, upon which is predicated the continued flow of both research grants and voluntary support. The disquiet created in 1981 when Harvard considered forming a commercial genetic engineering company, and its rapid decision to resist this temptation, illustrates the weight of these values. Alumni dependence, and hence the weight of alumni interests in institutional decision making, also vary considerably across these universities. For the half that are alumni dependent (alumni support >$800 per student) this principally means maintaining a particular emphasis upon undergraduate teaching and the residential college. The other half of the represented universities that are not alumni dependent (alumni support <$600 per student) tend to depend upon external support generated from their roles as regional research centers. This is the case with all but one of the "A2" universities, including even Chicago, which plays an indisputably national role in graduate training.[36]

The one orientation conspicuously lacking among private research universities is that of service, in the sense used here of supplying the educational requirements of a local population of students or fulfilling the training needs of employers. By choosing to fill their limited places with the best available students, these schools seek to optimize rather than maximize their educational outputs. In doing so they fulfill the function for which they are far better suited, that of setting high standards for the academic community as a whole.

Liberal Arts Colleges: Higher Education with a Difference

Liberal arts (LA) colleges were the original organizational form for higher education in the United States, but they have also managed to fill an important role in the age of the university. The ideal that they represent, it has just been noted, continues to exert a powerful influence on many research universities. The LA colleges themselves contribute irreplaceable elements of pedagogic excellence and cultural diversity to the system as a whole. In 1970 the Carnegie Council identified 572 LA colleges, which comprised more than three-quarters of all private degree-granting institutions and enrolled 26 percent of private-sector students. In the decade since, these schools have expanded moderately at the same pace as the private sector as a whole.[37] The occasional shuttering of one of the weaker colleges has tended to divert attention from the robust health of many others. Apparently, to paraphrase Daniel Webster's famous words, there are still those who love these little colleges.[38] Just who "they" might be is an important factor in the life of each college.

The most distinguishing feature of LA colleges is their dominant emphasis on undergraduate education. They have few or no graduate students, and except for sporadic small grants they do not participate in the federal funding of academic science (see figure 4). After this short list of common characteristics, however, a chasm develops between the schools that were designated LA1 and LA2 in the Carnegie Classification. That division was made chiefly on the basis of student-body quality as reflected in each college's selectivity. It can also be observed in figure 5 that there are significant differences in wealth between the two categories. But, beyond these objective factors, there are pervasive differences in atmosphere and orientation.

LA1 colleges have basically adapted to the age of the university by becoming "university colleges," designed to prepare a high proportion of their students for postgraduate training in university graduate or professional schools.[39] For this reason they share the same commitment to academic values that is found in research universities, but without the heavy emphasis on faculty scholarship. Although these values are seldom entirely absent in LA2 schools, they tend to be diluted by an admixture of nonintellectual values emanating from the sponsoring organization, the local community, or the vocational concerns of parents and students. This dichotomy is accompanied by a difference in the kind of people who "love these little schools" enough to contribute to them. Those colleges that best exemplify the university college ideal are overwhelmingly supported by their alumni, and this gives the LA1 colleges higher levels of voluntary support and higher per-student expenditures. Since they are by definition more selective, this creates a general correlation between selectivity and alumni giving: the higher the median composite SAT scores for a college, the higher per-student alumni contributions are likely to be. LA2 colleges typically depend upon voluntary support for a non-negligible portion of their revenue, but the amount derived from their alumni tends to fall well below the 26 percent average for all colleges.

In general LA1 and LA2 colleges share little common ground.[40] The former constitute a major tributary to the academic mainstream of American higher education. They please their alumni by recruiting able students and giving them the kind of close personal instruction that can provide the basis for later postgraduate academic success. Their alumni respond by providing the margin of support that is necessary to maintain the quality of their programs, and often by sending their sons and daughters there as well. LA2 schools, regardless of their attraction or aversion to the academic mainstream, are perforce oriented toward external constituencies. Not only do these groups provide a needed financial cushion, but they are also likely to be their chief source of students.

Among LA1 colleges there are a dozen that epitomize this type in terms of their affluence, the powerful loyalties of their alumni, and their level of selectivity. Thus, they might be called LA1+. Ten of these LA1+ schools are rather closely bunched in the "B1" area of figure 5; two others—Swarthmore and Wellesley—differ from these others only in being even wealthier. Five of the twelve are women's colleges (Wellesley, Smith, Mount Holyoke, Wells, and Agnes Scott); and another four only recently became coeducational (Vassar, and the formerly all-male Amherst, Williams, and Bowdoin). Thus, it would seem that single-sex institutions have had a special capacity for instilling a deep and lasting sense of community among classmates.[41] The three longtime coeducational colleges (Swarthmore, Oberlin, and Grinnell) seem to depend upon distinctive traditions of excellence to elicit a comparable degree of loyalty.

The area in figure 5 between "B1" and "B2" is rather sparsely populated. Few institutions are fortunate enough to receive a tuition value of voluntary support in excess of $2,500. Two that do (Wesleyan and Bryn Mawr), but with considerably less alumni dependence, also bear a greater resemblance to universities than do most liberal arts colleges. Pomona and Claremont Men's college are similar in being wealthy, highly regarded colleges with weak alumni giving. Significantly, they form part of the Claremont Group, which, if unified, would constitute a research university. A large number of colleges could be identified that derive more than half of their voluntary support from their alumni, but are somewhat less wealthy than the LA1+ schools (tuition value = $1,000–$2,500), including Haverford, Bennington, Mills, Goucher, and Sarah Lawrence. For these five schools, at least, it seems likely that the causes of alumni generosity are the same as for the LA1+ colleges. In a sense, then, the distribution of LA1 colleges can be envisioned as a continuum, but as one moves on figure 5 below the $2,000 level for tuition value, and toward a percentage of alumni giving under 45 percent, the density of institutions thickens.

The ten colleges that define the area "B2" of figure 5 are intended to represent the remaining (nearly one hundred) LA1 colleges, but their characteristics must be taken more as an ideal-type than an average. A substantial number of these colleges could be found that are less alumni-dependent than average, either because they are comparatively young, have failed to mobilize their graduates, or have depended upon the patronage of a few benefactors. Leaving these considerations aside, some generalizations can be made about this group, if accompanied by the blanket qualification that exceptions will always exist. Although schools like Carleton and Reed have national reputations, these LA1 colleges are far more likely to have statewide or regional recognition and drawing power. Distinctiveness constitutes one of their outstanding attributes, but the differences become less stark and the organizational sagas less vivid after the first dozen or so most unusual schools. Almost all of the LA1 colleges were founded with a religious affiliation, but their commitment to keep pace with the academic mainstream has produced an overwhelming trend toward secularization in the twentieth century. This has occurred even where church affiliations have been retained, as has been common in the South, and also among the comparatively few Roman Catholic LA1 colleges. Perhaps ten LA1 colleges might be identified in which religious commitment plays a central and inescapable part in the educational process, but these exceptions, such as Earlham and Berea, depend heavily upon external support. The voluntary support that the typical LA1 college receives is vital for its existence, but does not allow the level of opulence prevailing at the LA1+ schools.

The dozen schools in the latter group had per-student expenditures averaging $9,150, with 38 percent of that being covered by voluntary support. The ten schools in "B2," however, spent $6,250 for each student, 22 percent of which came from voluntary support.

The LA2 colleges are undoubtedly the most difficult to generalize about, partly because they are the residual category for small institutions in the Carnegie Classification, and partly because there are so many of them (approximately 450). They might be divided into one hundred Roman Catholic colleges, probably four-fifths of which are for women; a large number of Protestant colleges, running the gamut from nominally church-related through Christian-committed to evangelical fundamentalist colleges;[42] twenty-five traditionally black four-year colleges; a few dozen struggling urban institutions; and a remainder of independent liberal arts colleges with educational aspirations more or less similar to LA1 colleges. If all these schools are, by definition, small and unselective, they are nearly all rather poor as well. But, as their representation on figure 5 ("B3") indicates, their poverty is generally assuaged by what is for them a significant amount of voluntary support. For this sample of schools the average per-student expenditure was about $3,500, and 16 percent of that came from voluntary support. When the individual types of LA2 colleges are considered, the different sources of this support are evident. The traditionally black colleges have long been dependent upon external gifts. The odd feature of this has been the reliance upon national fund-raising sources for these extremely localized institutions. Most colleges sponsored by Catholic teaching orders exist on scant resources indeed; but they, of course, are undaunted by poverty, and also benefit from a nonmonetary subsidy from the involvement of the religious. Church-related colleges, and especially those that can be described as Christian-committed, can rely upon existing denominational organizations to contact sympathetic donors. Evangelical Protestants, in particular, have no lack of flair for fund raising—or else Oral Roberts University would not be one of the growth industries of Tulsa. The support of the faithful for these schools has allowed them to keep tuition low, and in some cases to begin building a significant endowment.

A number of LA2 colleges could be found in the borderline territory between "B2" and "B3" of figure 5, but few of them are pure liberal arts colleges, and the odds are greatly against any of them rising to LA1 status. To do so would require simultaneously becoming more affluent and more selective, a difficult feat for tuition-dependent institutions. Moreover, movement in recent years has tended to be away from the ideal of a liberal arts college. LA2 colleges wishing to sustain or enhance their drawing power have had little choice but to adopt a greater vocational or service orientation. Many of them now might better be described, somewhat illogically, as small comprehensive colleges,[43] because of these additional functions that they have sought to fulfill.

The broad spectrum of liberal arts colleges offers a bewildering variety of alternatives for undergraduate education. The LA1 colleges, above all, offer a different way to navigate the academic mainstream. They provide a more intimate and supportive instructional environment than large universities, as well as the choice between myriad cultural overtones. Cultural pluralism is even more important in the case of LA2 colleges with religious commitments. They more or less reconcile higher education with the great diversity of religious conviction across American society. Only among those institutions that have become, in effect, small comprehensive colleges is it difficult to perceive a distinctive role. Despite this partial exception, there can be little doubt that the private liberal arts colleges do more than any other type of institution to create diversity within American higher education.

Large Urban Private Universities: Serving the Multitudes

Urban private universities are not readily recognized as a distinct category in the United States, but this type of institution has in the past been widespread internationally. In those European countries where state universities were not located in major cities, the initiative of local civic boosters made higher education available, as was seen in the cases of Stockholm and Gothenburg. Before 1960 state legislators in the United States had a decided bucolic bias in the placement of colleges. Only two of the flagship state universities, Minnesota and Washington, are located in major metropolitan centers. Thus, the original development of urban higher education largely took place under private auspices. In some cases small, originally sectarian colleges grew with their cities; in other cases universities were started from scratch to meet the needs of the population. As described earlier, the universities that were fortunate enough to have large endowments became research universities, but the rest quite naturally assumed a service orientation. This meant the ready incorporation of vocational programs and a tendency to be inclusive rather than exclusive in student admissions. This makes the mission of these universities closer to that of the public sector than any of the types previously discussed.

For the Swedish examples just mentioned, this "publicness" of function ultimately spelled the end of private control. This same process occurred in the United States as well, but in a highly selective manner. Private universities in Houston, Kansas City, Buffalo, Pittsburgh, and Philadelphia (Temple) became state-controlled during the 1960s. Given the absence in these cases of any compelling rationale for independence, joining the public sector promised rapid growth, improved facilities, higher salaries across the board, and an end (or so it seemed then) to chronic financial difficulties.[44] Where there was a viable rationale for independence stemming from either religious ties or a strong research tradition, no such transitions occurred. The rather late development of the state system of higher education in Ohio exemplifies this crucial distinction. Where it was feasible, municipal (Cincinnati, Akron, Toledo) or private (Youngstown) universities were incorporated into the state system, but in those cities with strong private institutions (Dayton, Cleveland) entirely new state universities were founded. The momentum of such conversions in the 1960s led Christopher Jencks and David Riesman to believe that this would be the fate of most large urban privates in the United States.[45] This has not happened, however, even though some schools would be willing to trade their independence for greater financial security.[46] How have these institutions been able to survive the vast expansion of the public sector within their domains? It has not been easy, but by utilizing the advantages available to them they have survived, and some have prospered, through the 1970s.

The distribution of urban privates in figure 5 lies in an unusual semicircle, which looks like a curved horn because of the logarithmic scale. The wealthiest institutions ("C1" and "C2": tuition values = $700–$1,200) derive relatively little from their alumni; the middle groups ("C3" and "C4": tuition value = $200–$500) have in the aggregate an average alumni dependency; and the poorest ("C5") have little voluntary support from any source. The difference in alumni-dependence between the first and second groups turns out in most cases to correspond with emphases on graduate vs. undergraduate programs. The Catholic universities are depicted in separate categories ("C2" and "C3") because they are such a large and important component of urban higher education, and because they have the most clearly defined target population.

Yet, on the basis of this data, they differed among themselves, and tended to cluster with the different types of nonsectarian universities. This in itself may be corroboration that Catholic universities merged with the broader stream of American higher education during the 1960s.[47]

The universities in "C1" and "C2" are, to varying degrees, what might be called "graduate service universities." Their undergraduate colleges are fairly large, but the overall size is limited by a moderate degree of selectivity. Median composite SAT scores are typically in the 1,000–1,100 range, and only about two of three applicants are admitted. Their graduate enrollments, however, tend to be disproportionately large, and concentrated in professional schools. Besides the elite professional schools of medicine and law, they tend to have a proliferation of additional professional schools like business, public administration, education, and social work. Their undergraduate colleges draw some students from beyond the metropolitan area, but the nonelite professional schools predominantly serve the local population, many of whom are part-time and evening students. Graduate service courses have been an important area of growth for all types of urban universities during the past decade. The graduate service universities have been quick to perceive and respond to these types of needs. Perhaps the prestige of their elite professional schools has enhanced the attractiveness of their other offerings, and thus given them an edge over less costly public sector competitors. Students of professional schools are less likely to become alumni contributors, but the services these universities perform for the surrounding community are usually recognized financially by local philanthropists and area corporations.

The prototype of the graduate service university would have to be New York University. Its graduate enrollment of twenty-one thousand is not only the largest in the country, but it is double the number of the school's full-time undergraduates. The University of Southern California, besides holding a national role in intercollegiate athletics, is very much a graduate service university for the Los Angeles area, with some 45 percent graduate enrollments in twenty separate graduate divisions. The University of Miami is a less obvious candidate, with only 20 percent graduate enrollments, but that is a relatively high level for its region. A case can be made for considering two "C4" universities with the three "C1" graduate service schools just named, despite their sparser resources. Boston University, with 40 percent graduate enrollments, and George Washington with 58 percent partly compensate for that lack with considerable research funding, and consequently cluster with the other graduate service universities in the lower half of "C" in figure 4.[48]

Among the Catholic universities in "C2," Saint Louis and the Catholic University of America would also fit the graduate service type, although the latter, in keeping with its original purpose, to some extent serves the entire national community of Catholics. The third school in this "C2" group, Georgetown, is unique not only in being the nation's oldest Catholic university. Its undergraduates are not recruited locally, and have far higher aptitudes than those of other urban universities—equal, in fact, to the LA1+ colleges. Its professional schools rank with the "A2" universities, meaning that they compete in the national market for graduating seniors more than they serve the enormous local demand in the District of Columbia. Georgetown, then, is a kind of hybrid: an elite undergraduate college, a financially weak research ("A2") university, and the quality leader for graduate service programs in one of the nation's largest markets for graduate credentials.

There are considerable similarities between the graduate service universities and those located in "C3" and "C4."[49] Both the level of selectivity and the absolute amount of per-student alumni support is approximately the same. This suggests that, excluding Georgetown, there is considerable similarity among the undergraduate colleges of all these institutions. Most likely these middle-level service universities are considered by many to have some qualitative advantage over their more inclusive public competitors. These universities emphasize graduate service programs to varying degrees. Both the University of Detroit and Fordham have more than 30 percent graduate students, but lack the level of research funding of Boston and George Washington. The chief difference, then, between these universities and the graduate service type would seem to be the latter's greater involvement in research and ability to attract considerably more external support.

The dozen institutions located in "C5" represent the extreme of tuition dependence in the private sector and a corresponding emphasis upon fulfilling unmet consumer demand for higher education within their localities.[50] They consequently tend to be characterized by a broad range of vocational programs and a relatively large proportion of part-time undergraduates. Since the margin of quality between these pure service universities and their public counterparts is small or nonexistent, they have to be both pragmatic and flexible to maintain a numerous clientele. This results in some novel programs, unorthodox scheduling, heavy advertising, and in some cases the proliferation of campuses or extension centers in order to remain close to the customers.[51] This profile fits some of these institutions better than others. The three Catholic universities, as well as Hofstra and American University, have undergraduate colleges much like the other urban privates; however, the remaining nonselective institutions (median composite SAT less than nine hundred) are almost all heavily part-time. These tuition-dependent universities are in many respects the antipode of the American collegiate ideal embodied in the alumni-dependent institutions. The very precariousness of their finances makes them responsive to a broad range of semiacademic public demands, to which they can often react more quickly than public institutions.[52] By accommodating such students they extend access to higher education to many who are uninterested in or unsuited for the academic mainstream, or whose circumstances preclude regular attendance. This makes them a source of innovation—not the type, to be sure, likely to please academic purists, but innovations that will succeed or fail by the test of the marketplace. The twelve institutions of "C5" alone constitute almost 9 percent of enrollments in the private sector. There can be little doubt that they, the most unloved of private schools in terms of voluntary support, have an important contribution to make to American higher education.

The Dynamics of the American Private Sector in the 1980s

The analysis of the magnitude and composition of voluntary support, together with student-body characteristics and the amount of federal support for academic science, has defined institutions along two important axes of orientation and behavior. One axis extends from a commitment to the disinterested pursuit of knowledge and the values of the academic mainstream at one extreme, to the provision of local service at the other. The second stretches from a dependence upon alumni support to a reliance upon voluntary support from sources unconnected with the school. The private research universities are above all dedicated to advancing knowledge and providing the best possible undergraduate education to a select group of students. In pursuit of these goals they set the academic standards for American higher education. The alumni-dependent universities in this class are committed to maintaining an intense collegiate life as an integral part of the undergraduate experience, while the others focus more exclusively upon superior disciplinary and preprofessional instruction. The external patrons of this latter group make no claim on these schools other than that they make academic excellence regionally available. By concentrating upon offering relatively unspecialized undergraduate instruction in highly diverse styles the liberal arts colleges eschew the extremes of both research and service. It is essential to the mission of the elite liberal arts colleges that their graduates be comparable to those of research universities, and that their alumni support them liberally in order to accomplish this. The LA2 colleges, on the other hand, are responsive to the cultural values of their external benefactors, and are also rather easily drawn into limited service commitments. The large urban private universities fulfill a variety of roles, but the weakness of alumni support pushes them toward a decided service orientation. The graduate service universities reconcile commitments to both research and service by segregating the researchers in their disciplinary departments and medical schools, while the service-oriented programs define the role of the nonelite professional schools. For the middle range of urban universities the linkage with the academic mainstream becomes more tenuous and the weight of professional education more dominant. Finally, the pure service universities are forced to find the tuitions on which they depend among those who are poorly served by more academically oriented universities.

The extreme heterogeneity of the American private sector, then, is shaped by a pattern of three underlying rationales for privateness. The nature and circumstances of individual institutions will be somewhat determined by whether a particular school aims to augment publicly supported higher education in quantity, in quality, or by offering a different style of instruction. These factors will also determine how private institutions relate to the challenges of the immediate future. Although the various segments of the private sector appear for now relatively secure in the fulfillment of their respective functions, there has been for some time an acute anxiety about what the future might bring.

Behind all future calculations regarding American higher education are concerns about a 15 percent decline in the size of the eighteen- to twenty-one-year-old population from 1980 to 1990. It is not yet known how this decline will affect college enrollments, and which institutions will be most affected. Different scenarios have been offered.[53] Optimists expect increased participation from underrepresented groups and a greater enrollment of adult students to buoy up college attendance. Pessimists fear that poor labor-market conditions for college graduates could exacerbate enrollment decline. For the private sector it is ominous to note that the demographic fall-off will be greatest in those states with the highest private enrollments. Regardless of which predictions turn out to be more accurate, the years ahead seem destined to provide a difficult environment for higher education. Facing this situation, the principal source of disquiet for the private sector is, as it has been for the past decade, the matter of pricing.

For the selective part of the private sector the problem is the logical fulfillment of the course of development begun in the 1950s. These colleges and universities consciously restricted their size, became more selective, and consequently focused their growing educational resources upon a carefully chosen body of students. This basic strategy has proven highly successful over the last generation. It is partly responsible for the high level of per-student expenditures in the private sector reported in table 7, and it has contributed to the excellence of many of the institutions described earlier in this chapter. However, this course greatly depended on attracting students who were both smart and wealthy. Fortunately for the private sector, superior academic achievement and high family income often go together. Nevertheless, students of this most desirable kind are definitely in limited supply.

One attempt to break down the population of high school graduates by income and ability found that just 9 percent of a typical cohort belonged in both the top quarter of academic ability (according to verbal SAT scores) and the top fifth of family incomes.[54] Both of these thresholds are significant. That income level roughly represents the point at which students might be expected to pay the cost of their college education at a selective private school without financial aid. And, although 25 percent of this high school class could be expected to eventually graduate from college, the minimum level of academic aptitude for acceptance at a moderately selective private college would be near the seventy-fifth percentile. This population of high school graduates, then, represents the core clientele for selective private colleges and universities. Yet, they provided only 13 percent of the college students from that cohort, and many from this group undoubtedly preferred to attend state universities. Other students were obviously needed to fill the places in the private sector. Before World War II many private colleges would have found additional students within the highest family-income quintile, with little regard for their academic abilities. The universal postwar acceptance of meritocratic standards, however, caused recruitment to be extended to high-ability students with lower family incomes. This, of course, was possible because of the increasing availability of student financial aid, at first supplied by institutions themselves and then chiefly from the public purse. Student aid consequently assumed a prominent role, and the entire system of student financial aid has been rapidly evolving since the beginning of the 1970s.

The qualitative improvement of selective private institutions that began in the 1950s resulted in relatively higher levels of tuition and increased per-student expenditures. Whereas expenditure levels were about equal for the two sectors in 1950, by 1964 the private sector was spending 20 percent more on each student.[55] Despite the introduction of limited federal programs of student aid in the 1960s, there was a widespread feeling by the beginning of the 1970s that more federal aid would be needed if the private sector were to maintain its existing position. Legislation in 1972 supplied that assistance in the form of an expanded federal commitment to student aid that balanced the interests of both the public and private sectors.[56] For the remainder of the decade, however, colleges were hit with steeply rising costs for energy, for books, and for people—in fact, for all the principal inputs to the educational process. Tuition charges, to some extent underwritten by student aid, escalated during these years in order to maintain the accustomed academic standards. In the last half of the decade a public clamor rose again, only this time the issue was more narrowly focused: middle-income students, it was now claimed, should be eligible for public student aid so that they might cope with the sharply rising costs of a college education. Congress responded to these entreaties by passing the Middle-Income Student Assistance Act of 1978. Basically, this legislation raised the income ceilings for some forms of student aid and eliminated them entirely for federally guaranteed student loans. In retrospect it also seems that this act represented the upper limit of a generation-long development in the financing of private colleges and universities.

The Middle-Income Student Assistance Act was a response to an ominous development: fewer and fewer families could afford the escalating costs of higher education, particularly private higher education. In the political parlance of the day this was called the middle-class squeeze, although it was really most applicable to the upper middle-income range. The unrelenting increases in tuition and financial aid, it was alleged, had created a situation in which only the wealthy and the publicly assisted poor could afford a private higher education.[57] This act shifted the calculus of costs once again by substantially enlarging federal financial aid programs, but in doing so it inevitably increased the private sector's reliance upon these funds. The appropriations for these programs, in turn, depend on the vagaries of the political process. The vulnerability of these programs soon became apparent. After 1980, limitations were placed on the Guaranteed Student Loan program, and the substantial amounts of student aid that had been provided through the Social Security Administration were eliminated altogether. Further changes in the composition of federal student aid are no doubt in store. The essential point, however, would be that the trajectory of ever-rising student financial aid that shaped the development of the private sector for the past generation now seems to have passed its apogee. In the years ahead private institutions may well have to expect students to pay more of the actual costs of their education.[58]

The changing conditions for student recruitment in the 1980s are not likely to affect all private institutions in the same way. Each different type of institution possesses strengths that vary with its principal function and reason for existence. The interaction between tuition hikes and student aid, above all, threatens to narrow the applicant pool for the selective private universities and liberal arts colleges. Their mission of providing "better" higher education requires both a high level of per-student expenditure and a student body of high average ability. An institution could not compromise either of these standards for long without changing its character. The elite institutions in this category are obviously in the strongest positions, and that would include all twenty-four of the research universities discussed in this chapter.

The private research universities often give the impression of being on the verge of financial crisis, an impression that has at least one element of truth. They are in fact engaged in a labor of Sisyphus to raise the enormous sums required to accomplish the many tasks to which they are committed, as well as others that they would like to undertake. Yet, their role as either national or regional centers of excellence offers them a stability that should largely insulate them from the trends buffeting the rest of American higher education. The reputations of their academic and preprofessional programs should allow them to continue to recruit their students from among the cream of high school graduates. Just as important, the visibility and tangible promise of their research roles will likely keep them near the head of the line to receive voluntary contributions from corporations, foundations, and individual philanthropists. As long as the federal government provides an adequate level of funding for the nation's basic scientific research, these private research universities will perpetuate their distinctive role of providing superior education on both the undergraduate and graduate levels.

If the applicant pool for selective private higher education shrinks during the 1980s, the effects are more likely to be felt in the ranks of the LA1 colleges. The elite of the group, identified here as LA1+ colleges, will continue to be the first choice of many talented students, and a significant number of other LA1 schools will no doubt also fill their entering classes with the accustomed type of student. But at some point down this rather ambiguous pecking order the sparseness of students may cause other LA1 schools to undertake the difficult changes that many LA2 colleges have already undergone. Alumni loyalties, as reflected in donations and matriculations of sons and daughters, may be a critical factor in determining which schools remain competitive in this group. The ideal of the American liberal arts college will continue to have a great deal to offer: individualized instruction and close personal involvement in campus life; an exceedingly pleasant four-year experience often in idyllic settings; a solid general preparation for graduate or professional school; and the beginning of a lifelong association with classmates and college. Still, this approach to a college education is a consumption good that not everyone wants or can afford. Both fashion and economics, then, will be involved in determining how many LA1 colleges can remain in this mold.

Elsewhere in the private sector future enrollment patterns may be much less affected by the factors just discussed. The futures of the many schools predicated upon offering cultural differences in higher education will depend on the continued social significance of the niches they represent. In one example, the traditionally black colleges have seen their mission narrowed with the widespread integration of southern higher education during the 1970s. But the majority of institutions in this category depend on religious commitments that show little sign of waning. For this part of the private sector taken as a whole, tuition is relatively low and access is quite open, so that all those choosing these particular alternatives for their higher education are likely to find a place.

The urban private universities have faced the difficult problem of having to compete with low-cost public rivals. Yet, many of these universities have defied the logic of their position, and succeeded in raising both their enrollments and the tuition revenues on which they depend.[59] The reasons for this are most likely similar to the reasons for the prominence of urban universities in mass private sectors: they are located in the midst of a concentration of population and employers, and they have had the organizational flexibility to offer programs adapted to people's needs. In the United States these factors allowed the urban private universities to capitalize on some of the principal growth areas of the 1970s—vocational undergraduate programs, graduate service courses, and the expanding participation of mature students.[60] These markets are likely to retain their importance in the 1980s, and, to the extent that they do, the urban private universities will continue to prosper. Even if they were to have some difficulty maintaining the academic core of their undergraduate colleges, their strength lies in the diversity of their offerings and the concomitant ability to compensate by developing emerging areas of student interest. If the experience of mass private sectors is any guide, then, the inherent advantages of an urban location may assume greater weight in the balance of the higher education market in the years to come.

The vitality of the American private sector has always rested above all on the multiple roles fulfilled by different sets and subsets of institutions. In the last generation its health has become dependent upon the higher-education policies of the federal government as well. In the following chapters these two themes will be pursued in more global terms. The topics of government financial assistance for private higher education and the place of privateness in higher education will be examined in the comparative context of the eight private sectors.

Chapter 6

Government Support for Private Higher Education

In most of the national systems examined in the preceding chapters, government financial assistance for private higher education has been one of the most dynamic and significant developments of the last two decades. The private universities of Belgium and the Netherlands became wholly funded by the state during this period. The huge private sector in Japan was bailed out of financial crisis by the establishment of institutional subsidies beginning in 1970. The United States federal government vastly expanded its contribution to higher education and made these funds available to both public and private institutions. Growing research spending and special help for institutional expansion in the 1960s were then followed by an enlarged commitment to student financial aid. In Sweden the sole remaining university-level private institution has long received government support in lieu of charging tuition. Finally, the two exceptions among the cases examined here support this fundamental trend. The French government has traditionally monopolized university degrees within the state faculties in order to preclude private competitors, but at lower levels of education, where public and private schools coexist, government subsidization programs are well established. The Philippines differs in being a developing nation with desperate educational needs in public schools at all levels. It has been able to spare no more than a pittance for aid to its numerous private colleges.

Great Britain presents a situation that is structurally dissimilar from these other nations, but quite relevant to the issue of government subsidization. In chapter 4 the state-supported British universities appeared from the singular perspective of the University of Buckingham as something like a public sector. Yet, they are each in fact juridically independent entities, free to do what they like (in theory) with the funds the government gives them. Moreover, the British method of allocating funds through the University Grants Committee can claim to be the most studied and most admired form of university subsidization in the world. The British example is too important to be ignored in any consideration of government support for independent institutions.

In the sections that follow, an interpretation will be offered for the quantum increases in the objective needs of higher education that have occurred since World War II, particularly since about 1960. Next, the underlying reasons that caused different governments to commit public funds to sustain private institutions will be examined. Then, the different forms of government support will be compared and correlated with the different kinds of relationships between the state and private sector. The final section will evaluate some of the consequences of these various forms of subsidization, and try to distill from these disparate cases some indications of how states generally might best provide financial help to nonstate colleges and universities.

The Rising Costs of Higher Education

A number of developments have contributed to the spiraling costs of higher education over the last generation. Most obvious would be the enormous growth in the numbers of students during these years. Expansion on a grand scale requires large capital expenditures, but raising capital is something that nonprofit organizations are ill-equipped to do. Generally they must rely upon philanthropy, government grants, or at worst, subsidized loans. Hence, growth has often brought problems for private higher education. The inability of Japanese private colleges to finance rapid growth brought on the crisis of the late 1960s; in Belgium total state support was needed to accomplish the massive, politically determined expansion of the private universities; and in Sweden and the United States the capital needs of growth have caused institutions to change from private to public control.

A number of factors associated with the research roles of universities have also been involved in the inflation of costs. The staggering expense of research in the physical and biomedical sciences is widely appreciated, but there is less of an awareness that changes in the technology and overhead requirements for scholarship in the social sciences and humanities have considerably raised the expense of those endeavors as well. The problem, however, is larger than the costs of research *per se*. It involves the commitment of the university to operate at or near the frontiers of knowledge. Sheer cognitive growth has caused the core disciplines to proliferate into specialties, which themselves have attained the status of autonomous disciplines. At the same time, entirely new areas of study have won rightful places in the curriculum. These developments have greatly extended the cognitive territory within the domain of higher education, all of which has required greater resources.

In addition, the argument exists that cost pressures in higher education are inherent to the nature of the industry. As a labor-intensive service industry with a fixed teaching technology, higher education has not been able to increase productivity significantly. This means that as other industries in the economy enhance their productivity, and raise wages as well, the unit labor costs of higher education will tend to be drawn upward.[1] Finally, it is relevant in this context that, despite varying degrees of market segmentation, mixed systems of higher education in developed countries possess numerous unifying forces. As a result the just-mentioned factors of physical growth, expansion of research, and rising unit costs impinge over the long run on both the public and the private sectors. The availability of public funds and their mode of disbursement strongly affect which sector assumes the developmental advantage and which is left struggling to catch up. This dialectic has at times been behind the growing needs of higher education, particularly in the private sector.

As valid as these foregoing reasons may be, they are still not sufficient to fully account for the persistent inflation of higher educational costs over this period. They do not, for example, explain why universities could not have refrained from burdensome capital investments, limited their commitments to research, and/or seriously undertaken to increase the productivity of their teachers. They do not, in other words, explain why universities acquiesced in the escalation of these costs. Nor do these particular items elucidate why higher education cannot be offered on a fee-for-service basis, so that the direct beneficiaries of these services could either shoulder the rising costs or, by refusing, restrain them. These hypothetical questions are indeed germane to this entire phenomenon, for they touch upon the elusive issue of the qualitative aspirations that motivate a good part of university behavior.

An oversimplified depiction of several of the peculiar characteristics of academic labor can illustrate the workings of qualitative incentives. Inherent to the Western conception of a university is the notion that those who teach there be capable of contributing to the advancement of learning, that they be trained as scholars in order to extend and interpret the knowledge base in their particular field.

This, of course, makes university faculty rather overqualified, strictly speaking, for their principal activity of teaching undergraduate students. When a significant part of their time is devoted to scholarly activities, they also become underutilized as teachers. Furthermore, the universities that carry the greatest prestige in the academic world are those whose faculties are in this sense the most overqualified and the most underutilized—and, not coincidentally, the most expensive as well. Does this mean that these high-cost institutions also provide the best education? What evidence is available suggests that they probably do, but this is really beside the point.[2] The academic reputations of universities are measured less by educational outcomes, which are difficult to document and interpret, than they are by inputs to the educational process. The "best" institutions tend to be those with the most renowned and highly paid faculties, the largest libraries, the most ample facilities, and the most select student bodies. Other competing institutions, to the extent that they are able, seek to emulate the most prestigious universities by expanding the quantity and quality of their inputs.

These institutional tendencies produce a situation that Howard Bowen has described as "the revenue theory of cost in higher education."

> The unit costs of operating . . . universities are set more largely by the amount of money institutions are able to raise per unit of service rendered than by the inherent technical requirements of conducting their work.[3]

Given university goals of educational excellence and institutional prestige, there is virtually no limit to the amount that can be spent toward these ends. Universities consequently raise all the money they can, and then spend all the money they can raise. The cumulative effect is to create powerful pressure for continually growing expenditures.

Bowen was focusing on the American system when he formulated this model, and the behavior of affluent research universities and liberal arts colleges, as indicated in the preceding chapter, amply demonstrates its relevance in that context. To extend this perspective to other systems, however, crucial structural variations must be taken into account. The United States and Japan possess hierarchical structures in which the capacity of different institutions, public or private, to tap funding sources varies enormously. Large numbers of institutions in both systems have little choice but to eschew the research-related standards of the leading universities in favor of more modest vocational or service-oriented goals. Japan differs from the United States in that national universities there set the standard for educational spending. European systems of higher education differ sharply in containing strong normative conceptions of what a university ought to be. Although these systems are not without gradations of prestige among universities, each and every one is expected to meet a high minimal standard that includes research as an important component. These conceptions are often manifested in tangible ways through unified systems of allocating students and, even more importantly, through the legal equality of national degrees. The *de jure* equality of such universities virtually requires a national policy of equal treatment. Consequently, measures to enhance the quality of university instruction—or, to maximize the revenues applied to university purposes—tend to be transmitted throughout the entire system.

The revenue theory of costs, Bowen is careful to point out, is only applicable to a short-run analysis. In the long run, expenditures on higher education are determined by the amount that society at large is willing to pay. Society, of course, means primarily those parents and students who are directly involved in higher education, various other private contributors, and especially the state. The mix of supporters will naturally vary from system to system, with the Japanese relying most heavily upon student fees, the United States best able to mobilize voluntary support, and European systems depending overwhelmingly on the public purse. Despite these differences there can be little doubt that for a period of time extending from the 1960s into the 1970s, with variations between countries, each of these societies greatly expanded the resources available to higher education. The building boom, the proliferation of academic research, the persistence of generous staffing ratios, and much more, were the overt manifestations of an internal university dynamic that seemed to have behind it the consensus support of the population, at least as expressed in democratically elected assemblies. The introduction or extension of university subsidization programs, then, constitutes a major component of this larger process.

The Decision to Subsidize Independent Higher Education

The increased funding of higher education during the 1960s and 1970s involved some significant changes in its relationship with government. These changes were most far-reaching in those liberal states, like Japan and the United States, that had traditionally pursued a comparatively laissez-faire policy toward higher education. These governments, were, of course, never entirely disinterested regarding higher education; rather they assumed an implicitly functional attitude toward it. The national governments took whatever measures were necessary to assure that certain needs for research and highly trained personnel were filled, but beyond these matters the consumer demand for higher education was allowed to be met by private parties or other governmental units. Interestingly, the very absence of inhibiting controls over higher education, combined with an ethic of personal betterment through educational attainment, produced the world's highest levels of cohort enrollment in these two countries.[4] However, it was precisely the dependence of so large a portion of the population on this service that made higher education an inextricable component of the social welfare of the nation. Government was consequently pressured to advance from a functional to a welfare approach to higher education in order to guarantee that availability of this opportunity would meet the quantity and the quality demanded. This pattern is most stark in Japan, but it can also be discerned amidst the many federal programs affecting higher education in the United States.

The Japanese system, it was seen in chapter 2, evolved away from the principle that the national universities were to serve the needs of the state while private institutions catered to the aspirations of individuals. This explicit dualism became untenable in the face of the financial crisis of the private sector in the late 1960s. The private universities, with 78 percent of the country's students, had to be kept viable in order to sustain the quantity of higher education which Japanese society had come to expect. Furthermore, additional resources were needed for qualitative improvements if that education was to retain its credibility. Government subsidies seemed the only solution, but such a step required an altered government orientation toward the private sector. The basic planning document of this period for Japanese higher education clearly enunciated the rationale for an expanded government role.[5] In general it argued that subsidies were justified by the important, if incalculable, social returns to higher education, whether public or private. It further asserted a government responsibility to work toward equalizing educational opportunity, implying that efforts be taken to raise standards in the private sector. Higher education was thus presented as an essential social service whose provision, given the existing structure of Japanese higher education, demanded a comprehensive policy of financial support and overall guidance for the private sector. It was this limited welfare approach to higher education that was implemented in the Private School Laws of 1970 and 1975.

The method chosen to subsidize private universities was, not surprisingly, the same indirect form that had been established previously to distribute relatively small sums of scientific aid. The expanded and reorganized Private School Promotion Foundation now became the conduit for regular subsidies designed to cover a significant portion of the operating budget of each private university.

The policy of the United States government toward higher education has been in some ways more obviously functional than Japan's. Since education as a whole is the responsibility of the states, the federal government needed only the service academies to meet its own special personnel needs. When it undertook to accomplish other national objectives related to higher education, it introduced specific programs that worked through the existing system of state and private institutions. While hardly being blind to the existence of two sectors, it has consistently followed a policy of nondiscrimination between them. Thus, the land grants provided by the Morrill Act (1862) for colleges "to teach such branches of learning as are related to agriculture and the mechanic arts" were channeled through the states to public and private institutions alike.[6] This principle persisted, although federal programs likely to benefit private colleges were virtually nonexistent until World War II. At that time universities were mobilized to conduct basic and war-related scientific research, and the continuation of many of these programs after hostilities ended became the basis for a permanent federal role as the patron of science on campus. A second federal intrusion was the G.I. Bill, created for the compensation and readjustment of returning veterans. The sheer magnitude of this program transformed the face of American higher education: more than two million veterans took advantage of the generous provisions of this legislation to obtain some college-level training, compared to a total prewar collegiate enrollment of just 1.3 million.[7] These developments established the federal government as a permanent presence in American higher education, but through the 1950s that presence remained limited. Federal funding programs were largely functional and indirect until stimulated by another challenge.

The Soviet launch of *Sputnik* in 1957 touched off a quantum leap in federal support for higher education. In the process the

original functional objectives of this policy were gradually transformed in the direction of a welfare commitment. The immediate
response was legislation dealing with the country's most pressing
scientific and educational needs: The National Science Foundation,
fount of funds for basic research, was expanded, and scholarships
were created to attract students into teaching and area studies.[8]
With the shift of power going to the Democrats in 1960, education
rose on the list of national priorities, just as the large cohorts of the
postwar baby boom began to reach college age. The first direct response to this was the Higher Education Facilities Act of 1963,
which provided federal matching grants for university construction.
With this measure, analysts of federal higher education policy have
noted, "the national defense rationale of federal higher education
policy receded, and the goal of equal educational opportunity began
to emerge."[9] Within the context of Lyndon Johnson's "war on poverty" this goal was specifically addressed in the next two years by
three programs of financial help for needy students. Under "work-
study" the government paid most of the cost of part-time employment in campus jobs; federal opportunity grants, also administered through the university, for the first time supplied outright
federal grants to needy undergraduates; and a program of federally
insured loans supplied an additional source of support. None of
these programs was sufficient in itself to finance a college education, nor were sufficient funds appropriated to meet the needs of all
low-income students. Still, the federal government had implicitly
committed itself to rectifying the effects of income disparities on
the opportunity for a college education. The form of that commitment remained consistent with liberal assumptions about the ap-
propriateness of individual sacrifices, in the form of part-time work
and loans, to attain that end. In the 1970s this commitment would
be broadened into a full-fledged welfare program.

The political machinations that led up to the passage of the
1972 Education Amendments might tend to obscure the consensus
then existing that the federal government should in some manner
substantially increase its support for higher education.[10] American
colleges and universities, particularly in the private sector, were
complaining of being squeezed by rising costs; and in the nation at
large there was widespread support for expanding and equalizing
access to higher education. The political judgment of Congress gave
precedence to the latter over the former. The result was the creation
of "Basic Educational Opportunity Grants" (BEOG, since renamed
"Pell Grants") to provide a basic, or floor, subsidy for all low-income

students. These were entitlements of sorts, but their magnitude depended upon the relationship between parental income and college costs, as well as the amount of money authorized for the program. The government would grant each student one-half of the estimated cost of attending college, taking into account an income-based expected parental contribution, up to a maximum originally set at fourteen hundred dollars. In addition, Supplemental Educational Opportunity Grants, awarded through the universities and also based on need, were retained up to a maximum of fifteen hundred dollars.[11] The provisions of the 1972 Education Amendments, together with all the other discrete programs, ratcheted the federal contribution to higher education upward. From 1956 to 1966 it quadrupled from $655 million to $3,500 million; in the next ten years it nearly quadrupled again to $12,500 million. This sum represented 38 percent of the operating budgets of all American colleges and universities combined (although not all of this went directly into college treasuries, since most was in the form of student aid).[12] The full implications of this system of funding will be considered further below; however, it is necessary here to note the impact upon the private sector.

Since the overall thrust of federal policy in higher education has consistently been to achieve specific objectives within the context of the existing system, the government has generally attempted to avoid actions that might distort the institutional balance. This concern has tended to work in favor of the private sector—the smaller and on the whole financially weaker part of the system. This solicitude was evident in the controversies surrounding the 1972 legislation, where educational "choice" served as the code word for preserving the interests of the private sector, and counterbalanced to some extent the political clout of "equality." "Choice" achieved some notable victories in this instance. The limitation of BEOGs to one-half of a student's actual cost (total cost minus parental contribution), for example, precluded any "free-rides" at low-tuition public colleges, while also spreading the fixed sum appropriated for these grants across a wider range of incomes. The supplemental grants were also important for private institutions because they particularly benefited schools with high tuition.[13] Together these measures tended to lessen rather than accentuate the tuition gap between public and private higher education for eligible students.

This situation illustrates how the expanded role of the federal government in equalizing educational opportunities has inevitably affected the relative pricing, and hence relative viability, of different types of institutions. It reveals as well the considerable ambiguity surrounding the American welfare commitment to higher education. Because of the extremely variegated nature of the system, the concept of equal opportunity must include the chance for poor students to attend those selective institutions with high costs and high potential benefits. Thus, for a given income level the amount of financial aid has to be variable according to the type of institution a student attends.[14] Furthermore, given the large discrepancies in cost, the point at which "need" ends and self-sufficiency begins is a complex, rather arbitrary, and ultimately political decision. In 1978, it was seen, Congress and the president agreed to extend this welfare commitment to middle-income families through federally guaranteed loans, but in 1981 this commitment was abruptly rescinded.[15] The welfare right of needy students to receive financial aid for their college education was definitely established in the 1970s, but only upon a foundation composed of individual responsibility, institutional interest, and national politics.

The United Kingdom differs markedly from the United States and Japan in having made an earlier and fuller transition from liberal to welfare state, and in having a university system pegged to a single high standard. Still, the University Grants Committee, as an indirect means for the national funding of universities, belies its liberal origins and bears some comparison with American and Japanese analogues. From the end of the nineteenth century the government accepted the existing university system, plus infrequent locally sponsored additions, as approximating the country's needs for higher (or degree-level) education. Accordingly, it subsidized the independent universities as circumstances required. World War I led to the formalization of this support in the UGC; World War II quickly produced the conditions for near-total institutional support from the national Treasury. Still, an explicit government commitment to supply as many university places as were demanded had to await the report of a special Committee on Higher Education chaired by Lord Robbins. The principal recommendation of the Robbins Report (1963) was that "courses of higher education should be available for all those qualified by ability and attainment to pursue them and who wish to do so."[16] Its acceptance immediately set off an unprecedented expansion in the number of university places, followed shortly by the reorganization and expansion of the nonuniversity sector. In a coeval development, the arrangements for student financial support were rationalized and liberalized so that more than 90 percent of British university students were able to claim some type of maintenance grant from the Local Education Authorities.[17] For the relatively few who were deemed qualified for degree-level study, the British government built and supported universities, and the local rate-payers paid the costs of attendance. The enormous increase in university expenditures that this entailed made the role of the UGC, as was seen in chapter 4, more activist and more controversial. But through the vicissitudes of educational policy two principles have been steadfastly maintained: the nearly total government provision of higher education (the University of Buckingham notwithstanding); and the preservation of rather elite universities for the limited pool of qualified students.

Belgium and the Netherlands also possess elite university systems, together with the welfare assumption that they should be open without significant cost to those eligible to attend. Direct grants from the government to the private universities in both countries have been increased since World War II and now constitute virtually their entire source of income. In the Swedish case direct subsidization of private universities in a welfare state assumes a different form. As explained in chapter 4, government payments to the Stockholm School of Economics are now governed by a negotiated contract. Since the state has only limited objectives in this relationship, it provides only partial support for the institution.

Forms of Subsidization

These six countries exhibit four different primary modes of subsidizing nongovernmental higher education. University support in the United States may be said to be indirect, since it is given in the form of financial aid to students,[18] or contracts to undertake specific research projects for federal agencies. Thus, excluding a few exceptional cases, there is no direct institutional support from the federal government.[19] In Japan and Great Britain, on the other hand, government funds are for general institutional support, but they are given indirectly through an intermediate body. In Belgium and the Netherlands government funds are simply granted directly to private universities, while in Sweden the direct grant is governed by a negotiated contract. Whether subsidization occurs directly or indirectly would seem to depend upon the relationship between the government and the parties being subsidized. And, with the exception of Sweden, the extent of government subsidization correlates roughly with each country's position on the continuum between liberal and welfare state.

In those countries employing direct methods of support, the private universities being subsidized are identified with specific constituencies whose relationship with the government is a relevant factor. In the consociational democracies of Belgium and the Netherlands this relationship is positive and trusting. Religious organizations and other voluntary groups are entrusted to perform a wide variety of social services with full government funding. This situation is most unlikely under circumstances where the interests of the private sponsoring groups are perceived to be at variance with the interests of the state. This was specifically the case between the business groups who founded and still sustain the Stockholm School of Economics and the social-democrat architects of the Swedish welfare state. Their relations were consequently governed best by a negotiated contract. By this means the state could be assured that its payments to the school in lieu of tuition would guarantee the meritocratic selection of students; or, that assistance to the school's library would ensure scholarly cooperation between it and the state universities.

Contractual arrangements have proven to be convenient for controlling the delicate relations between Catholic schools and secular states. France managed to resolve decades of rancorous conflict over private schooling on this basis. The Debré Law (1959) established two kinds of contracts that private schools could sign with the Ministry of Education: basically, in return for a government subsidy covering part of their educational costs the schools agreed to abide by certain standards in force in the public sector.[20] The French have consistently excluded higher education from such contracts for reasons that are peculiar to their system, but this need not be the case elsewhere. When Catholic higher education was again permitted in Portugal after the passing of the Salazar regime, for example, a form of contractual subsidization directly inspired by French practice was introduced.[21] The principle of general institutional support on a contractual basis, then, can be applied to either singular institutions or, through standardized contracts, to an entire class of institutions. In essence it involves granting limited governmental support in exchange for limited concessions. These arrangements thus protect the autonomy of private schools, while also circumscribing the obligations of government.

In the three countries that utilize indirect subsidization, the sector receiving government funds is large and variegated. The private sector in Japan, the universities of Great Britain, and both sectors in the United States are identified with the general provision of higher education in their respective countries, not with any specific group. They are thus politically neutral, and are supported to varying extents by the national governments as part of the overall commitment to enhance the public weal. Although it may be imperative in each system to treat all institutions equitably, the size and inherent diversity of these sectors make it unlikely that national purposes would be best served by treating them equally. These systems consequently face a problem in determining how national aid should be apportioned among institutions.

In both Great Britain and Japan this issue was first handled by creating an intermediate body to determine the distribution of state subsidies. The University Grants Committee ascertained the needs of British universities, and then reconciled those needs with the sum granted by the Treasury. In Japan the Private School Promotion Society used to channel limited amounts of government loans and scientific aid to what it considered the most appropriate private colleges. Both bodies exercised considerable discretion in their awards. This was inherent in their function, as they were established as autonomous bodies precisely so that they could exercise their independent judgments in ways that legislatures cannot. However, as the UGC block grants came near to being the sole source of university revenues, and as university expansion diminished, much of their discretion was inevitably lost. To a large extent they simply passed along the bills for the fixed and unalterable costs of university operations. Conversely, changes in the status quo enhance the role of expert judgment. In 1981 the UGC was forced to make some of the most far-reaching decisions concerning British universities since the post-Robbins expansion. Faced with apportioning a 17 percent cut in the university appropriation over the next three years, the UGC chose, in a most controversial decision, to protect as best it could the prevailing university ideal. It consequently imposed a disproportionately large share of the cuts upon the weakest, least popular universities, and it recommended that these budgetary cutbacks be accompanied by enrollment reductions. Educational standards were thus preserved at the universities judged to be most successful, but at the cost of severe hardship for the others. The merits of this approach have been, and will continue to be, debated at great length.[22] More relevant here is the fact that, faced with an inevitably painful decision, the UGC opted for unequal treatment of institutions—a course of action likely to be chosen only by a body with both independence and great confidence in its own expert judgment.

The increased government funding of private higher education in Japan in the 1970s has involved a more formal and more irrevocable diminution in the discretion of the intermediate body. The Private School Promotion Foundation, successor to the Society, has seen its freedom of judgment, insofar as grants are concerned, replaced by the complex formulas explained in chapter 2. The inherent function of the intermediate body has not been altered—merely codified. Given the size and variety of the Japanese private sector, compared to the forty-four universities of Great Britain, it would hardly seem advisable to rely upon the informed judgment of a single body to make differential funding decisions. Yet, differential treatment is undoubtedly necessary if progress is to be made on the Ministry of Education's objective of raising standards in the private sector.

In the United States intermediate bodies like the National Science Foundation and the National Institutes of Health are utilized to bring expert judgment to bear on the distribution of research funds.[23] Government aid to higher education in the United States is nevertheless indirect in an entirely different sense. Because the federal structure allocates responsibility for education to the separate states, Washington pursues its chief interests in higher education by either purchasing the services it desires, such as scientific research, or by subsidizing "needy" students in the interests of equalizing educational opportunity. In the first case the university itself is subsidized only insofar as it is paid to do something—attempting to create new knowledge—that it considers intrinsically desirable in any case. Overhead expenses, equipment purchases, and the buying of faculty time provide some additional benefits for the recipient, but these are essentially incidental to the principal transaction. Such grants allow universities to fulfill an aspect of their purpose for which their own resources are insufficient. In the case of student aid, federal funds have become an additional factor in the complex open market of American higher education. It is in this market that students must weigh the relative advantages of different types of institution, differing standards of instruction, at different levels of price. Federal student aid enters this complex matrix by affecting relative prices. Its primary effect has been to increase the number of participants by allowing low-income students to afford college in the first place, or by making it possible for nonaffluent students to attend relatively expensive institutions. The secondary effect, especially important for private institutions, has been to allow colleges and universities to institute larger tuition increases. With the government subsidizing the most price-sensitive students, private schools naturally have greater freedom to increase charges to those who can better afford to pay.

The two principal types of federal aid to higher education in the United States, then, both provide institutional support in a second-hand manner. Federal support for science not only accomplishes its intended purpose of advancing knowledge, but it allows universities to expand their research function and to maintain a larger and more specialized faculty in the process. Federal aid to students serves to diminish inequality of opportunity, but also results in greater institutional revenues. Compared to the other countries with indirect government support, only research funding depends upon qualitative distinctions between institutions, analogous to those made by the intermediate bodies of Japan and Britain. As for student aid, it works directly through the system of tuition finance, rather than parallel to it as in Japan. That these forms of government assistance seem so appropriate to the American system is actually beside the point: American colleges and universities have in fact been shaped by adapting to these sources of revenue, as was seen in the previous chapter. If one looks at the practices of the individual states, however, it becomes apparent that other measures are also possible.

In many ways the higher educational systems of the individual states provide a more apt comparison with the other national systems that have been considered here. In all but one state (Wyoming), state-funded and private colleges and universities coexist; and, as of 1977, thirty-nine states had aid programs that benefited the private sector.[24] The best way to summarize this complicated picture is to note that there are basically four kinds of student aid and two types of grants for institutions. The different state legislatures have enacted numerous variations on these basic themes, and have united them in different combinations. The oldest state programs for students tend to take the form of competitive academic scholarships. A number of states then introduced financial aid for needy students at roughly the same time as the federal government. Special concern for the health of the private sector and the implications of the tuition gap led to the establishment of some "tuition-offset" grants that provide equal sums to all in-state students in private colleges within the state. Finally, many states have supplemented such programs with need-based student loans. As for institutional aid, it is either functionally targeted for specific purposes or general in nature. Much of the specific institutional aid is directed toward the expensive and politically popular health fields. While several states offer token amounts of general institutional aid, usually for enrolling certain types of student, New York State distributes the most significant amount for this purpose. There an outright grant is made to the state's independent colleges and universities based upon the number and type of graduates each institution produces.[25]

The most generous programs of state aid to private higher education have been shown to occur in those states having large private sectors that also enroll a large number of in-state students.[26] This strongly suggests that the principal motivation for these programs is simply to provide for the welfare of state citizens: these states have acted to preserve the private sector in much the same way that Japan did, because a significant portion of the population was dependent on it. To justify these subsidies it is often noted that a student transferring into the public sector costs the state more than one subsidized in a private institution. Nevertheless, the intended effects of these programs have been both to provide incremental revenues to the private sector and to preserve the status quo. In the mid-1970s all forms of state aid to private higher education averaged $290 per full-time student, or 1.9 percent of private-sector revenues. In half the states, aid averaged over $100 per student; in twelve it exceeded $400.[27] Student aid, comprising almost two-thirds of the total, was primarily directed toward tuition. Thus, like federal financial aid programs, it sustained the existing tuition-pricing mechanism for higher education. Where the ceilings for such aid are relatively high, as in California and Illinois, such grants undoubtedly allow some students to attend private schools who could not otherwise afford to do so. Tuition-offset grants are more directly beneficial to private institutions by permitting higher tuition. Largely because of these two types of programs the majority of state student aid flows into the private sector— something that is not the case with federal student aid. State aid to institutions also implicitly maintains the status quo by eschewing any qualitative criteria that might distinguish between institutions.[28] Grants are made according to mechanical formulas based in some form or other on student counts. In this respect institutional aid only confirms the welfare thrust of state aid to private higher education. Beyond supporting needy students, the underlying purpose is simply to ensure the continued provision of these educational services by marginally increasing the revenues of independent institutions.

Each of the four modes of subsidization examined here seemed specifically adapted to the particular relationships existing between national governments and the private schools requiring support. This does not necessarily mean, however, that these modes could not be adapted to different circumstances. The next section will attempt to assess the strengths and the weaknesses of these different modes in order to reach some conclusions about the public support of independent higher education.

Consequences of Government Funding

It was seen in the first part of this chapter that the amount of higher education a nation provides, the standards to which it is held, and the relative responsibilities of public and private sources for its support are highly interdependent features of educational systems. European nations have preferred university education to be of uniformly high quality. This has, perhaps inevitably, been accompanied by a high degree of government financial responsibility; and, those university sectors have been restricted in size as some of the more practical tasks of advanced education have been assigned to less costly and less demanding nonuniversity institutions.[29] Japan and the United States have left considerable responsibility for higher education in private hands, and have achieved quite high rates of participation, but with variable levels of quality. Comparing the impact of government financial support across such markedly different types of systems presents a problem of finding fairly neutral standards for evaluation. There are, however, certain general qualities that would be widely regarded as desirable in the relations between universities and governments. They would include: sufficient *stability* in funding patterns to permit rational decision making beyond the short-term; *efficiency* in the transmission of funds to their designated purpose, along with *effectiveness* once employed for those purposes; and preservation of university *autonomy,* or at least the avoidance of governmental intrusions that are detrimental to the educational ends of the university. These criteria will be employed to evaluate the four modes of government subsidization that have been exhibited in these six countries.

Stability is scarcely an issue when appropriations for higher education are rapidly expanding, as they were in most countries through the 1960s and into the 1970s. It became a problem when high inflation began to erode the real income of universities, and when government austerity policies forced nominal cutbacks as

well. In some ways it is worse for universities to expand and contract than never to expand at all. Stagnant salaries and blocked
career lines cause differentially greater losses among the young and
the talented, and persistent retrenchment inhibits adaptation to
changing conditions. Still, the risks of fiscal uncertainty have to be
borne by someone, and the mode of subsidization largely determines
the relative burdens of government and universities.

Where funding is indirect the state has the greatest leeway to
determine what it needs and what it can afford in terms of higher
education. Global sums may be appropriated and distributed by an
intermediate body according to established criteria. When such
fiscal government control can be coupled with medium-range guarantees for universities, both sides can have a relatively stable context for financial planning. This was the case with the late and
lamented quinquennium grants of Britain's University Grants
Committee, which were widely regarded as an ideal vehicle for government support. But they could not survive the high inflation and
tenacious economic difficulties that have plagued Britain since the
late 1960s. Since then, planning has been scaled back to three-year
periods at best, with liberal modification periodically made for inflation and changing circumstances. The reductions for the triennium
1981–84, already mentioned, were a shock that perhaps reveals the
nature of these arrangements more clearly than the expanding budgets of the halcyon days ever could. The Conservative government
of Margaret Thatcher made the political decision to reduce university appropriations substantially, but left to the UGC the more difficult and unpopular task of applying the knife. In this situation even
the legendary buffer between universities and Parliament could do
little to cushion the impact of government fiscal policy. Still, even
though its policy of protecting certain universities at the expense of
others generated great controversy, it seems better on the whole to
have these painful decisions taken by a body of sympathetic academics. By making intelligent distinctions between universities, instead of lapsing into the less controversial course of shared misery,
the UGC probably preserved stability as well as was possible under
such difficult circumstances.

The university subsidies distributed by the Private School Promotion Foundation in Japan might be described as "relative entitlements": every private college, unless disqualified for malfeasance, is
entitled to receive a subsidy for their operating expenses, but the
value of that subsidy is relative to the overall funding for this purpose. Thus, the government has control over the global expenditure,

just as in Britain, while each institution is assured of its relative share of the subsidy. The Private School Law of 1975 authorized the government to pay up to 50 percent of the operating expenses of each private college; the government chose a 40 percent level of subsidization; and reductions caused by the funding formulas reduced the actual level to about 30 percent. These two stages of deflation have given the government rather close control over these expenditures. The 40 percent level could be adjusted upward or downward, although to do so would constitute an educational policy decision of the highest order. Once this figure is set the subsidies are in fact entitlements; however, the classic way in which entitlement obligations are manipulated is through the adjustment of regulations. In this case the formulas and base figures are sufficiently complex to assure considerable latitude of interpretation. As discussed in chapter 2, the 1980 subsidy proposal from the universities was reduced 12 percent by the Ministry of Education, and that proposal was in turn sliced by 11 percent in the Ministry of Finance. Thus, bureaucratic control over this expenditure is maintained. Japan, of course, has not had to reduce relative spending on higher education, as have many Western nations. Should the need arise, however, there is little doubt of the government's capacity to do this.

Indirect funding of higher education takes its most flexible form under the disparate programs utilized in the United States. When funding research, for example, the government is actually purchasing thousands of discreet services involving medicine, agriculture, basic science, or humanities. Through the budgetary process global sums are allocated to the agencies responsible for distributing these grants, and these sums are annually adjusted according to relative priorities and fiscal constraints. The enormous uncertainty of this process does not unduly disturb the operations of colleges and universities. Rather, it has encouraged them to treat research as a luxury instead of a necessity. Research funds are consequently regarded as "soft money," i.e., not part of the "hard" recurring budgetary obligations of the institution. The various student-aid programs are also malleable. In most cases a total sum is appropriated, but the income-based sliding scales and various ceilings make the grants infinitely adjustable according to the money available. Given the piecemeal nature of this support, even major reductions such as the 1982 cutbacks are diffused throughout the system. There is no doubt that American higher education is poorer as a result, but it is virtually impossible to determine what, in terms of research not performed or instruction not received, has been lost.

The effects of uneven funding patterns on directly funded systems are more evident. Contractual arrangements need not be considered here, since the obligations of both sides are fully specified. However, the parallel private sectors of Belgium and the Netherlands offer cases of unintended and unwelcome consequences stemming from total dependence on government funds. In the simplest and starkest terms, the patterns described in chapter 3 showed these private universities being granted the right to total government support in the absence of very effective government control over the extent of that support. The result was a golden age of expansion accompanied by an unsustainable acceleration of expenditures. The governments of both countries inevitably reacted, each in its own fashion, to contain these entitlements within nets of restrictive regulation. The consequences for the universities have been twofold. First, the governments have become deeply involved in internal university affairs, affecting institutional autonomy in ways that will be explored below. More germane to the general question of stability, the cycle of rapid expansion followed by retrenchment has proved costly to the long-range interests of these private institutions. The private universities, particularly in Belgium, find their budgets completely committed to ongoing obligations. Without gainsaying the impressive facilities and ample faculty salaries that have been the direct result of such government support, it should nevertheless be recognized that the private universities of Belgium and the Netherlands have paid a high institutional price in return.

The issue of effectiveness of government aid to higher education is to a large degree a peculiarly American concern in the present context. In all the other systems being considered the principal form of government aid flows ultimately into university coffers in order to partially or fully finance the general operating budget. Federal aid in the United States, in contrast, is intended for purposes that can be isolated and evaluated. Beyond this difference, however, there is some common ground. Different criteria of subsidization can establish incentives for institutions to behave in such ways as to maximize their revenues—to exhibit what is sometimes called strategic behavior. Thus, it is possible to examine how strategic behavior conforms with the original intention of a program. But first the effectiveness of the American programs will be considered.

Federal practices of research funding in the United States have compiled a remarkable success record since World War II, whether judged by the number of Nobel laureates, by the sheer quantity of research, or by the international prestige of graduate programs. Beyond the amount of funds made available, there are at least three aspects of this process that probably enhanced that success. The evaluation of research proposals through the peer-review system undoubtedly produced more objective and tough-minded judgments than those likely to have been made within individual institutions. The funding of proposals for rather short periods of time puts researchers under considerable pressure both to produce results and to develop ideas for further proposals. Finally, funding through the various federal agencies is on a prioritized basis, so that projects are accepted up to the point at which funds are exhausted, according to their relative potential for scientific advancement. Theoretically this would mean that each succeeding grant would be less vital than the one before. Perhaps for this reason American scientific output has held up rather well despite the stagnation in real federal appropriations for basic science since the late 1960s.[30]

Compared with other nations, the peer-review system as it operates in the United States depends first upon the existence of a large, decentralized system of higher education and secondly upon an exceedingly strong disciplinary organization. The size and scope of higher education produces considerable competition, while effective academic disciplines greatly facilitate objective and impersonal judgments about recondite topics. The other nations considered here all award some research and development money on a competitive basis, but in none of them does this process become one of the driving mechanisms of the higher education system. This is partly because competitive awards are overshadowed by distributions based upon considerations of institutional equity. Pressures for more equitable spreading of federal research and development money periodically surface in the United States Congress, but they have yet to erode the peer-review system.[31]

The competitive awarding of federal research funds for specific purposes constitutes a rather efficient utilization of government funds, even though there is some nonproductive effort required for formulating grant proposals and accounting for grant expenditures. The same cannot be said for the other principal form of federal support for higher education, student financial aid. In this case the principal goals of these programs—equalizing the opportunity for higher education and preserving freedom of choice—are essentially ideological. There is general agreement that the financial condition of the private sector has improved since the passage of the Educational Amendments of 1972, but it is difficult to say what contribution that legislation has made, and at what cost. Aid to students is actually an inefficient conduit of federal funds to institutions of higher education because much of the money merely replaces private funds that would have been expended for the same purpose. One study estimated that an overall student-aid subsidy to the private sector of $1,262 million in 1975–76 produced additional institutional revenues of only $370 million; or, 71 percent of the government's expenditure merely replaced the private funds of students.[32] Of course, such an estimate does not include additional private funds received through higher tuition charged to unaided students. Private institutions may have been strengthened in this case at higher private *and* public cost.

This same issue assumes greater magnitude in European countries where aid for student living expenses is far more extensive, and where tuition pricing mechanisms are absent. One survey of practices in several of these countries concluded that higher education was oversubsidized because "equity considerations have usually taken precedence over efficiency considerations." It was consequently urged that steps be taken to increase private contributions through tuition.[33] Even though these programs are consistently justified through the rhetoric of equity, it has already been argued here that they are essentially welfare programs. It is inherent to welfare programs that, to some extent, they displace private funds that otherwise would have been expended for food, health care, etc. This is intentional: the basic function of welfare is to improve the quality of the recipient's life by lessening hardship and assuring a secure and adequate flow of necessary goods and services. Whether or not higher education should be one of those necessary services, just who should benefit from these subsidies, and to what extent, are all fundamental issues for each society. But that does not mean that these issues are always squarely faced. In the American case the Educational Amendments of 1972 were a political compromise that attempted to harmonize the sometimes conflicting objectives of numerous constituencies inside and outside of higher education. In the end the most expedient solution was to pump additional funds into the existing higher education market through the tuition pricing mechanism. The result, then, was a sizable welfare commitment that only partially increased the revenues of American colleges and universities.

Japan is the one country in this study that has evaded this efficiency problem by restricting all student aid to loans, and by funneling subsidies straight into the treasuries of private universities. The striking feature of the Japanese legislation, as explained in chapter 2, is the introduction of institutional incentives to improve quality. As proxies for quality, the amount of each university's subsidy is based upon their maintaining their authorized size, lowering student-teacher ratios, and spending to improve educational facilities. An institution with an operating budget of 1,000 million yen, for example, could at current funding levels qualify for a subsidy as high as 520 million yen, or as low as 200 million yen, depending on how well they meet the Ministry of Education's standards. This approach has both benefits and drawbacks. It is a noncoercive method of affecting university behavior, and one that is relatively easy to monitor as well. Above all, it creates a means for treating the many private universities both equitably and unequally. Negatively, one might note that the proxies for educational quality are not the real thing. Progress along those officially sanctioned lines will probably produce positive effects in the long run, but can do little to alter the current pedagogical traditions and the manpower-screening functions of Japanese higher education. These last two factors may prove to be more powerful determinants of educational quality than the inputs measured by the Ministry of Education. Also, incentives based upon rather crude indices have a tendency to generate other unforeseen and usually unwelcome forms of strategic behavior. In this case, since almost all colleges were above their authorized student populations, it proved to be in their interests to raise tuition and to devote the extra revenues to additional educational resources. As a result, both the social and the private costs of private higher education in Japan rose rapidly during the 1970s. Despite these inherent difficulties, Japanese practices deserve high marks as an intelligent approach to the problem of subsidizing the private sector, and one which manages to place educational considerations in the forefront of university policy.

Educational considerations have hardly been paramount in the controversies over subsidizing private universities in Belgium. The Belgian legislature made accountability its principal concern when it granted private universities ostensible funding parity with state universities. This meant basing subsidies on explicit objective criteria, and then closely monitoring university expenditures with government delegates. The norms that were instituted for almost every category of university expenditure, however, were almost certainly counterproductive in the short run. Universities that exceeded the norms for, say, square meters of cafeteria space per student, were obviously constrained; but those below such norms felt entitled to immediately expand to the allowed level. In this way the strategic behavior of the private universities pushed government financial commitments far beyond expectations during the years of the "golden age."

If the Belgian universities lack incentives to economize, this does not distinguish them from institutions in many other systems. It was seen in chapter 4 that such charges were part of the critique of British universities that lay behind the independent college movement. Such allegations have recurred periodically, usually accompanied by charges that secure funding through the UGC tends to make British universities complacent and unresponsive. There is some truth to these arguments, but the British have historically claimed that security is a proper condition for pursuing intellectual endeavors. Since British universities are generally considered to maintain the highest systemwide standards in the world, their government subsidies would seem to be employed effectively.[34] The basis of the security and autonomy of each British university is the block grant awarded by the UGC, but in fact their vaunted autonomy is constrained by several other features inherent to the system. First, the UGC itself provides a "Memorandum of Guidance" to each university, based in part on prior understandings, that specifies numerous aspects of university policy. Universities invariably conform, albeit voluntarily. Second, there is considerable peer pressure in the status-conscious British academic community, which is made all the more acute by such practices as exchanging external examiners. Compared to other national systems, British academics know their counterparts at other universities very well. Third, there is a pervasive underlying competition between British universities. Perhaps this is most obvious in the recruitment of students, but it also involves to a lesser extent the award of government research grants and the appointment of faculty. These external controls allow British universities relative freedom to make their own decisions, while recognizing a powerful motivation to maintain high standards.

A good deal has already been said about the relative autonomy of universities receiving government support, but this important issue requires specification before it can be evaluated in relation to the different modes of subsidization. National governments have legitimate interests in higher education that extend beyond keeping track of how public money is spent. Generally these include many of the typical functions of universities, such as performing research or training competent professionals. But, regarding the matter of how universities choose to perform these functions, the institutions themselves may legitimately expect the liberty to make decisions (about who will teach what, to whom, and how) at the appropriate levels by the individuals directly involved. This simple dichotomy obviously fits the real world rather imperfectly. What a university does cannot always be separated from how it does it, and the legitimate interests of both governments and universities can overlap and conflict. Nevertheless, this simple dichotomy between what and how will be useful for signaling when government intrusions are actually inimical to the ends of the university.

The contractual relationship between the Swedish government and the Stockholm School of Economics is perhaps the simplest situation to analyze. Although the social responsibilities of institutions usually take priority over autonomy in that country, the long-term contract the school negotiated has done little to infringe upon its internal sovereignty. Its social responsibilities, on the other hand, are guaranteed by the presence of a government appointee as chairman of its Board of Governors. In the case of this singular institution, then, it has been relatively easy to protect the respective interests of both parties.

The indirect funding mechanisms of Great Britain and Japan each represent different kinds of government intrusion into university affairs. The "Memorandum of Guidance" that accompanies a university's block grant spells out the expectations on which that grant was made, including the number of students that will be enrolled, the proportion of scientific students, and other important particulars. Within the context of this virtually obligatory "guidance," British universities possess an extraordinary degree of self-government. Furthermore, it is the faculty who largely govern the universities, a fact that is certainly germane to the persistence of high academic standards. While there has been an undeniable tendency for UGC guidance to become more restrictive over the last two decades, a tendency that has ironically reached its extreme under the laissez-faire government of Margaret Thatcher, the autonomy of British universities essentially remains intact.

Japanese private universities are also highly autonomous in their internal affairs, but it might be said that the government has created a more restrictive context for them than that existing in Britain. This is largely the result of the Ministry of Education's historical concern over the competence of a low-quality private sector. This is most apparent in the substantial degree of regulation over the curriculum, which on occasion places a damper on innovation. It is nevertheless true that in most developed systems of higher education strong informal tendencies exist toward standardization of the curriculum across institutions. The extensive regulations would seem to be vestiges of the system's past that are increasingly anachronistic under present conditions. In this light, the incentives built into the current subsidy formulas may represent a more subtle and effective way to influence the behavior of independent institutions than overt regulation. These formulas were intended, and from all indications have succeeded, in changing the internal priorities of universities, which have for the most part limited enrollments and increased overhead expenditures. In Japan and Great Britain—and Sweden as well—the subsidized universities basically retain control over their own internal affairs. Complications, however, are present in the other three cases.

The basic problem in Belgium is that the elaborate government funding formulas have badly encumbered the internal flexibility of the private universities.[35] Norms that were established only for funding purposes were quickly transformed into imperative administrative guidelines. This situation has been most serious in matters of teaching and research personnel, where the existing allowable ratios would permit few foreseeable new appointments for years to come. These detailed norms have pushed the government into university administration, but they have not provided a smooth and efficient system of university finance. The government delegate charged with overseeing this process at each private university can interpret the complicated regulations narrowly or sympathetically. The delegate's rulings are often appealed to the Ministry of Education, and sometimes beyond. It is not unusual for the legitimacy of a university expenditure to ultimately be decided in the courts—years after the fact. This has produced an acrimonious relationship between the private universities and the Walloon or Fleming ministries of education. The universities, in attempting to maximize their subsidies, tend to do what the ministries least want them to do; the ministries, preoccupied with the need to control expenditures, are unable to give priority to the higher education needs of the country. As a result, it has been exceedingly difficult for the private universities of Belgium to adapt since the new arrangements were put in effect.

The universities of the Netherlands have always enjoyed a high degree of autonomy, and this has not been appreciably damaged through the process of government subsidization. The private universities submit their budget proposals directly to the Ministry of Education. From that point, until a final budget is approved, a good deal of haggling can take place over the inclusion or exclusion of certain items. The university is then held closely accountable for spending within the categories specified, but this presents few problems because the budget is essentially a university creation. The concern for university autonomy in the Netherlands is focused more on the legal framework for higher education than on the funding process.[36] Public and private universities are completely equal before the law. In the 1970s the Dutch Parliament passed legislation that reorganized university government, restricted student admissions, shortened degree courses, and changed university research commitments. Each of these controversial actions has affected the way in which universities perform their essential tasks. The Dutch case seems to demonstrate that private universities can be directly dependent on the government for their entire financing without necessarily sacrificing their autonomy, although the highly individualized treatment that each university receives could only occur in a rather small system. Ironically, though, the greatest threat to autonomy has come not from control of the purse strings, but from the state's legal power to determine the conditions under which universities operate.

The United States would seem at first glance to be the most impervious to government intrusions on university autonomy. Not only does the federal government have no direct responsibilities for higher education, but its expenditures are intended for specific purposes that do not touch the overall operations of institutions. The major federal programs pertaining to higher education—from the Morrill Act (1862), through the GI Bill (1944) and the National Defense Education Act (1958), to the Educational Amendments of 1972—all brought infusions of federal funds in the name of some overriding public purpose. Beginning in the late 1960s this pattern was given an entirely new twist when universities were required to take actions in pursuit of government social objectives for which no separate funding was involved. Instead, failure to comply would result in the withdrawal of all federal funds from existing programs. This approach was used to force institutions of higher education to conform to a number of different regulations, but the case that most compromised institutional autonomy was undoubtedly the set of procedures required for the policy of affirmative action. There can be little doubt that these regulations accomplished their purpose of skewing the process of academic appointments, chiefly for the benefit of women and blacks.[37] In doing so they intruded into an hitherto sacrosanct area of institutional sovereignty, making gender and race play a role in hiring decisions that were ideally to be based solely upon academic merit.[38] These effects were in part due to the large and influential constituency supporting the expansion of employment for women and minorities. From their point of view this social objective was far more important than the principle of institutional autonomy, which they, in any case, regarded as a shield that had been used to conceal discriminatory practices. The particular strength of these groups on campus made it extremely unlikely that universities would resist these regulations. Within this climate a very zealous regulatory bureaucracy in Washington was able to weave some rather general executive orders and favorable court rulings into a set of requirements that considerably altered procedures of faculty selection.[39]

These pressures seem to have abated somewhat since the end of the 1970s for reasons that are not yet entirely evident. Possibly, the affirmative action demands of the 1970s for colleges and universities will appear in retrospect as an incident of bureaucracy run amuck, rather than a permanent erosion of institutional autonomy. Nevertheless, two of the underlying conditions that made this situation possible will undoubtedly persist in the relationship between the federal government and higher education. The first is the insistence that colleges and universities should be subject to the same degree of regulation as all other federal contractors. The second would be the legitimacy of imposing regulations upon higher education for attaining ulterior and unrelated social objectives. The spokesmen for higher education in the United States have yet to make a unified and coherent case to the legislators and government officials responsible for these policies. Such an argument would not claim that universities should be immune from all federal regulation, for that would convince no one in Washington, but that the inner core of academic functions should be protected from incursions of government authority. Unless such a case is made, and made cogently enough to impress politicians, institutional autonomy in the United States will continue to run the risk of being subordinated to one overriding national priority or another.

Conclusions

The different experiences of these six countries in subsidizing higher education have each produced mixed results. It would be unlikely in any case that the procedures adopted to meet the particular needs of one system could be easily transferred to another. The modes of financing independent institutions obviously vary according to the nature of the private sector, the degree of government subsidization, and the relationship between the state and the recipient. Nevertheless, it is possible to draw some general conclusions about which arrangements work better than others, and why.

In the preceding discussion of subsidization the conclusion was consistently reached that indirect methods were more satisfactory than direct allocations. Indirect procedures gave the government greater control over the global level of expenditures. They also permitted a decentralization of financial control to the institutional level. Such arrangements seem to vest different responsibilities in their appropriate spheres: government exercises its political responsibility in determining the level of public spending allotted to higher education; institutions largely determine how the funds available can be best utilized for educational purposes. Furthermore, the separation of university and state by an intermediate body has considerable utility. Legislators and bureaucrats are usually poorly situated to make intelligent decisions about specific matters in higher education. The judgments of legislators, no matter how well intentioned, are prone to ideological factors, political compromises, and plain ignorance. As a result, major pieces of educational legislation, like the Educational Amendments of 1972 or the Belgian reform of 1971, have been enacted largely in response to immediate pressures that virtually precluded serious consideration of what their long-range consequences were likely to be. The reforms passed by Dutch lawmakers during the 1970s present even more discouraging evidence about the possibilities of solving university problems in a political arena. As for government bureaucrats, the inherent tendency of most agencies is to regulate and regularize, and this makes them particularly insensitive to university claims for independence. For this reason an adversarial relationship is likely to develop over issues of regulation when government agencies and universities are brought into too close contact. This has been the case in Belgium and the United States; but not in Sweden, where the conflicting perspectives of the government and the Stockholm School of Economics have been controlled by a different type of separation resulting from a negotiated contract.

Of course, universities and governments must continuously interact, especially where government funding is involved; thus the issue is really how best to facilitate this. Here the evidence suggests that higher education is justified in expecting what is sometimes regarded as special treatment. Other industries with unique operating conditions, such as banking or the merchant marine, usually have special government organs to deal with their interests and problems. Such organs of government designed for the needs of higher education have been seen to be highly effective in the cases of the British University Grants Committee and the agencies that disburse research funds in the United States. Nor is it accidental that academics are strongly involved in their operations. The interests of higher education can also be handled knowledgeably by civil servants who have specialized knowledge in this area. The protracted budget negotiations between universities and the state in the Netherlands are conducted by a permanent professional staff in the Ministry of Education that has great understanding of university issues, and ministry officials in Japan work closely with university organizations and the Private School Promotion Foundation to formulate policy toward the private sector in that country. Conversely, it is widely believed that the functioning of the UGC was somewhat impaired when it was joined to a Department of Education and Science dominated by nonuniversity interests. The point here is simply that the necessary interaction between government and universities is best mediated through people familiar with the conditions and mores of academic life.

Qualitative distinctions are inherent to the enterprise of higher education, whether involving the grading of students, evaluation of colleagues, or the conventional wisdom concerning institutional differences. The capacity to make qualitative judgments between institutions would also seem to be a prerequisite for an intelligent funding policy.[40] Certainly in large systems of higher education there is a functional need to treat institutions unequally in order to produce the degree of specialization required for excellence and the amount of diversity needed to accommodate multiple social purposes. Treating institutions unequally calls for establishing procedures that are methodical, fair, and also insulated from the political process. Great Britain accomplishes this in the university sector through the expert judgment of the UGC; Japan uses objective weighted funding formulas designed to discriminate between institutions on the basis of qualitative criteria; and federal programs in the United States support quality through research grants and access through student aid. Small systems that are committed to institutional equality, such as those in Belgium and the Netherlands, would readily admit that in consequence they pay a high price in extra overhead expenditures—primarily in overstaffing and in the duplication of academic facilities. The maintenance of institutional equality almost invariably produces strains at other points of an educational system, because such a policy tends to deny natural allocative mechanisms created by meritocratic competition and institutional adaptation to changing social demands.

This overview of different forms of government funding has drawn a relatively simple picture. Government subsidization of independent institutions seems to operate most satisfactorily when the independence of those institutions is respected. This is best accomplished through the utilization of intermediate bodies composed of people from, or closely connected with, the academic world. Such bodies should not be reluctant to treat institutions differently according to their capabilities and their roles within the educational system. This prescription could, of course, be applied to the public as well as the private sector, but this relatively optimistic assessment of the capacities of individual colleges and universities to chart their own destinies is particularly relevant to private higher education. It implies that individual institutions will, at least in the aggregate, make intelligent decisions about how to operate within their particular niche in the educational system, and that government forms of assistance should not short-circuit their ability to do so. Organizational freedom is thus one of the ultimate rationales for privateness in higher education.[41] But it is not one that should be accepted *a priori*: it should be scrutinized against the preceding case studies of private higher education in eight nations.

Chapter 7

Privateness in Higher Education

Typical judgments about private higher education tend to be impressionistic and categorical: private colleges "are free to pursue excellence"; "cater to the rich"; "are sources of innovation"; or "provide diversity." Such sentiments are tenuous generalizations at best, based upon a small subset of private schools. The essential purpose of this study has been to supply knowledge of private higher education that was empirical and, of necessity, relative. The task remaining is to transcend this relativity to some extent by developing a cross-national understanding of the general characteristics and limitations of private sectors. In order to do this, private higher education will be viewed in turn from three different perspectives.

The section that follows will first review these eight private sectors in their own specific contexts. Particular attention will be paid to the way in which underlying values, sectoral structure, and standards of conduct have shaped the actual performance of private sectors. In the next section a crucial distinction will be made between those private institutions that seek to compete and be judged as part of the academic world and those that relate primarily to constituencies outside of higher education. These two perspectives on private sectors provide the background needed for evaluating private higher education, in the following section, according to the qualities of diversity, adaptation, quality, and privilege that have been considered throughout this study. It will here become apparent that private control of colleges and universities possesses neither absolute virtue nor absolute evil. Trade-offs exist on numerous issues, and different societies choose to emphasize different results. Nevertheless, as argued in the final section, private higher education would still seem to have a capacity to make positive contributions to the goals of higher education and to the realization of an open, pluralistic society.

Privateness in National Contexts

Basic characteristics of higher education systems might be categorized analytically into three levels. Most abstract would be the normative level, in which a nation's political culture, its values regarding education and social position, and the ethos of the academic community all compose the general normative environment surrounding higher education. The second level, that of structure, has been defined in this study by the way in which different systems divided tasks between public and private sectors. The third level would encompass the actual conduct of higher education, which varies between national systems according to legislative fiat, administrative customs, and financial arrangements. Examples from the preceding case studies illustrate how developments at each of these levels have affected the circumstances of private higher education.

The normative environment of higher education was transformed by the sea change from liberal to welfare states in Europe and the United States. More specifically, changes in the normative environment were seen to have affected the balance between public and private sectors in nineteenth-century France and in postwar Sweden. On the other hand, consensus over preserving the existing public/private structure in Japan and the United States caused the implementation of important measures of government financial assistance for private institutions. The conduct of higher education undergoes continual adjustment, but laws such as the one establishing the National Collegiate Entrance Examination in the Philippines, or the law on university governance in the Netherlands, abruptly alter institutional behavior. Taken together, norms, structure, and conduct depict a unique context for each national system. By reviewing these eight countries through this analytic lens, judgments can be made about the performance of private sectors.

The mass private sector of Japan has historically served to expand access to higher education while also staying closely attuned to employment opportunities in private industry. It has fulfilled the first of these functions with such success that Japan now vies with the United States for the honor of being the most highly educated democratic nation. The second of these roles has kept Japanese private universities rather closely bound to the credentialing function of higher education. Broad access inevitably compromises academic standards, as reflected in the fact that the less selective half of Japanese higher education consists entirely of private institutions. It should not be overlooked, however, that quality private universities exist at all levels within the upper half of the institutional hierarchy. Thus, the private sector has also expanded the availability of higher education comparable in quality to that given in the public sector. The inception of public subsidies in 1970 seems to have greatly strengthened the private sector in general. The incentives built into the subsidization formulas have produced additional educational resources for the better private universities, while placing considerable pressure on inferior institutions to raise their standards. One result has been to shut off expansion, as marginal students have chosen to attend nonuniversity technical schooling instead of weak university programs. Since these technical programs often have superior occupational prospects, no loss of social opportunity would seem to be involved. Perhaps the principal drawback of the new financial arrangements has been that they have led, somewhat paradoxically, to a sharp rise in student fees which, should it continue, could threaten the relatively broad social representation that the private sector has achieved. More fundamental problems facing Japanese higher education encompass both public and private sectors. They would include the "exam hell" pressure generated by exclusive reliance upon standardized testing for selection, a tradition of lax pedagogy, credentialism, and weakness in graduate training and disciplinary organization. These aspects of Japanese higher education, however, are linked to some deeply ingrained features of Japanese society, and consequently can be dealt with only to a limited extent within the confines of the educational system.

The performance of private higher education in the Philippines must be considered as part of the economic realities of a developing nation, and not by the standards of the other, affluent countries in this study. The private sector as a whole accomplished a remarkable feat of expansion in the generation after World War II as burgeoning demand created opportunities for profitable investment by proprietary institutions. Nevertheless, the majority of the private institutions that made this expansion possible were badly deficient in physical facilities, libraries, laboratories, and, most crucially, adequately trained teachers. The Ministry of Education of the Philippines, like that of many other less-developed nations, has consistently attempted to compensate for these glaring weaknesses through a surfeit of regulation. Such devices as rigidly specified course contents and required class attendance, however, affect the formalities of higher education without touching the inner content. Worse, they stifle better institutions while scarcely improving poorer ones. By the 1970s the private sector of the Philippines seemed ripe for a consolidation that would produce greater meritocratic differentiation between institutions, especially by strengthening the standards of middle-ranking universities. The possibilities for such a differentiation were enhanced when the National Collegiate Entrance Examination (NCEE) provided a national standard for evaluating secondary school graduates. In addition, private accrediting and assistance organizations exist to encourage this kind of development. However, the financial controls that were placed on private higher education seem to have virtually frozen the sector in its current mold, while gradually starving it of the funds necessary to cope with rising price levels. The consequences have probably been most dire for attracting and retaining qualified faculty. With more than 80 percent of the nation's college students, the Filipino private sector today fulfills an irreplaceable role in meeting the national demand for higher education, and will undoubtedly continue to do so for the foreseeable future. Although the present circumstances leave much to be desired, the current extensive structure at least holds the possibility that positive changes in the economic and political environment could lead to rapid and significant improvements in the capabilities of private higher education.

The parallel sectors of Belgium and the Netherlands present examples of private higher education that has become totally reliant upon funding from national governments. This situation is largely a by-product of the cultural pluralism that pervades the social institutions and political life of both countries. Only within such a context, it would seem, is it possible to successfully press the claim that universities controlled by subcultural groups should receive treatment equal to those of the state. The relative financial security of these arrangements has nevertheless only been attained at the cost of some independence and vitality for each private sector. In this respect the two systems have had rather different experiences.

The private sector of the Netherlands is relatively small and represents cultural cleavages that have lost much of their emotional significance, although not their institutional importance, in the last half of the twentieth century. Private universities have consequently been virtually assimilated with the public sector for most matters of higher education policy. During the 1970s private and public universities were equally buffeted by government efforts first to democratize, then to rationalize, and finally to economize Dutch higher education. The private universities of the Netherlands still retain complete sovereignty over matters pertaining to their philosophical outlook, but in all other respects they have become indistinguishable from those of the state. Belgian private universities, by way of contrast, still reflect latent conflicts in Belgian society between Flemings and Walloons, statists and liberals, or Catholics and free-thinkers. Although these rivalries tend to compartmentalize the intellectual life of the nation, they also seem to produce a high degree of vitality and responsiveness in private institutions. Perhaps as a result the private universities increased their share of student enrollments during the past decade. Undoubtedly the most negative feature of government funding has been the constraints created by close financial accountability; and these have been made more painful by the government's continuing financial plight. The large private universities of Belgium, in particular, find themselves with obligations outstripping their means, and no discretionary funds for additional programs. For the past half-century they have repeatedly looked to the state to solve their financial difficulties, but, in light of the current difficult economic circumstances, they will have to utilize their remaining independence in order to fashion resourceful solutions to these problems.

The official government disposition toward higher education in France has remained remarkably constant through the nineteenth and twentieth centuries. Feeling an overriding responsibility for both the unity of French culture and a high standard of competence in the learned professions, the state has essentially monopolized these functions within a centralized system of public faculties and national degrees. The private sector in France has consequently grown organically over time on the periphery of the state system by accommodating those tasks that fell outside of the state's self-defined mission. The French Catholic Church, in an unsuccessful challenge to the state's monopoly, had to settle for truncated institutes instead of the church-controlled universities originally envisaged. Yet, these institutions have grown over time to serve the Catholic community in a variety of ways. They have cultivated traditions of Catholic scholarship in selected areas, provided numerous possibilities for complementing study for national degrees, established a number of *grandes écoles* for advanced vocational education, and cultivated areas connected with the traditional pastoral functions of the church. The French schools of commerce and management began by teaching their subjects at the subbaccalaureate level, but have since developed to the status of *grandes écoles*. Although similar programs have been introduced in state faculties following the reorganization of universities begun in 1968, the schools in the private sector retain the advantages of established reputations and close connections with private industry through chambers of commerce and industry. The French private sector has been allotted an admittedly minor part in that country's higher education, but, significantly, that role is greatest in areas of vocational education where the public sector has been acknowledged in recent years to be most deficient. For at least some people, then, its minor contribution to French higher education has indeed been an important one.

Also on the periphery of dominant public sectors are three singular private institutions described in this study. As common ground among these unique examples, one can look at the niche occupied by each in its educational system, the relative distinctiveness and isolation of each, and the consequences stemming from these situations.

The Ecole Libre des Sciences Politiques was clearly the most separated from the mainstream of academic life, and it was also the one school in this trio that came closest to monopolizing a single function. In its early years its relative independence undoubtedly worked to its advantage, and its success in sending graduates to the *grands corps* was to some extent merited. But in the longer run the absence of meaningful competition and its exclusive orientation toward a single social stratum produced an intellectual ossification that extended from the school to that portion of the governing class that it aspired to shape.

The Stockholm School of Economics has not been able to monopolize its field in recent years, but it has remained preeminent through the strength of its continued achievements. Although it has always been closely identified with particular elements of the Swedish business community, it has also had to adjust to government domination of higher education. In its recent history it has adapted to both these facets of its existence. The school has conformed to Swedish norms concerning the social responsibility of educational institutions in such matters as universalistic standards of admission and appointment, and cooperation with the rest of the academic community. At the same time it has revitalized its services to Swedish business by developing a variety of new programs. As a result, the Stockholm School of Economics has confidently been able to defend its unique position as Sweden's only private university-level institution.

The school that claims that same distinction for Great Britain can only hope to attain so enviable a status in the future. Compared with the two other singular institutions, the University of Buckingham has yet to achieve a distinctive and prestigious niche in British higher education, nor has it managed to establish a sustaining relationship with a group of external supporters. Instead it is something of a school of convenience, meeting the needs of certain Malaysian, Nigerian, and British students, and receiving sporadic financial support from ideological sympathizers. Its weaknesses, however, should be seen in relation to the formidable problems of starting from scratch and competing with an entrenched and dominant system of state-funded universities. In only a few years the University of Buckingham has made conspicuous progress, and its greatest trials may now be behind it. If its chronic capital shortage can be overcome, the high morale of the UB faculty and staff and the working of the higher education market may assure not merely that Buckingham survives, but that it will eventually succeed in shaping and fulfilling a distinctive role.

The tremendous variety of American private colleges and universities can be related to three broad currents that have shaped the country's system of higher education prior to the twentieth century. An indigenous tradition of education in the liberal arts was supplemented by an emphasis on research and graduate training that derived from the influence of German universities. At the same time pragmatic attitudes facilitated the incorporation of numerous applied fields into the university curriculum. This evolution encompassed both public and private sectors; but even though the same courses are taught and the same degrees granted in both sectors, private institutions have been able to define their missions more narrowly and more effectively. Liberal arts, research, and local service were the three major orientations of private colleges and universities described in chapter 5. The research universities have succeeded in setting a high standard of academic achievement; the liberal arts colleges in myriad ways have concentrated on the intellectual development of undergraduates as a foundation for later learning; and the large urban service universities have proven themselves adept at responding to the training needs of their surrounding populations. Much of the excellence and the vitality of the American private sector can be ascribed to the pervasive competition that exists among the nation's three thousand institutions, competition for students, for research funds, and for voluntary support. To flourish in this environment requires that private institutions define their tasks carefully and fulfill them well.

The variety of purpose of American private colleges and universities corresponds with different patterns of financial dependence. Tuition provides a significant portion of revenues for all private schools, but many of the Liberal Arts 2 colleges and large urban universities rely almost totally upon this one source of income. Most colleges now attempt to cultivate alumni giving, but none quite as successfully as the leading Liberal Arts 1 schools and the Ivy League. The research universities in general maintain their expensive commitments to scholarship with the assistance of voluntary support from foundations and corporations, as well as through research funds from the federal government. Since the mid-1960s all private institutions have benefited from the growth of substantial federal programs of student aid involving direct and indirect grants, subsidized loans, and work-study programs. Their dependence upon these programs to sustain existing tuition levels has created a source of perpetual uncertainty. The continual adaptations that this uncertainty stimulates have become an inherently dynamic feature of the American private sector. As private colleges and universities face a rather bleak future, which threatens to combine smaller college-age cohorts with a diminished flow of federal funds, they may find that their ingrained capacity to adapt and change will ultimately become their greatest asset.

Privateness and Academic Integration

The private colleges and universities of these eight countries were founded for a great variety of purposes, and since their beginnings many have developed new and different functions. Clearly, their common attribute of privateness signifies less about the nature of these individual institutions than other salient characteristics. One of the variables that strongly affects the role and the significance of privateness is a school's degree of "academic integration"—the extent to which an institution identifies with and behaves according to the academic values embodied in international subject disciplines and usually exemplified by a nation's leading universities.

The basic academic values associated with the ideal of the university are widely shared across national systems. Without denying that different forms of university prestige exist within different countries, or that university organization varies considerably from one country to the next, it is still possible to posit a relevant academic ideal-type. It would have the following minimal attributes:

1. To an important extent the institution would be devoted to disinterested learning and the creation of new knowledge within academic disciplines.
2. Its faculty would be largely full-time, and have professional qualifications equivalent to the Ph.D.
3. Its students would be full-time as well, and they would be recruited from among well-prepared secondary school graduates.
4. It would possess most of the physical appurtenances of an institution of learning, such as a permanent campus, library, laboratories, etc.

These characteristics are in fact important variables within academic systems. The more research a university produces, the higher the qualifications of its faculty and students, and the more extensive its facilities, then the more prestige it is likely to attain within the academic community. The private institutions that have been examined in this study vary enormously in the degree to which they approximate this ideal—in the degree to which they have become integrated into the academic portion of their respective higher education systems. Thus, the degree of academic integration is the single most telling factor in the organizational behavior of private colleges and universities.

It was argued in the preceding chapter that the pursuit of academic distinction requires resources transcending the needs of instruction *per se*. Academic integration consequently implies a perpetual appetite for the type of students, faculty, and facilities that set the standards for high academic status. Since access to these kinds of resources differs widely between mass, parallel, and peripheral private sectors, academic integration entails various issues depending on the type of system. Overall, then, the conditions for the academic integration of private institutions will vary according to their underlying function in the higher education system, their relationship with the public sector, and the relative availability of public and private resources.

In the mass private sectors of Japan and the Philippines private institutions in essence serve the "overflow" from the comparatively small public sectors. The numerous institutions of such sectors naturally vary widely with respect to size, tasks, clientele, and the amount of resources that they can bring to bear for the purpose of instruction. These private sectors consequently tend to be inherently hierarchical, and it is the degree of academic integration that an institution is able to achieve that largely determines its place in the hierarchy. The strongest private colleges and universities in Japan and the Philippines are almost comparable to the best of the public sector, and definitely superior to the average public institution. The majority of private schools, however, simply lack the wherewithal to come close to matching the academic resources of the public sector. Nor are they able to ignore the standards prevailing elsewhere in their systems. Despite the specialized tasks of some private schools, like women's colleges or technical colleges, these systems possess relatively unitary standards of academic quality—standards that are enforced formally to varying degrees by the ministries of education, and informally by the effects of the institutional prestige hierarchy. The subsidization of private colleges in Japan was begun, in a sense, to strengthen academic integration, and many of the higher education regulations in the Philippines have been less costly efforts to achieve that same purpose.

The large urban private universities of the United States resemble mass private sectors in also exhibiting variable degrees of academic integration. A few have managed to become academically eminent Research 1 universities, but far more have had to rely upon their service roles to attract students. While the latter commonly make a virtue of a necessity in their publicity campaigns, it would be mistaken to assume that they are actually repudiating the academic definition of quality. Despite the enormous variety of American higher education, the unitary standard of academic quality became more powerful and more pervasive during the course of the 1960s.

If academic integration is a problematic goal for private institutions in mass private sectors, it is a necessary condition for their counterparts in a parallel private sector. The underlying assumption is that higher education, like education at the primary and secondary levels, should be a public service, but that it should be privately controlled in order to protect the cultural heritage of certain segments of the population. The logic of this position requires complete equality between the public and private sectors, thus implying the full academic integration of private universities. In Belgium and the Netherlands, of course, full state financing of private universities was eventually required to bring this about.

Historically, a similar situation has arisen where communities made provisions for locally available higher education through private or municipal means without ever considering it anything other than a public service. The British civic universities, the universities of Stockholm and Gothenburg, and certain American city universities fit this description. The logic of their position dictated that they remain roughly abreast of prevailing standards; i.e., that they be integrated with the wider academic community. In the absence of any compelling justification for remaining private, however, academic integration eventually meant absorption by the state. Stockholm and Gothenburg were formally nationalized; the British civic universities became part of a nationally financed university system without any change in their independent charters; and many American urban universities joined the public sector to become the nuclei of sprawling new state universities.

Private institutions in peripheral private sectors are not intended for general public purposes, but rather for specific functions, and sometimes for specific, limited constituencies. In these cases academic integration may be impossible, undesirable, or merely a secondary consideration, depending upon the circumstances of each institution. The schools of economics and the schools of commerce in Europe illustrate two divergent courses, even though their special missions and their historical origins were quite similar. The Stockholm School of Economics and its kindred institutions achieved complete academic integration because their subject matter became a part of the university curriculum. The schools of commerce, however, with their somewhat more practical orientation, have remained on the margins of the academic world. External ties remain important in both these cases, but for the Stockholm School of Economics they are balanced by scholarly cooperation with Swedish universities. The French schools of commerce, in contrast, are funded through local chambers of commerce, and are only indirectly under the jurisdiction of the Ministry of Education.

By far the most widespread type of private college intended for special constituencies are, of course, those sponsored by religious denominations. Close church ties have usually conflicted with academic integration, given the underlying trend toward the secularization of higher education in the twentieth century. Many of the leading American private colleges and universities dropped their religious ties early in the century; others retained church affiliation, but deemphasized its actual significance. Thus, the colleges that have resisted this trend are a distinctive lot. They have largely eschewed academic integration in order to preserve and propagate the beliefs of their specific clienteles. They consequently depend upon those constituencies for the recruitment of students and the provision of voluntary support. In general this pattern seems more common for small colleges, particularly many of the Liberal Arts 2 colleges in the United States. Larger universities appear far more likely to succumb to the pull of secularization and academic integration, although there are some notable exceptions like Brigham Young University. The same would be generally true for Roman Catholic institutions of higher education. Most Catholic universities have largely accepted the secularization of a substantial portion of the curriculum, and have thus been receptive toward academic integration. The exception here would be the Catholic universities of France, which for the last century have faced legal impediments to any meaningful integration with the state-controlled university system. In general, however, it has usually been the smaller Catholic colleges that have kept closer to the faith and more dependent on the faithful.

For private higher education in general, academic integration becomes a crucial variable for evaluating the role and the significance of private control. In those systems where private institutions are integrated, the most important single factor determining the behavior of individual colleges and universities will be the prevailing mores, customs, and practices of the national academic community. In other words, basic goals and standards will be largely the same in both the public and the private sector. Privateness, nevertheless, may be a factor in an institution's relative access to the resources needed to attain those goals. Thus, private institutions may do better or worse than average, depending upon their abilities to secure the resources for supporting the high overhead costs of academic research. Where an institution finds itself in the academic hierarchy, then, will be determined in large measure by its financial circumstances rather than by the fact of its privateness.

The situation differs for those private schools for whom academic integration is a secondary consideration. This is generally the case when privateness is organically related to special missions or constituencies. Direct links through trustees or sponsoring organizations typically exist between such schools and the groups that they serve, usually guaranteeing that these institutions will respond first and foremost to the needs of those constituencies. Their organizational behavior will be more distinctively private than their academically integrated counterparts who pursue many of the same objectives as public institutions. This distinction is highly relevant when measuring the performance of private sectors according to our criteria of diversity, adaptation, quality, and privilege.

The Pros and Cons of Privateness

The benefit most commonly attributed to private sectors has undoubtedly been that of providing diversity—affording numerous alternatives for the pursuit of advanced education. Diversity, however, is a nebulous concept. While it is regarded as a positive quality in some systems of higher education, it can be viewed rather suspiciously in others. Nor is it a quality pertaining only to the private sector. Public sectors often contain, whether through historical accident or by design, a considerable variety of institutional types. The states of California and New York, for example, when expanding their systems of higher education, consciously attempted to create institutional diversity. But government institutions must bear the pressures of both democracy and bureaucracy, and over the long run these pressures are likely to have some effect. Specifically, state systems of higher education tend to be drawn away from the unusual, and particularly from the unfashionable, toward greater parity and regularity in their organization and financing. In contrast, a private sector consists of multiple organizational centers, each to some extent feeling and responding to different sets of pressures.

Diversity and Innovation

Diversity arises naturally in private sectors from the varied purposes for which these institutions were founded, and from the independence that private control allows in the pursuit of these ends. The private schools in the eight countries covered by this study have differed along numerous dimensions. Some private institutions have chosen to be relatively small, catering to an academic elite; others have worked to grow as large as possible. One considerable class of private schools has specialized in training for specific professions, notably engineering, business, and home economics for women. Another type of school, defined in culturally exclusive terms, meets the particular needs of different religious faiths. Schools can manage to acquire a particular socioeconomic identity, with some catering to the scions of the affluent, others offering evening courses to part-time working students. Some institutions emphasize their differences in style of instruction—in the distinctive way they manage to conduct their students to the common

242 / Private Sectors in Higher Education

goal of a university degree. Yet, it is worth pointing out that this great variety of institutional species may be less diverse than would first appear. Curriculum is one thing that is unlikely to exhibit significant variation within systems of higher education. Often it is closely specified by a ministry of education, but a prevailing consensus within an academic discipline can informally accomplish the same purpose. At times prestigious institutional models exert a strong influence to conform upon the rest of the system, and this type of pull would not necessarily contradict some of the sources of diversity just mentioned. More generally, however, higher education systems possess quite powerful norms about what is and what is not fitting behavior for an institution. To transgress these norms can call into question the very legitimacy of the education an institution provides. Diversity and uniformity, then, are different facets of a private sector that will vary from one national system to another.

Academic integration provides a major element of uniformity to those private institutions that give it high priority, but a common academic orientation does not necessarily preclude dimensions of diversity. In the hierarchically structured systems of higher education (mass private sectors and the United States), hierarchy itself probably accounts for the most significant differences between institutions. Universities fortunate enough to be at the top of the pyramid are able to devote themselves to academic excellence. This is most obvious in the case of the private research universities in the United States, which not only present exceptional educational resources to their highly select students, but also set a standard that the outstanding public research universities must emulate. In Japan the leading private universities have been increasing their selectivity relative to the national universities—in effect, broadening the peak of the hierarchy there. And the leading colleges of the Philippines offer students educational programs that are roughly comparable with higher education in developed nations. The existence of these three sets of private institutions quite clearly enriches the higher education systems of their respective countries. But then, what distinctive contribution do their less distinguished counterparts make to their respective private sectors?

Japan and the United States, of course, enroll the highest percentage of current cohorts in higher education, and the Philippines has unusually high participation for a developing nation. In Japan and the Philippines the private sector is responsible for these high enrollment rates, and historically this has been true in certain regions of the United States. The diversity provided by less selective private colleges has undoubtedly enhanced access to higher education in these three societies. Moreover, the less rigorous standards of these institutions assure that students are not only admitted, but that they have a realistic chance of graduating as well. This contrasts sharply with some systems of higher education where relatively open admissions are combined with a high rate of attrition. Of course, it is just this feature of hierarchical private sectors that offends academic purists, or those accustomed to the European university standard. Nevertheless, these systems do extend access to higher education. It would be difficult to argue that these greater educational opportunities do not, *in the aggregate* and *over time,* have positive effects upon the personal development and occupational chances of their students. This line of reasoning cannot be extended too far, however. At the bottom of academic pyramids lie mediocre institutions with programs of questionable worth.

A second axis of diversity derives from functional specialization. Many private colleges were begun for specific purposes and have not evolved beyond them toward comprehensiveness. The Japanese private sector best illustrates this point with three out of every five institutions being single-faculty colleges, but this same tendency is evident in the Philippine private sector as well. It is undoubtedly sensible for private colleges with limited means at their disposal to specialize in this way. Limiting their scope ought to allow them to maximize their competency. However, one might still question whether or not this considerable variety of institutional form actually contributes to the diversity of the system. Particularly in a system like the Japanese, where the individual faculties are the most important institutional units, a freestanding faculty of commerce may have few significant differences from one that forms a part of a larger university. And the differences that do exist may not be advantageous, to judge from the clear preferences of Japanese students for larger institutions. On balance it might be said for Japan that the technological colleges, especially those closely connected with industry, and the women's colleges do contribute to the diversity of the entire system, but that the other single-function colleges do little to enhance choice in this particular respect.

The situation is rather different with regard to liberal arts colleges. Although they evolved as a distinctly American form of higher education, American influence carried them to Japan and the Philippines where they now form, respectively, a minor and a major component of those private sectors. Since the content of a liberal arts curriculum is far more fluid than that of most special-purpose colleges just discussed, liberal arts colleges have considerably more latitude to differ significantly from one another. Each tends to have a distinct personality derived from its particular origins, its instructional style, physical setting, and the cultural overtones of the curriculum. Because of the relevance of cultural elements, the roles of liberal arts colleges vary somewhat according to national culture. In the United States those liberal arts colleges that are most academically integrated are also largely secularized; that is, they have dropped much of the cultural coloration associated with their original church affiliation. Conversely, those colleges that remain strongly identified with a particular religion or culture contribute to diversity in precisely that way, but often at the expense of their academic status. This dualism does not hold for Japan and the Philippines. Christian liberal arts colleges such as International Christian University and Kobe College in Japan have managed to be prestigious and selective, and the two most eminent private colleges in the Philippines are both operated by religious orders. In Japan the relatively small number of liberal arts colleges provides an alternative to the typical literary faculties, while in the Philippines the many liberal arts colleges present qualitative and cultural differences among themselves.

The issue of private sector diversity is considerably altered in parallel private sectors. Cultural pluralism, or the accommodation of major cultural cleavages, was the rationale for the arrangements that have evolved in Belgium and the Netherlands. Politically potent communities in these two countries have demanded, and been granted, universities of their own that were "just as good as the state's." For that reason these private universities closely resemble those of the state. The Netherlands is the extreme in this respect—the nadir of private sector diversity, one could say. And perhaps for that reason important changes in Dutch higher education are initiated in the national legislature instead of at the institutional level. In the Belgian private sector there is more desire on the part of private institutions not only to be independent, but to express their individuality. This stems from a greater degree of institutional competition, which itself reflects the contentiousness in Belgian society between Flemings and Walloons, and between Catholics and free-thinkers.

Finally, diversity is inherent to peripheral private sectors because they exist largely to provide something that is not available in the dominant public sector. The French private sector illustrates well the range of possibilities. It contains institutions oriented to the special cultural requirements of French Catholics. It also has vocationally oriented schools for subjects such as commerce that are not—or have not been until very recently—taught in the national universities. A third type of private preparatory school is to some degree a product of the importance of examinations in the French academic culture. In fact, wherever examinations are used to determine important life chances, whether educational opportunities or vocational credentials, a field is created for private initiative, quite often inspired by the profit motive. For-profit educational ventures in this case are able to compete with nonprofit or public rivals because they will be judged upon a single, unambiguous result. Thus, besides the French private schools of this type, one could point to the *jukus* of Japan and numerous American examples that endeavor to help either high school students improve their scores on the Scholastic Aptitude Tests, law school graduates pass their bar examinations, or aspiring real estate agents gain their licenses.

The singular institutions that have been examined in this study present particularly strong testimony of the benefits of diversity. Both the Ecole Libre des Sciences Politiques and the Stockholm School of Economics managed to excel in the roles they fashioned for themselves. It is immaterial that one was nationalized and one retained its independence, since both originated as privately sponsored efforts to supply public needs that the respective states were not at the time willing to fulfill. The University of Buckingham has attempted to fashion a similarly distinctive niche for itself, and has succeeded in creating several original, albeit minor, contributions to higher education in the United Kingdom.

The possibilities for diversity in a given system of higher education are first circumscribed by structure, then powerfully affected by national cultures, and finally limited by the material circumstances of a given institution. For this reason it has been difficult to make explicit comparisons of diversity across systems without artificially focusing on a single dimension at a time. Moreover, diversity is a static concept—the anatomy of a system at a particular point in time. Yet, private sectors are diverse because independent institutions, acting independently over time, tend to fulfill the possibilities that structure, culture, and circumstances allow. Doing this means fulfilling the multiple needs of students, parents, employers, and the considerable demands of the academic system itself. This, in turn, calls for continual adaptation to the changing requirements of external constituencies, labor markets, and the knowledge base of higher education. Thus, adaptive innovation forms the dynamic counterpart of diversity within private sectors.

Not that higher education is all that prone to change. Academic institutions in general tend to exhibit inertia unless induced to do otherwise. Such inducements to change might be generalized into four broad categories: internal competition between institutions for students, faculty, gifts, or glory; external stimuli from outside the higher education system; political actions taken by government; and proactive or anticipatory planning. Any institution, public or private, might be affected by each of these four kinds of change; but private institutions are especially responsive to the first two types, and public ones are more subject to the latter two. This is simply because the multiple centers of control in private sectors allow more rapid and more various responses to the exigencies of competition or stimuli. The reverse would hold for public sectors which, in addition, are under direct governmental authority and are obviously more likely to become the object of centralized planning. Institutional competition and external stimuli, then, are the principal incentives for adaptive innovation in the private sector.

Competition characterizes entire systems of higher education, not just private sectors. The nineteenth-century German university system was noted for institutional competition, even though it was comprised exclusively of state universities. In general, however, large private sectors are associated with competitive conditions. Hierarchical systems, of course, are inherently competitive, but the development of the relatively flat Belgian system has also exhibited considerable competition. What institutions compete for naturally varies with their position in their national system; what causes them to change or remain the same will vary accordingly.

At the top of the academic hierarchy, institutions compete to attain and to sustain academic excellence. The chief dynamic element in this competition is the constantly growing knowledge base on which higher education is predicated. Universities are obliged to add courses and to expand departments in order to incorporate new specialities, or to add entirely new departments when the occasion calls for it. However, this strong orientation toward frontiers of knowledge is generally accompanied by the widely acknowledged phenomenon of academic conservatism. Concentrating their attention on cognitive developments can make such universities oblivious to many of the other more mundane functions that higher education fulfills, and actually disdainful of some of the instrumental forms of knowledge that are readily taught at less rarified institutions. Moreover, when these institutions are threatened with change in such related areas as student recruitment or university governance, they often invoke the need to sustain academic excellence as a defense of existing practices. Academic conservatism and knowledge-driven innovation seem to reinforce one another, judging from the example of American research universities. This is, of course, their great strength; but it can only be considered a virtue in pluralistic systems where different sorts of institutions can be relied on to sponsor other forms of innovation.

It is more difficult to generalize about the middle ranges of the academic hierarchy. Private institutions there utilize advantages of style, location, and specialization to establish and maintain niches for their existence. Competition is implicit in such an environment, but the institutions that are successful over the long run are the ones that cultivate a secure and dependable clientele. To do so may require strategic innovations, but it usually also demands a great deal of constancy. Changes that might attract additional support must be weighed against the possibility that they could alienate a portion of those already in the fold. Institutions in this middle range can rarely stand still for long. They must continually adapt in order to maintain or enhance their academic credibility, while continuing to provide the kinds of services needed by their clientele. Despite such changes, however, these institutions derive much of their strength from the stability inherent in their distinctive roles.

The most intense competition for student enrollments exists at the bottom of academic hierarchies. Here are the tuition-dependent institutions for whom prosperity, or even survival, ultimately depends upon attracting sufficient numbers of students. Should their popularity wane, they have few other resources to fall back upon. This type of university has consequently been most innovative in creating new programs, and least inhibited by concern for the academic respectability of new educational services or customers. Some of the large private universities in this category have grown into educational conglomerates in this fashion. For good or for ill, these institutions most clearly exhibit the connection between independent control, a competitive environment, and adaptive innovation.

Private institutions having nonacademic orientations are likely to innovate in response to those external groups upon which they depend. Competition may sometimes be a factor, but by their very nature these institutions succeed by fulfilling the well-defined functions for which they are suited. Professional schools will feel the need to innovate in order to keep up with changes in the fields they teach. Institutions oriented toward religious or cultural purposes are likely to be responsive to their supporters in a different way. The overriding purpose of such schools is usually to promote the intergenerational perpetuation of their particular beliefs within the context of higher education. Their aim is consequently stability rather than change. Such institutions are naturally open to types of innovation that do not interfere with their fundamental beliefs— and may occasionally be highly imaginative regarding innovations that might further those beliefs—but on the whole, these, the most private of the colleges and universities covered in this study, are also the most conservative and least innovative.

The evidence from these eight private sectors presents a complex picture of diversity and adaptive innovation, but it nevertheless lends overall support to the conventional association between these qualities and private higher education. Yet this still leaves a larger question concerning the importance of diversity and innovation for the social functions of higher education. In the context of the United States' highly pluralistic and dynamic society the advantages are usually justified with two different but compelling arguments—one organizational and the other normative. Organizationally, the advantages of redundancy are evident when different units in a system are accomplishing similar tasks in dissimilar fashion.[1] If one approach develops problems, others are likely to be able to either assume the burden or indicate possible solutions. Such a process implies the existence of systemwide learning among and within institutions, so that success will be rewarded and imitated, while failure will be gradually eliminated. This would create a capacity for adaptive change within the system considerably greater than the propensity to innovate among individual institutions. The normative argument is based upon the value of choice in a democratic society. A larger variety of institutions simply allows individuals more opportunity to find the kind of higher education that is compatible with their beliefs and appropriate for their aspirations. These features of the American system have been described as the "benefits of disorder"—structural and functional advantages that flow from the multifaceted evolution of American higher education in the near absence of central direction.[2] It does not necessarily follow, however, that these qualities would be similarly appreciated in other societies.

The great pluralism of American society and the prevailing individualism of American culture make diversity a virtual necessity, but some of the other countries studied here, notably Sweden and

Japan, are much more homogeneous. This tends to make them dis-trustful of diversity and rather skeptical toward the possible seren-dipity of disorder. Many Swedes feel rather uncomfortable about an educational anomaly like the Stockholm School of Economics. The political culture of Sweden is strongly committed to the position that deliberate planning with extensive consultation of all con-cerned will ultimately produce the most rational social action. In the case of the recent reorganization of Swedish higher education, known as the U-68 Reforms, this painstaking process took nine years. Despite the imperfections of the final result—and the inevita-ble intrusion of political factors into this type of decision—it would be difficult to convince most Swedes that a laissez-faire situation would have produced a better reform. In France the relatively low degree of homogeneity in the nation has historically led the state to compensate with highly centralized organs of government, includ-ing the university system. In part this reflects a widely shared sus-picion that privately controlled institutions will be employed for the advantage of private parties, as was clearly the case in the rela-tionship between the old Ecole Libre des Sciences Politiques and the *grands corps*. It has been seen in the case of Japan that the higher education preferences of a highly homogeneous society, plus the pressure exerted by the Ministry of Education, have been lessening the diversity inherent in such a large private sector. Yet, the minis-try has been simultaneously encouraging diversification by approv-ing only new faculties that promise programs not otherwise avail-able. Thus, there is a desire for both a greater variety of vocationally oriented programs and a rather tightly controlled order in Japanese higher education. In general, then, it would seem that there is far less tolerance of diversity and much less appreciation of adaptive innovation as a mode of academic change in these three countries than one finds in the United States.

Quality and Privilege

The issue of private sector diversity just examined also touches fun-damental questions of social values. A high degree of diversity in a system of higher education inevitably means considerable in-equality as well: institutions will differ in their capacity to provide quality instruction, and this will be translated into unequal oppor-tunities for students. The different countries of this study differ markedly in their perceptions of these two problems of mediocrity and privilege.

Large hierarchical private sectors inevitably face the problem of low-quality schools in the lower portion of the academic pyramid. It has been pointed out that such institutions, usually the most zealous in the recruitment of students, significantly expand access to higher education. However, it is not possible to determine to what extent these gains are cancelled out by the inferiority of the instruction provided. In every country there exist implicit normative standards, in addition to the legal requirements for accreditation, and institutions suspected of failing to meet these standards are likely to be regarded with disdain, if not ostracized completely, by the rest of the academic community. The United States, which has had the world's largest system of higher education in this century, has generally shown considerable tolerance for inferior institutions in both the public and private sectors. Mediocre colleges have been no less inevitable in the mass private sectors of Japan and the Philippines, but in both those countries a central ministry of education has in recent years attempted to systematically upgrade the weaker institutions. In western Europe, where a single university standard has prevailed, the intolerance of mediocrity has stood as one of the most powerful arguments restricting private initiatives in higher education. Historically there have been many reasons for this, including the influence of the German idea of a university, the bifurcated structure of secondary schooling, and the close connection between university credentials and government employment. The structural consequence for the five European nations considered here has been the segregation of many types of advanced vocational instruction into a nonuniversity sector. The recent trend toward lessening that separation, which has been taken furthest in the Swedish U-68 reform, does not signify a more liberal attitude toward qualitative diversity. Quite the opposite, it represents a conscious commitment to make opportunites in higher education more equal for all participants.

When equality in some form (equal opportunity, equal treatment, equal results) becomes a goal of higher education, a strong presumption is created against private control of institutions. In Belgium and the Netherlands this presumption has been overridden by the strength of cultural pluralism; in countries with peripheral private sectors the animus against private control forms part of the rationale for the dominant scope of the public sector. Opportunities within higher education nevertheless cannot be equalized without a vast reordering of the occupational structure.[3] For that reason all developed nations have adopted meritocratic procedures for a reasonably just allocation of these unequal opportunities. These procedures are naturally incumbent upon institutions in both sectors. Of course, it is widely recognized that meritocratic procedures do not equalize the social incidence of higher education: student from upper social backgrounds have numerous advantages in this type of competition. But this fact, too, affects both public and private higher education. The question of privilege in private higher education thus only arises when private control can be associated with special advantages that violate the established procedures or tacit assumptions of meritocratic competition—when one student displaces another who would be considered more deserving according to universalistic criteria.

This study has encountered three clear instances where privilege might be linked with privateness: the monopolization of opportunities to enter the *grands corps* by the Ecole Libre des Sciences Politiques; the recently created medical and dental colleges of Japan that charge exorbitant tuitions; and, in a social context quite different from the developed countries, the predominance of a social elite in the leading colleges of Manila. Had this study delved more deeply into the history of the American private sector it would have encountered discriminatory admissions practices in prominent private universities.[4] Both Japan and the United States, in addition, contain numerous private colleges that cater to social elites, although they are not literally exclusive, since they cost no more than other good private schools, nor do they, like the schools in Manila, possess the academic superiority to assure postgraduate preferment. In order to make the connection between privilege and privateness it is useful to consider these cases from three perspectives.

First, these situations reflect existing social relations within their respective countries. The institutions thus function as intermediaries in one stage of the intergenerational transfer of wealth and position. To point this out is not to condone these institutions, but rather to underline that they are not independent agents. In the absence of accompanying social changes, their outright elimination would alter only the details of this process, not the final result.

Second, patterns of privilege are fundamentally incompatible with the prevailing meritocratic assumptions of all highly developed systems of higher education. The resulting tension works against privilege in the long run. The Ecole Libre des Sciences Politiques came under strong political pressure in this century, and would most likely have been nationalized in the 1930s had it not been for the international crisis. The Japanese medical colleges in question are regarded in higher education circles there as a scandal for the private sector. They are likely to feel consistent bureaucratic pressure to conform with the rest of the system. As for the prestigious American private universities, they have long since shed overtly discriminatory admissions practices. In fact, they have moved so far in the opposite direction that they now give special consideration to certain groups that are likely to be at a disadvantage in the normal meritocratic competition. As for the Philippines, the establishment of the National Collegiate Entrance Examination holds at least the possibility of strengthening meritocratic practices in years to come.

Third, the degree of privilege should be evaluated in relation to the magnitude of the potential rewards. The "preppie" colleges of the United States and Japan, for example, do not seem to represent undue privilege in spite of their social character, because they provide their students with no unwarranted advantages over other college graduates. The right to practice medicine, of course, is a coveted opportunity everywhere, as well as a publicly sanctioned position; but the extravagantly priced medical education offered by the new Japanese colleges has been notoriously ineffective in preparing its graduates for the rigorous state licensing examinations. In this case there would seem to be limits to the educational benefits that wealth can buy. Indeed, those institutions that can promise their students the largest and surest rewards are also the institutions that adhere most strictly to meritocratic practice—and this is obviously why their graduates are so valued. Thus, for the mature educational systems covered in this study it would seem that when a private institution acquires the capacity to dispense significant social opportunities, it relinquishes the right to restrict arbitrarily public access to them. Prevailing social standards of equitable treatment ultimately limit privilege in these private sectors.

The Merits of Private Higher Education

Viewed abstractly the features of private education that have just been discussed could appear as a series of trade-offs. A high degree of diversity will allow greater student choice and a broader range of tasks in higher education, but at the price of some cultural fragmentation and incoherence. A rapid pace of innovation may keep a system abreast of a changing environment for higher education, but it is also likely to erode established curricula with time-tested value and to introduce programs of dubious merit. It is easy to deplore low standards in higher education, yet most people would support the increased access that they permit. Similarly, it is natural to laud the excellence that selective, well-financed institutions can achieve, while at the same time feeling uncomfortable about the unequal opportunities that inevitably result. From this perspective it is evident that a theoretically optimal mix of these qualities cannot be prescribed. Furthermore, given the variable relationships between types of private higher education and the consequences for the educational system, it would seem even more obvious that no optimal division of higher education between public and private sectors can be recommended.

In fact, all that has been said in this book should serve to emphasize that private control over institutions of higher education cannot be construed as a determinative social arrangement. Rather, it is one that is largely shaped by more fundamental social, political, and economic realities. These more comprehensive forces can be credited in a general way with shaping educational systems in which the public-private balance is but one component. This does not mean that private sectors should be regarded as being socially inert—mere consequences rather than causes of the developments surrounding them. Instead it would suggest that the immediate influence of the existence of private sectors is exerted within the educational system itself, and only then at times to society at large. Nevertheless, some general conclusions stand out from this study about the positive contributions that private sectors can offer.

Private sectors play an important role maintaining the cultural pluralism of certain societies by providing a means for the expression and perpetuation of private collective interests. Moreover, outlets such as these are an indispensible component of a free society. Many political regimes in the world today strongly oppose pluralistic alternatives, insisting instead on the cultural hegemony of the ruling government. These countries, quite naturally, have no toleration for private sectors. For religious groups, in particular, control over their own institutions of higher education has offered an invaluable haven against the perils of minority status or the pervasive influence of a secular state. However, this study has encountered the same freedom being utilized by free-thinkers in Belgium, nationalists in the Philippines, and Western-oriented liberals in Japan. In a different way the openness of higher education to private initiatives has created new educational opportunities for formerly excluded segments of the population. This has been most obvious in the creation of private women's colleges in several countries, but earlier this century it would also apply to Catholic universities in American cities. The situation of professional groups seeking to promote their interests through higher education involves social changes of a different kind. The penetration of education for business or commerce into the postsecondary realm was largely the result of private initiatives taken by groups eager to promote the status of their profession. Although recent years have seen considerable efforts to promote vocational higher education in the public sectors of France, Sweden, and in American community colleges, it seems far more likely that initiatives privately generated within a profession will signal propitious conditions for the receptivity of programs by students, and the acceptance of graduates by employers. To the extent that private higher education embodies private collective interests, then, it expresses natural forces existing in open societies.

Private sectors also have a substantial contribution to make to the private interests of individuals. Private institutions in all of the countries studied here have either marginally or substantially increased the range of possibilities for potential students. The benefits of greater choice, like the advantages of open entry for private groups, will in most systems be utilized by a minority. However, the benefactors will be precisely those people whose preferences differ from the majority that has preponderant influence over the nature of the public sector. Thus, in these cases as well, the existence of private higher education enhances the freedom and openness of a given society. The situation is somewhat different in mass private sectors, where the majority of students rely upon private institutions. Ample choice may be an important aspect of these systems, but they chiefly benefit from the third general contribution of private higher education.

Privately controlled institutions have a capacity to mobilize private resources for the ends of higher education. These resources are not always different from those tapped by public sources, but their net effect is to augment total investments in higher education. As a result, these extra commitments tend to increase the total quantity of higher education in some cases, and to augment its quality in others. It is no accident that the two most extensive systems of higher education, those in Japan and the United States, both rely heavily upon private resources. Japan accomplishes this through its mass private sector, and the Philippines has achieved a remarkable level of enrollment through a similar structure. The United States, it should be remembered, had by far the largest system of higher education in the world *before* the great expansion of its public sector; i.e., when it was still relying heavily upon private institutions to provide access to higher education. It is not difficult to account for this phenomenon: the perceived private returns to higher education are a continual inducement for individuals to commit their own funds when a subsidized place in the public sector is not available to them. In addition, tuition-dependent institutions have a continual incentive to recruit the clientele that will provide their financial sustenance. Private institutions are often particularly adept at mobilizing human resources as well—inspired founders who assemble the human and material commitments necessary to launch and sustain a college, or dedicated teachers and administrators who work long hours for comparatively little pay. Of course, this would not be valid for all private institutions; but few would doubt that the abilities of many private colleges and universities to inspire deep loyalties within their employees is a key ingredient in their effectiveness.

Finally, to varying degrees, private sectors are able to bring the resources of private philanthropy to bear on higher education. This has been important in the history of the three singular institutions examined in chapter 4; it has also figured in the development of Belgian and Dutch private universities; and it may well become more significant for the Japanese private sector in the near future. Even more to the point, private giving was seen to play a unique and irreplaceable role in sustaining many American private colleges and universities. In this case privately donated funds have allowed the private sector to contribute to serving some of the public responsibilities of higher education. These would include not only the funding of basic research, but also furthering the welfare of needy students through private scholarship funds. In sum, the existence of a private sector tends to expand the social resources available to higher education. During the great postwar expansions of government commitments to higher education this may have seemed like a matter of small and declining importance, but in the current environment of government financial austerity this facet of private sectors could be crucial to the future well-being of higher education as a whole.

In the final analysis, private higher education should not be perceived as an end in itself, or as an inherently superior way of organizing the tasks of higher education. It has, however, been a widely utilized vehicle for achieving certain general objectives in higher education, and these efforts in themselves have produced the above-mentioned benefits for the educational system and for society. In keeping with this, future actions bearing on the public-private structure in any country should not be predicated on insulating certain institutions, or protecting the private sector for its own sake. Rather, the concern should be to devise policies that will preserve and enhance the demonstrated benefits that privately controlled higher education can bring to a system of higher education, and to the society it serves.

Notes

Foreword

1. See Charles E. Lindblom, *Politics and Markets: The World's Political-Economic Systems* (New York: Basic Books, 1977).
2. See James Douglas, *Why Charity?: The Case for a Third Sector* (Beverly Hills: Sage Publications, 1983).
3. See Burton R. Clark, *The Higher Education System: Academic Organization in Cross-National Perspective* (Berkeley and Los Angeles: University of California Press, 1983).
4. Daniel J. Levy, *The State and Higher Education in Latin America: Private Challenges to Public Dominance* (Chicago: University of Chicago Press, 1986).

Chapter 1

1. Cf. David W. Breneman and Chester E. Finn, Jr., eds., *Public Policy and Private Higher Education* (Washington, D.C.: The Brookings Institution, 1978).
2. Outside of the United States Japan is the only country covered in this study for which there is a scholarly literature dealing specifically with problems of private higher education. This work has been utilized in chapter 2. An international study of private higher education should complement this volume by covering conditions in Latin America: Daniel Levy, *The State and Higher Education in Latin America* (Chicago: University of Chicago Press, 1986). Recent work by Estelle James has focused primarily, but not exclusively, on private primary and secondary education. Her basic findings are presented in "The Public/Private Division of Responsibility for Education: An International Comparison," 1984. Mimeo. Similarly inclusive is Guy Neave, "The Nonstate Sector in the Education Provision of Member States of the European Community" (Brussels: Report to the Education Services of the Commission of the European Community, 1983).
3. Two somewhat more complicated public-private structures will not be considered here. In India numerous private colleges are affiliated with major state universities—a pattern that harks back to former British arrangements for external degrees, but today is more akin to mass private sectors. In Latin America private sectors have grown in some countries as a refuge

257

from uncontrolled growth and politicization in the national universities. See Levy, *State and Higher Education*.

4. There are no clear ground rules for determining the most highly educated society. In terms of current student cohorts, Japan and the United States compare as follows: Japan graduates more of its youth from high school (90 percent vs. 75 percent); about the same proportion graduate from college in each country; however, the United States has a considerable advantage in graduate education and in adult education. Roger Geiger, "The Limits of Mass Higher Education," Yale University Institution for Social and Policy Studies Working Paper, YHERG-41 (February 1980).

5. E.g., John R. Silber, "Paying the Bill for College: The 'Private' Sector and the Public Interest," *Atlantic* 235 (May 1975): 33–40.

6. With respect to the United States, see John S. Whitehead, *The Separation of Church and State: Columbia, Dartmouth, Harvard and Yale* (New Haven: Yale University Press, 1973).

7. Henry Hansmann, "The Role of the Non-Profit Enterprise," Yale University Institution for Social and Policy Studies Working Paper, PONPO-1 (April 1978).

8. Burton R. Clark, *The Higher Education System: Academic Organization in Cross-National Perspective* (Berkeley and Los Angeles: University of California Press, 1983).

9. One important input to quality in higher education is the ability level of the students: however, the higher the price of the education, the fewer topnotch students who will be able to afford it. A second important input is the scholarly attainments of the faculty: but top faculty are able to demand teaching positions that generously subsidize their scholarly activities.

10. Proprietary higher education is discussed in chapter 2 of this volume.

11. Burton A. Weisbrod, "Toward a Theory of the Voluntary Nonprofit Sector in a Three-Sector Economy," in *The Voluntary Nonprofit Sector* (Lexington, Mass.: Lexington Press, 1977), pp. 51–76. Education is technically not a pure collective good, but a "quasi-public good," which is parcelled out and from which some people can be excluded. See James, "Public/Private Division."

12. In particular, the desire for *better* higher education than that available in the public sector may provide an additional rationale for private higher education. See chapter 5 in this volume; and, with regard to Latin America, Levy, *State and Higher Education*.

13. Thomas Kuhn, *The Structure of Scientific Revolutions*, 2d ed. (Chicago: University of Chicago Press, 1970); *The Essential Tension* (Chicago: University of Chicago Press, 1977), p. xix.

14. Charles E. Lindblom and David K. Cohen, *Usable Knowledge: Social Science and Social Problem Solving* (New Haven: Yale University Press, 1979), p. 74.

15. Arend Lijphart, "Comparative Politics and the Comparative Method," *American Political Science Review* 65 (1971): 682–93; Dennis J. Palum-

bo, "Comparative Analysis: Quasimethodology or New Science?" *Comparative Urban Research* 4 (1973–74): 37–53.

Chapter 2

1. The mass private sector of Brazil is analyzed in Daniel Levy, *The State and Private Higher Education in Latin America* (Chicago: University of Chicago Press, 1986). The Belgian private sector is covered in chapter 3 of this volume.

2. On the role of education in Japanese society generally, see Edwin O. Reischauer, *The Japanese* (Cambridge: Harvard University Press, 1977), pp. 167–78. The importance of an indigenous educational tradition is stressed in Ronald P. Dore, *Education in Tokugawa Japan* (Berkeley and Los Angeles: University of California Press, 1965); and Thomas P. Rohlen, *Japan's High Schools* (Berkeley and Los Angeles: University of California Press, 1983), pp. 45–76.

3. Ikuo Amano, "Continuity and Change in the Structure of Japanese Higher Education," in *Changes in the Japanese University,* ed. William Cummings, Ikuo Amano, and Kazuyuki Kitamura (New York: Praeger, 1979), pp. 10–39.

4. Michio Nagai, *Higher Education in Japan: Its Take-off and Crash,* trans. Jerry Dusenbury (Tokyo: University of Tokyo Press, 1971), p. 55.

5. Nagai, *Higher Education,* p. 21.

6. In 1905, for example, twenty state *senmongakku* graduated 2,939 students compared with 683 graduates produced by the two imperial universities (Amano, "Continuity and Change," p. 16). See also Ikuo Amano, *Kyusei senmongakko* (Old-style special schools) (Tokyo: Nippon Keizai Shimbunsha, 1978).

7. Nagai, *Higher Education,* pp. 28–33.

8. Amano, *Senmongakko,* pp. 55–71.

9. Nagai, *Higher Education,* p. 32.

10. Amano, "Continuity and Change," p. 21.

11. Ibid., pp. 21–22; Akira Ninomiya, *Private Universities in Japan* (Tokyo: Private Universities Union of Japan, 1977), pp. 3–4.

12. Amano, "Continuity and Change," p. 26.

13. Nagai, *Higher Education,* pp. 42–44.

14. John E. Blewitt, S. J., ed. and trans., *Higher Education in Post-War Japan: The Ministry of Education's 1964 White Paper* (Tokyo: Sophia University Press, 1965), pp. 77–80.

15. Amano, "Continuity and Change," pp. 33–34.

16. T. J. Pempel, "The Politics of Enrollment Expansion in Japanese Universities," *Journal of Asian Studies* 33 (1973): 67–86.

17. *Higher Education in Post-War Japan,* pp. 80–85.

18. The rationale for this policy is presented in the Ministry of Education paper, "Demand and Supply for Graduates from Secondary Schools and Universities" (1961), which projected a deficit of 170,000 science and en-

gineering graduates for the 1960s. Pempel suggests that Japanese business interests were the motive force behind this policy in "Politics of Enrollment Expansion."

19. Shogo Ichikawa, "Finance of Higher Education," in *Changes in the Japanese University,* pp. 40–63.

20. Ninomiya, *Private Universities,* p. 28. Note that tuition and fees vary greatly between faculties, with medicine by far the most expensive subject. However, within the same subjects there is comparatively little variation between institutions—an unusual feature of a large, stratified private sector.

21. Hiromitsu Muta, "Kyōiku shishutsuno futan kubun—Kōtō kyōiku no baai" (Sources of expenditures for higher education) in *Kyōiku ni okeru saiteki shigen haibun ni kansuru kisōteki kenkyū* (Allocation of educational resources in Japan), ed. Shogo Ichikawa (Tokyo: National Institute for Educational Research, September 1978), pp. 51–102.

22. Shogo Ichikawa, "Kyōiku shishutsuno jisshitsuka to yoin bunseki" (Real educational expenditures and factors in its increase) in *Kyōiku ni okeru,* pp. 11–50.

23. Jyoji Kikuchi, "Shiritsu daigaku gakusei nōfukin to kakei futan" (Expenses and fees for private university students) in *Shiritsu daigaku no shakaiteki kōzō* (Social structure of private universities) (Tokyo: National Institute for Educational Research, 1978), pp. 199–215.

24. Michiya Shimbori, "The Sociology of a Student Movement: A Japanese Case Study," in *Students in Revolt,* ed. S. M. Lipset and P. Altbach (Boston: Beacon Press, 1970), pp. 283–309.

25. Ichikawa, "Finance," p. 60.

26. Beresford Hayward, "The Social and Economic Issues of Japanese Educational Policy," in *Reviews of National Policies for Education: Japan* (Paris: Organization for Economic Cooperation and Development [OECD], 1971), pp. 153–62.

27. Blewitt, "Higher Education in Post-War Japan," pp. 87–88.

28. Ichikawa, "Kyōiku shishutsuno," p. 39.

29. OECD, *Japan,* pp. 75–79.

30. Ministry of Education, "Basic Guidelines for the Reform of Education: Report of the Central Council for Education" (Tokyo: Ministry of Education, 1972).

31. Student activism after 1967 focused increasingly on external political question in contrast to earlier protests over issues within the universities. This coincided with a shift in protest to the national universities. The government reaction, the University Control Bill of August 1969, was far more prominent and controversial than the law on private school finance, although its chief provisions for closing obstreperous campuses were never exercised.

32. Cf. the arguments of Ronald P. Dore in OECD, *Japan,* pp. 115–23.

33. Unless indicated otherwise, all figures on enrollments are from the

Statistical Abstract of Education, Science and Culture (Tokyo: Ministry of Education, 1979).

34. In 1978 required donations were prohibited, but private medical and dental faculties responded by sharply raising their charges to the astronomical levels cited (1981 tuition and entrance fees from *Daigaku juken annai*, 1981). See Ishikawa, "Finance," pp. 57–58.

35. On university entrance exams, see Rohlen, *Japan's High Schools*, pp. 77–110.

36. Ikuo Amano, *Henkakuki no daigakuzō* (University in transition) (Tokyo: Nippon Recruit Center, 1980), pp. 152–65.

37. *Keisetsu jidai*, August Supplement, 1972 and 1980. The improvement in the relative position of private colleges is discussed by Chuichi Nakamura, *Shiritsu daigaku: Sono kyozo to jitsuzo* (Private universities: Images and facts) (Tokyo: Toyokeizai Simposha, 1980).

38. Japanese universities were recently categorized as follows:

	Public	Private
Research Universities	19	5
Doctoral Granting Universities	20	101
Semidoctoral Granting Universities	21	14
Master Granting	42	43
Undergraduate Universities	23	155
Total	125	318

Tominaga Keii, ed., *Daigaku hyoka no kenkyu* (Evaluation study of Japanese universities) (Tokyo: University of Tokyo Press, 1984).

39. Morikazu Ushiogi, *Gakureki shakai no tenkan* (Change in a credential society), pp. 48–60. The five high schools studied by Rohlen sent the following percentages of their graduates on to universities: 100 percent, 72 percent, 62 percent, 6 percent, and 2 percent: *Japan's High Schools*, p. 44.

40. The phenomenon of *ronin* bears some resemblance to the recruitment to the *grandes écoles* of France, which requires one or two years of study in a special preparatory class before the competitive entrance examinations are taken (see chapter 4 in this volume). The result of this mode of recruitment in France has been pronounced social inequality. See Pierre Bourdieu and Jean-Claude Passeron, *Les héritiers* (Paris: Les Editions de Minuit, 1964).

41. Jyoji Kikuchi, "Kyōiku kikai to shigan haibun," (Opportunity for education and allocation of resources) in Ichikawa, *Allocation*, pp. 147–216.

42. William K. Cummings, *Education and Equality in Japan* (Princeton: Princeton University Press, 1980), pp. 223–27. Also, see note 45 below.

43. Reischauer, *The Japanese*, pp. 160–62.

44. Cummings, *Education and Equality*.

45. Discussion of this point usually focuses on the University of Tokyo— a rarefied institution virtually in a class by itself (see Cummings, *Education and Equality*, pp. 225, 227; Rohlen, *Japan's High Schools*, pp.

86–91). Figures for average family income (1976) show national university students at ¥3,760,000; private university students at ¥5,041,000; and University of Tokyo students at ¥5,170,000. See Nippon Shiritsu Daigaku Renmei (Private Universities Union of Japan), *Ibarano michi—Kyōgaku jyōken no kaizen to zaisei no akka* (Improvement of education and research conditions and deterioration of financial conditions) (Tokyo: 1980 White Paper on Financial Conditions), p. 29.

46. The *yobikos* constitute an educational system in microcosm, with different schools specializing in different levels of preparation. Some prepare only for a single faculty entrance exam, such as Tokyo Law. One result of the sophisticated testing and preparation is that students are directed toward institutions within their capabilities.

47. On the "occupational downgrading" of college graduates, see M. Ushiogi, "The Japanese Student and the Labor Market," in *Changes in the Japanese University,* pp. 107–26.

48. Most lists of these imperfections would include "exam hell" and the pressure it places on adolescents; the stultifying effects of examinations upon curriculum; the inefficiency and inequality of *yobikos;* and the exorbitantly priced new medical schools discussed above.

49. Isao Amagi, *Higher Education in Japan: Problems and Prospects* (Tokyo: Institute for Higher Education, 1977).

50. Private School Promotion Foundation, *Shiritsu daigaku to keijyohi hojokin toriatsukai yorko, haibun kijyun* (Rules and standards for government subsidies for private university operating costs, fiscal year 1979). There is a third stage of determining the subsidy that involves only punitive adjustments for such causes as financial mismanagement, defaulting on loan repayments, and campus closings due to student unrest. In 1979 three colleges were receiving no subsidies as a result of these provisions.

51. Interview with Akio Ishida, Secretary General, Private Universities Union of Japan, Tokyo, October 15, 1980.

52. The Association of Private Universities (Nippon Shiritsu Daigaku Kyokai), consisting predominantly of the smaller and younger colleges, has taken a position in favor of further expansion; but the Private Universities Union (Nippon Shiritsu Daigaku Renmei), made up of the older and more prestigious universities, endorses qualitative improvement at existing enrollment levels.

53. Ministry of Education, *Kōtō kyōiku no keikakuteki seibi ni tsuite* (Report on higher education planning) (Tokyo: Ministry of Education, 1979). Decentralization was deemphasized after the "oil shock" of 1973.

54. Ikuo Amano, "Stability and Change in Japanese Higher Education," Report to the Second Hiroshima Seminar on Higher Education (Hiroshima: Hiroshima University, 1980).

55. Roger Geiger, "The Limits of Mass Higher Education: A Comparative Analysis of Factors Affecting Enrollment Levels in Belgium, France, Japan and the United States," Yale University Institution for Social and Policy Studies Working Paper, YHERG-41 (February 1980).

56. Ministry of Education, *Shiritsu gakko no zaimu jyokyo ni kansuru chosa ho kokusho* (Research report on the financial conditions of private schools, 1978) (Tokyo: Ministry of Education, 1979).

57. Average salaries of private university teachers have risen to exceed their public counterparts since the advent of government subsidies: Estelle James and Gail Benjamin, "Public versus Private Education: The Japanese Experiment," Yale University Institution for Social and Policy Studies Working Paper, PONPO-81 (May 1984).

58. E.g., the 1980 White Paper on Financial Conditions of the Private Universities Union: "Improvement in Education and Research Conditions and Deterioration of Financial Conditions" (Tokyo: Private University Union of Japan, 1980).

59. Amano notes in "Stability and Change" that the number of eighteen-year-olds in the greater Tokyo area can be expected to increase by 60 percent between 1980 and 1991.

60. There has been at least one current of criticism to the current development toward centralized control. If students were subsidized instead of institutions, this argument runs, the market would again be ascendant in higher education, and the independence of private institutions would no longer be threatened. Although some form of student subsidy is possible in the future, it seems unlikely to this observer that the ministry would relinquish the forms of control that it has established. See Private Universities Union, "1980 White Paper on Financial Conditions"; and Shogo Ishikawa, *Shidai jyosei no arikata* (Methods for government support of private universities), Kokko jyosei ni kansuru shiritsu *Daigaku kyojukai* 13 (1980).

61. *UNESCO Statistical Yearbook, 1970.*

62. Nena Vreeland et al., *Area Handbook for the Philippines,* 2d ed. (Washington, D.C.: Government Printing Office, 1976), p. 156. Perhaps one indication of the absence of cultural obstacles to education is the fact that women at times outnumber men in Philippine higher education. Muslim Mindanao in the south is a partial exception to the general Filipino desire for education, and it lags behind the rest of the country on most indices of educational development.

63. Since 1970 the Philippine Ministry of Education has reclassified public postsecondary institutions: whereas in 1970 there were 37 government and 597 private colleges, the figures for 1980 show 309 government versus 775 private. The enrollment breakdown has not been available, but under the new form of bookkeeping the proportion of private students would undoubtedly be less. Cf. *1983 Philippine Statistical Yearbook* (Manila: National Economic and Development Authority, 1983), pp. 464–65.

64. Arthur L. Carson, *The Story of Philippine Education* (Quezon City: New Day Publishers, 1978), pp. 181–82.

65. Ibid., pp. 106–19; Antonio Isidro and Maximo D. Ramos, *Private Colleges and Universities of the Philippines* (Quezon City: Alemar-Phoenix, 1973), pp. 14–25.

66. Carson, *Philippine Education,* p. 136.

67. Paul P. Zwaenepoel, *Tertiary Education in the Philippines, 1611–1972: A Systems Analysis* (Quezon City: Alemar-Phoenix, 1975), pp. 60–67.

68. Vreeland, *Handbook,* pp. 107–10.

69. These and the following enrollment figures in this section, unless otherwise indicated, are from the *1979 Philippine Statistical Yearbook* (Manila: National Economic and Development Authority, 1979).

70. Besides the University of the Philippines, Manila has two more specialized schools, the Philippine College of Arts and Trades and the Philippine Normal College, both of which were founded in 1901 and raised to college status in the 1950s. A municipal university, Pamantasan ng Lungsod ng Maynila (University of the City of Manila) was started in 1967 and became a university in 1976. Like the UP, this is also a selective institution.

71. Zwaenepoel, *Tertiary Education,* p. 644.

72. Ibid., p. 641.

73. Evelyn Chih-hua Miao, "The Structure and Performance of Proprietary Institutions of Higher Education in the Philippines" (Ph.D. diss., University of Wisconsin, 1971), p. 77.

74. The following information was derived from the University of the East, College of Arts and Sciences, *1979–80 Bulletin of Information;* and *Profiles of Philippine Universities and Colleges* (Manila: Philippine-American Educational Foundation, 1975), pp. 427–36.

75. Cf. *Profiles.*

76. Ibid. One sample survey found that 90 percent of the students at these two schools came from the wealthiest decile of the population: "Equalization of Educational Opportunities," *FAPE Review* 9, no. 3 (January 1979).

77. The issue of trust and other reasons for the suitability of nonprofit organizations for certain industries has received extensive discussion in the growing basic literature on nonprofits. See Henry Hansmann, "The Role of Non-Profit Enterprise," *Yale Law Journal* 89 (1980): 385–901; James Douglas, "Toward a Rationale for Private Non-Profit Organization: A Review of Current Theory," Yale University Institution for Social and Policy Studies Working Paper, PONPO-7 (April 1980); and Giandomenico Majone, "Professionalism and Non-Profit Organizations," Yale University Institution for Social and Policy Studies Working Paper, PONPO-24 (October 1980).

78. A proliferation of proprietary colleges in Turkey during the 1960s provides an interesting comparison with the Philippines on this point. These colleges were confined to areas of immediate practical applicability, namely, business, journalism, engineering, chemistry, dentistry, and pharmacy. See Ayse Oncu, "Higher Education as a Business: Growth of a Private Sector in Turkey" (Ph.D. diss., Yale University, 1971), p. 62.

79. Cf. "Financing of Private Education," *FAPE Review* 10, no. 1 (July/October 1979): 90–112.

80. Miao, "Structure and Performance," chapter 2.

81. Miao, "Structure and Performance," pp. 1–15; Zwaenepoel, *Tertiary Education,* pp. 149–50, 333n, 500–501.

82. Miao, "Structure and Performance," p. 150.

83. Zwaenepoel, *Tertiary Education,* p. 150.

84. Ibid., pp. 336–39; Isidro and Ramos, *Private Colleges,* pp. 168–200.

85. Isidro and Ramos, *Private Colleges,* pp. 51–52.

86. Isidro and Ramos, *Private Colleges,* pp. 164–67; Zwaenepoel, *Tertiary Education,* pp. 65–66.

87. Isidro and Ramos, *Private Colleges,* pp. 44–46; Zwaenepoel, *Tertiary Education,* pp. 149–53.

88. "Financing of Private Education," pp. 90–112. The average return on equity for Manila proprietary schools, 1972–77, was 6.37 percent; for nonmetro Manila, 7.29 percent.

89. Department of Education and Culture, *Technical Report on the 1975 National College Entrance Examination* (Manila: 1977).

90. Department of Education and Culture, "Post-secondary Freshman Enrollment, 1973–74 to 1977–78" (mimeo, n.d.).

91. Based upon a sample of 106 colleges with enrollment of 336,000 in 1977: "Financing of Private Education," p. 127.

92. Ibid., p. 119. Based upon a sample of twenty colleges with enrollments 197,000 in 1977.

93. Department of Education and Culture, "1979 Statistical Bulletin" 5, no. 1, pp. 23–24.

94. This interpretation of enrollments is pieced together from a) the samples cited in notes 91 and 92 above; b) the *Philippine Statistical Yearbook*; and c) enrollment figures from several large universities.

95. Regional disparities in NCEE results, and especially the advantage of Metro Manila students, have provoked considerable criticism. Political pressure has been building to place the cut-off scores on a regional basis. Also, irregularities caused the 1978 NCEE to be entirely invalidated.

96. I would like to thank Mr. Adriano Arcelo, Vice President of FAPE, for his assistance in providing this and other information.

97. Isidro and Ramos, *Private Colleges,* pp. 4–6.

98. Two FAPE-sponsored policy studies have recommended mandatory forms of student financial assistance: *Quantum Leap for Private Higher Education* (Manila: FAPE, 1978) suggests that a percentage of all future tuition increases be reserved for this purpose; and "Equalization of Educational Opportunities," *FAPE Review* 9, no. 3 (January 1979) advocates a socially graded tuition schedule that would charge wealthy students more and indigent students less.

Chapter 3

1. Arend Lijphart, *Democracy in Plural Societies: A Comparative Exploration* (New Haven: Yale University Press, 1977), pp. 25–103.

2. For the development of Belgian higher education see Roger Geiger, "Universities and the State in Belgium: Past and Present Dimensions of Higher Education in a Divided Society," Yale University Institution for Social and Policy Studies Working Paper, YHERG-29 (November 1978).

3. Frans van Kalken, "L'Université Libre Bruxelles" in *Histoire des Universités Belges* (Brussels: Collection Lebegue and Nationale, 1954), pp. 5–6.

4. Roger Geiger, "Two Paths to Mass Higher Education: Issues and Outcomes in Belgium and France," Yale University Institution for Social and Policy Studies Working Paper, YHERG-34 (April 1979). For the expansion problem see Geiger, "Universities," pp. 28–32; and Christian Dejean and Charles-Louis Binneman, *L'Université belge: du pari au défi* (Brussels: Editions de l'Institut de Sociologie de l'Université Libre de Bruxelles, 1971).

5. Organization for Economic Cooperation and Development, *Towards Mass Higher Education: Issues and Dilemmas* (Paris: OECD, 1974), p. 181.

6. On the Louvain crisis see Dejean and Binneman, *L'Université belge;* Geiger, "Universities," pp. 32–35; and Jef Verhoeven, "The Belgian Universities under Crossfire: Linguistic Communalism, Bureaucratization and Democratization," in *Universities, Politicians and Bureaucrats: Europe and America,* ed. Hans Daalder and Edward Shils (Cambridge: Cambridge University Press, 1982), pp. 125–72.

7. William Ancion, "Le système de financement et de contrôle en vigeur en Belgique" (Paper for OECD Meeting, Paris, February 1978).

8. Geiger, "Universities," pp. 49–62; "Changing Demand for Higher Education in the Seventies," *Higher Education* 9 (1980): 255–76.

9. Ancion, "Le système de financement et contrôle."

10. E.g., "If the state or private universities complain of having been the victims of a policy of budgetary austerity, it is precisely because until the present they have lived too liberally, carried along by lavish budgets and the dispersion of new faculties to the four corners of the country." Joseph Michel, Minister of French Education, quoted in *Le Monde de L'Education* (September 1977), p. 29.

11. Ignace Hecquet et al., "Planifier sans planifier: le cas de l'université Catholique de Louvain" (Paper for OECD Meeting, Paris, August 1979).

12. Ancion, "Le système de financement et contrôle."

13. Arend Lijphart, *The Politics of Accommodation: Pluralism and Democracy in the Netherlands,* 2d rev. ed. (Berkeley and Los Angeles: University of California Press, 1975), pp. 16–68.

14. Hans Daalder, "The Netherlands: Opposition in a Segmented Society," in *Political Oppositions in Western Democracies,* ed. Robert Dahl (New Haven: Yale University Press, 1966) pp. 186–236.

15. R. A. DeMoor, "Diversification in Dutch Tertiary Education," *Paedagogica Europaea* 10, no. 1 (1975): 73–86.

16. Cf. Roger Geiger, "European Universities: The Unfinished Revolution," *Comparative Education Review* 22 (1978): 189–211.

17. Lijphart, *Politics of Accommodation,* esp. chapter 10; Hans Daalder,

"The Dutch Universities between the 'New Democracy' and the 'New Management': Ten Years of Development," in Daalder and Shils, *Universities, Politicians and Bureaucrats pp. 173–232.*

18. Arend Lijphart, "Dutch Universities in the Seventies," *International Council on the Future of the University Newsletter* 4, no. 1 (November 1977); Maurice Punch, "Dutch Sociology and University Reform" (Paper presented to the British Sociological Association Annual Conference, April 1980).

19. For a detailed analysis see Daalder, "Dutch Universities."

20. Ibid.

21. J. J. Donner, "De Vrijheid van het bijzonder wetenschapplijk onderwijs" (The freedom of private scientific education) (Doctoral thesis, VUA Law Faculty, 1979). The controversial 1975 Act has been replaced by more recent legislation with the same intention (1980), scheduled to take effect in 1982.

22. For background see OECD, *Science Policy in the Netherlands* (Paris: OECD, 1972).

23. Daalder, "Dutch Universities"; Punch, "Dutch Sociology and University Reform."

24. These and all following enrollment figures for Belgium are from the respective *Rapports annuels* of the Bureau de Statistiques universitaires (Brussels: Foundation Universitaire); for the Netherlands, The Netherlands Central Bureau of Statistics, *Statistical Yearbook of the Netherlands, 1983* (The Hague: Staatsuitgeverij, 1984), p. 106.

25. These advantages are considerable in the light of the heavy load of courses, large lectures, and 50 percent failure rate which characterize the first candidature in most institutions: See Geiger, "Universities," pp. 56–62.

26. *Contours of a Future Education System in the Netherlands: Discussion Memorandum* (The Hague: Ministry of Education and Sciences, 1975).

27. Provisions for part-time university study has long been advocated in Belgium (e.g., Counseil nationale de la politique scientifique, *Une nouvelle strategie universitaire* [Brussels: 1976]), but the Belgian practice of awarding credit for a year's work as a unit has proved a formidable obstacle (Geiger, "Universities," pp. 75–82). Individual universities have recently been informally modifying this format to provide more flexible programs.

28. Hecquet et al., "Planifier," pp. 14–21.

Chapter 4

1. A. Aulard, *Napoléon Ier et le monopole universitaire* (Paris: Colin, 1911).

2. Roger Geiger, "Prelude to Reform: The French Faculties of Letters in the 1860s," in *The Making of Frenchmen: Current Directions in the History of Education in France, 1679–1979,* ed. Donald Baker and Patrick Harrigan (Waterloo, Ontario: Historical Reflections Press, 1980), pp. 337–62.

3. Ibid.

4. George Weisz, *The Emergence of Modern Universities in France, 1863–1914* (Princeton: Princeton University Press, 1983), pp. 98–107.

5. In 1870 a government commission led by François Guizot strongly recommended freedom of higher education. Foremost among liberal spokesmen for this position were Edouard Laboulaye and Emile Beaussire.

6. Louis Liard, *L'Enseignement supérieur en France, 1789–1893*, vol. 2 (Paris: Colin, 1894), pp. 297–334.

7. For the first model French Catholics consciously looked toward Belgium, where examining juries for state and private universities were at that time mixed. See Albert Duruy, "La Liberté de l'enseignment," *Revue des deux mondes,* February 1, 1870. The second model would be similar to the system that emerged in the Netherlands as a consequence of *verzuiling* (see chapter 3 in this volume).

8. Victor Duruy, *L'Enseignment supérieur devant le sénat* (Paris: 1868).

9. Weisz, *Emergence,* pp. 102–7.

10. Liard, *L'Enseignement supérieur,* pp. 317–21.

11. For the development of state higher education, see Weisz, *Emergence,* passim; and Roger Geiger, "Reform and Restraint in Higher Education: The French Experience, 1865–1914," Yale University Institution for Social and Policy Studies Working Paper, YHERG-2 (October 1975).

12. Liard, *L'Enseignement supérieur,* pp. 324–33.

13. Enrollment figures have been compiled from *Statistique de l'enseignement supérieur,* Paris: 1878, 1888, 1898; and *Annuaire statistique de France.*

14. *Journal officiel. Documents parlementaires—Sénat* (March 23, 1914), pp. 538–63. For the impetus behind this commission, see *Revue internationale de l'enseignement* 43 (1902): 207–58.

15. On the development of applied scientific institutes in provincial universities and the heavy involvement of private philanthropy, see George Weisz, "French Universities and Education for the New Professions, 1885–1914: An Episode in French University Reform," *Minerva* 17 (1979): 98–128.

16. Elie Bertrand, *L'Enseignement technique en Allemagne et en France* (Montpellier: 1913), pp. 325–33; Auguste Foubert, *L'Enseignement commercial supérieur en France et à l'étranger* (Paris: 1922).

17. Bertrand, *Enseignement technique,* pp. 329–30.

18. Including Guizot, Laboulaye, Beaussire, and Hippolyte Taine.

19. On the Ecole Libre des Sciences Politiques, see Pierre Rain, *L'Ecole Libre des Sciences Politiques* (Paris: Fondation nationale des sciences politiques, 1963); Eugene d'Eichtal, "Nos grandes écoles—L'Ecole Libre des Sciences Politiques," *Revue des deux mondes,* 1927, pp. 535–53; Thomas Osborne, "The Recruitment of the Administrative Elite in the Third Republic: The System of The Ecole Libre des Sciences Politiques, 1870–1905" (Ph.D. diss., University of Connecticut, 1974).

20. For the social context of the Ecole, see Osborne, "Administrative Elite."

21. Rain, *L'Ecole Libre.*

22. Osborne, "Administrative Elite."

23. This is in striking contrast to the complete reliance on universalistic criteria in the functional successor to the Ecole, the present Ecole nationale d'administration. There students are admitted by *concours,* and choose their starting positions in the state administration by rank order in their graduating class.

24. Commercial education was organized on a private basis in a number of French cities (eleven schools with two thousand students in 1899). However, this could not be considered higher education at this time. An effort to organize commercial studies within the law faculties failed badly before World War I. See Weisz, "French Universities."

25. *World of Learning, 1979–80,* p. 470.

26. *Nouvelles de l'Institut Catholique de Paris,* October 1979, pp. 99, 127; "Les dossiers de l'etudiant," *Les Universités,* no. 10 (June 1979): 31.

27. Ministère des Universités, *Statistiques des enseignements,* 5.1, 1976–77, p. 27.

28. Ibid., pp. 7–8; "Les dossiers de l'etudiant," *Les Grandes Ecoles,* no. 12 (November 1979): 21–54.

29. *Les Grandes Ecoles,* pp. 38–39.

30. Ibid., p. 159.

31. ESSEC was for a long time only distantly connected with the Institut Catholique de Paris. It relocated itself in a newly constructed campus at Cergy-Pontois outside of the capital. However, the financial strain of the new campus proved too great for ESSEC's tuition-dependent revenues. In 1981 France's second-leading business school ironically faced bankruptcy. It was rescued by becoming associated with the Versailles Chamber of Commerce and Industry, thereby making its status the same as the other schools of commerce discussed below.

32. *Les Grandes Ecoles,* p. 13.

33. Yvette Ménissez, *L'Enseignement de la gestion en France* (Paris: La documentation française, 1979), pp. 138–39.

34. Ibid., pp. 71–73, 150–51. Eighteen universities currently possess such institutes.

35. Ibid., pp. 135–37.

36. Louis Lévy-Garboua, "La sélection dans l'enseignement supérieur française: une synthèse des travaux récents" (Paris: OECD, 1977).

37. Roger Geiger, "A Retrospective View of the Second-Cycle Reform in France," Yale University Institution for Social and Policy Studies Working Paper, YHERG-18 (August 1977).

38. Les Dossiers de l'Etudiant, *Les Etudes Supérieures Courtes,* no. 8 (February/March 1979): 38.

39. François Orival, "Quelques rappels quantitatifs concernant l'evolu-

tion de l'enseignement supérieur français," in Gérard Lassibille et al., *De l'inefficacité du système français d'enseignement supérieur* (Paris: Centre Nationale de la Recherche scientifique, s.d.), pp. 1–22; also, Roger Geiger, "Two Paths to Mass Higher Education: Issues and Outcomes in Belgium and France," Yale University Institution for Social and Policy Studies Working Paper, YHERG-34 (April 1979).

40. *Les Etudes Supérieures Courtes,* pp. 29–30.

41. The Swedish Monarchy also established universities at Abo and Dorpat in the seventeenth century, and another was founded in Oslo in 1811. None of these areas, of course, are still part of the Swedish state.

42. W. H. G. Armytage, *Civic Universities* (London: Ernest Benn, 1955).

43. Within a generation schools of economics were established in: London (1895), Leipzig (1897), St. Gallen, Switz. (1898), Cologne (1901), Frankfurt am Main (1901), Berlin (1906), Mannheim (1907), Helsinki (1909, 1911), Munich (1910), Rotterdam (1914), Copenhagen (1917), and Tilburg (1927), besides the Swedish schools in Stockholm (1909) and Gothenburg (1923). And this is by no means an exhaustive list.

44. Total enrollments increased as follows: 1945: 14,854; 1950: 17,859; 1955: 22,645; 1960: 37,405; 1965: 68,691; 1970: 124,381. Rune Premfors and Bertil Ostergren, *Systems of Higher Education: Sweden* (International Council for Education Development, 1978), p. 201.

45. Lars Gurmund, *Gothenburg University—A Dispersed Institution* (Gothenburg: Gothenburg University Press, 1977).

46. Interview with H. Cramer, President of Stockholm College from 1950 to 1958, March 27, 1980.

47. Rune Premfors, "Analysis in Politics: The Regionalization of Swedish Higher Education" (Paper presented at "The Urban University in Comparative Perspective," conference held at the City University of New York, March, 1982).

48. Strictly speaking, the Stockholm School of Economics is the sole private university-level institution of higher education in Sweden; however, since the U-68 Reform there is no longer any official distinction between university and nonuniversity sectors. There are also three privately controlled schools of nursing and one private school of social work.

49. The following draws in part on interviews with Rector Per-Jonas Eliaeson (March 27, 1980) and Professor Erik Dahmen (March 25, 1980) of the Stockholm School of Economics.

50. Buckingham's uniqueness lies in the fact that it offers a university degree, as will be explained below. Other private colleges prepare students to sit for external degrees from the University of London, and at least half a dozen institutions award degrees of American universities. The peripheral private sector in Britain naturally includes a variety of specialized institutions, some of which, like the school of the British Architectural Association, are university level, and some of which are not. The latter are covered in *Independent Further Education* by Gareth Williams and Maureen Wood-

hall (London: Policy Studies Institute, 1979), the scope of which transcends postsecondary education.

51. John H. Van de Graaff, "Great Britain," in Van de Graaff et al., *Academic Power: Patterns of Authority in Seven National Systems of Higher Education* (New York: Praeger, 1978), pp. 83–103. The polytechnics in Britain are directly under the control of the Department of Education and Science, and are consequently regarded as the "public sector."

52. Van de Graaff, *Academic Power*, p. 210; Organization for European Cooperation and Development, *Educational Expenditures in France, Japan and the United Kingdom* (Paris: OECD, 1977).

53. Robert O. Berdahl, *British Universities and the State* (Berkeley and Los Angeles: University of California Press, 1959), pp. 20–47.

54. Ibid., passim; A. H. Halsey and M. A. Trow, *The British Academics* (Cambridge: Harvard University Press, 1971), pp. 84–99; and Graeme C. Moodie, "Academics and University Government: Some Reflections on British Experiences." (Mimeo, n.d.)

55. *British Academics,* pp. 68–121.

56. Ibid., pp. 81–82. Generally, as access to higher education expands, the proportion of commuter students increases.

57. Van de Graaff, *Academic Power,* pp. 209, 217.

58. Moodie, "Academics and University Government."

59. Ibid. For a more benign view, see the memoirs of the then Chairman of the UGC, Lord Wolfenden: *Turning Points* (London: The Bodley Head, 1976), pp. 147–62.

60. E.g., "the UGC's autonomy and hence the autonomy of its parts—the separate universities—are now gone. The systematising, homogenising and centralizing forces of British society are engulfing the universities. For the present all political parties support and indeed encourage this tendency": Harry S. Ferns, "Towards an Independent University," Institute of Economic Affairs, Occasional Paper no. 25, 2d ed. (London: 1970), p. 31.

61. *The Times,* 27 May 1967; reprinted in Joyce Pemberton and John Pemberton, *University College at Buckingham: A First Account of its Foundation and Early Years* (Buckingham: Buckingham Press, 1979), pp. 13–14.

62. Max Beloff, "British Universities and the Public Purse," *Minerva* 5 (1967): 520–32.

63. Ferns, "Independent University."

64. Reprinted in ibid., pp. 35–39; and in Pemberton and Pemberton, *University College at Buckingham,* pp. 187–90.

65. Pemberton and Pemberton, *University College at Buckingham.*

66. Sydney Caine, *British Universities: Purpose and Prospects* (London: The Bodley Head, 1969), pp. 208–12.

67. Pemberton and Pemberton, *University College at Buckingham,* p. 21; Ferns, "Independent University."

68. Max Beloff, "Starting a Private College: A British Experiment in Higher Education," *American Scholar,* Summer 1979, pp. 395–403. An-

other way in which the legitimacy of the new college was buttressed was by establishing two Advisory Councils. The Academic Council consists of about forty distinguished British academics, and judges the adequacy of the college's academic program. The International Council of about fifty scholars from around the world is available for consultation as needed.

69. *The Economist,* February 19, 1983, p. 63; *The Times Higher Education Supplement,* April 1, 1983, p. 8. Maintenance grants to defray student living expenses and fees are provided by Local Education Authorities. Prior to the government's decision to include the UB, some LEAs had independently agreed to support UB students.

70. *The Times Higher Education Supplement* (February 25, 1983); Pemberton and Pemberton, *The University College at Buckingham,* pp. 91–106.

71. Beloff, "Starting a Private College," p. 400.

72. "The University College at Buckingham, Annual Report: 1980" (April 1981).

73. James Douglas and Peter Wright, "English Charities: Legal Definition, Taxation, and Regulation," Yale University Institution for Social and Policy Studies Working Paper, PONPO-15, n.d. As of April 6, 1981, the tax relief for charitable contributions has been liberalized, but the process remains cumbersome: basically, the individual or corporate donor must sign a contract, or covenant, to make a charitable contribution for at least four years with after-tax money; the Treasury then reimburses the receiving charity for up to 30 percent of the tax that had been paid on that contribution. The 1981 changes also now offer additional relief for individuals in higher marginal tax brackets.

74. Max Beloff has written,

> My own greatest disappointment has been that our experiment has failed to attract any of the great American foundations. . . . Of the famous international foundations, only Volkswagen in Germany has shown a benevolent and constructive interest in our affairs. Apart from this gift, money for American books given by three smaller U.S. foundations, and one large benefaction from the Sultan of Brunei, almost all the money that has been raised for us has come from within the United Kingdom—and for the most part from individuals and corporations. Most of the British foundations which have supplemented government expenditures on state-financed institutions have played safe by remaining aloof. "Starting a Private College," pp. 402–3.

75. I would like to thank UCB Registrar, Mr. Simon Ellis, for these and the following Fall 1981 enrollment figures.

76. Interview with Mr. Simon Ellis, September 7, 1981. Also see *The Times Higher Education Supplement,* April 1, 1983.

77. A program of business studies has been under "active consideration" at the UCB: "Annual Report, 1980"; interview with Professor Alan Peacock, Principal of the UCB, September 7, 1981.

78. *The Times Higher Education Supplement*, August 7, 1981.

79. Max Beloff has written of this situation, "nothing in the original ideas of the founders was further from the truth than the notion that independence in itself would be so appealing an idea that good British students would flock to the banner once unfurled." "Starting a Private College," p. 400.

Chapter 5

1. National Center for Education Statistics, *Digest of Education Statistics, 1981* (Washington, D.C.: Government Printing Office, 1981), pp. 120–24.

2. See Burton R. Clark, *The Higher Education System: Academic Organization in Cross-National Perspective* (Berkeley and Los Angeles: University of California Press, 1983).

3. Christopher Jencks and David Riesman, *The Academic Revolution* (Chicago: University of Chicago Press, 1977), pp. 257–70.

4. For-profit higher education in the United States is nearly all narrowly vocational. With the exception of a few schools of law or business it has virtually no overlap with the nonprofit private sector which is the sole concern of this chapter.

5. Jencks and Riesman, *Academic Revolution*, pp. 270–76. Enrollment figures are from the *Digest of Education Statistics, 1981*, and refer to only degree-credit enrollments.

6. Any complete interpretation of enrollment fluctuations would have to take into account changes in demography, tested academic abilities, sex ratios, racial composition, full-time vs. part-time attendance, plus the impact of the graduate job market and the military draft. Some of these issues are discussed in Roger Geiger, "Missing Students: The Causes of Declining Participation Rates of White Males in American Higher Education," *Change* (December/January 1978/79): 64–65; and "The Limits of Mass Higher Education: A Comparative Analysis of Enrollment Trends in Belgium, France, Japan and the United States," Yale University Institution for Social and Policy Studies Working Paper, YHERG-41 (February 1980).

7. Estimated degree-credit enrollment, 1975–79: *Digest of Education Statistics, 1981*, p. 92.

8. *Chronicle of Higher Education*, October 14, 1981, p. 10.

9. For an analysis of voluntary actions in the nonprofit sector of the economy undertaken from a similar perspective, see Burton Weisbrod, "Toward a Theory of Voluntary Nonprofit Sector in a Three-Sector Economy," in *Altruism, Morality and Economic Theory*, ed. E. Phelps (New York: Russell Sage Foundation, 1975) pp. 51–76.

10. David Riesman offers many insights on this topic in *On Higher Education* (San Francisco: Jossey-Bass, 1980).

11. Roger Geiger, "Hierarchy and Diversity in American Research Uni-

versities," in *The University Research System,* ed. Bjorn Wittrock (forthcoming); and see notes 33 and 34 below.

12. Cf. Carnegie Council on Policy Studies in Higher Education, *A Classification of Institutions of Higher Education,* rev. ed. (Berkeley: Carnegie Foundation for the Advancement of Teaching, 1976). The material that follows is based upon an analysis of financial and enrollment data for selected representative research universities, liberal arts colleges, and urban universities. Because of the marked asymmetry of these three categories different methods of selection were employed for each. For private research universities, only 24 institutions met the criteria, and all were examined. Among Liberal Arts 1 colleges, the wealthiest dozen according to per-student voluntary support were analyzed, and nine others which in some way approach this dozen have also been mentioned. A group of eleven other LA1 colleges was selected to represent the remainder. Eight colleges were selected to represent the hundreds of LA2 colleges. Since "large" and "urban" are relative concepts, the twenty-eight large urban private universities examined represent the largest urban or urban-Catholic institutions for which data was available. All institutions used are identified in the text or notes.

13. Educational and general expenditures for the public and private sectors were, respectively, $4,378 and $5,965, compared with total expenditures including hospitals, independent and auxiliary operations of $5,372 and $8,210: *Digest of Education Statistics, 1981,* p. 149.

14. National Institute of Independent Colleges and Universities, "The New Economics of Independent Higher Education" (NIICU, 1985). On the issue of the tuition gap, see Michael S. MacPherson, "The Demand for Higher Education," in *Public Policy and Private Higher Education,* ed. David W. Breneman and Chester E. Finn, Jr. (Washington, D.C.: The Brookings Institution, 1978), pp. 143–96.

15. NIICU, "New Economics."

16. Susan C. Nelson, "Financial Trends and Issues," in Breneman and Finn, *Public Policy,* pp. 63–142; and Chester E. Finn, Jr., *Scholars, Dollars and Bureaucrats* (Washington, D.C.: The Brookings Institution, 1978), pp. 45–104.

17. David W. Breneman and Susan C. Nelson, *Financing Community Colleges* (Washington, D.C.: The Brookings Institution, 1981), p. 128.

18. Jencks and Riesman, *Academic Revolution,* pp. 270–76.

19. National Science Foundation, *Federal Funds for Research and Development, 1980* (Washington, D.C.: Government Printing Office, 1981), pp. 24–25; also, Geiger, "Hierarchy and Diversity."

20. Robert K. Merton, "The Matthew Effect in Science," in *The Sociology of Science,* ed. Norman Storer (Chicago: University of Chicago Press, 1973), pp. 439–59.

21. See esp. Merle Curti and Roderick Nash, *Philanthropy in the Shaping of American Higher Education* (New Brunswick, N.J.: Rutgers University Press, 1965).

22. The distribution of endowment wealth across the private sector is quite unequal. For example, Harvard's $1,500 million endowment alone constitutes about 10 percent of the endowment of all private colleges and universities. Since a significant proportion of endowment income must be reinvested to protect its purchasing power against inflation, only about 5 percent of the total value is available each year to support the current operations of the school. On this basis the 1979–80 income for four-year private institutions was about $750 million, which compares with annual current gifts to the same schools of $2,050 million. Council for Financial Aid to Education, *Voluntary Support of Education*, 1979–80 (New York: CFAE, 1981).

23. CFAE, *Voluntary Support*. All further data on voluntary support will be from this source unless otherwise indicated.

24. Roger L. Geiger, *To Advance Knowledge: The Growth of American Research Universities in the Twentieth Century, 1900–1940* (New York: Oxford University Press, 1986).

25. Earl F. Cheit and Theodore E. Lobman, *Foundations and Higher Education: Grant Marking from the Golden Years through Steady State* (Berkeley: Carnegie Council on Policy Studies in Higher Education, 1979), pp. 33–35.

26. *The Chronicle of Higher Education,* May 18, 1981 and December 9, 1981. Corporate support averaged less than 16 percent of total giving to higher education in the 1970s, but had risen to 20 percent by 1981–82: CFAE, *Voluntary Support 1981–1982,* p. 72.

27. A recent guide for prospective college students reflected this perspective perfectly: it gave each school reviewed three equally weighted ratings—for academics, for quality of life, and for social life. Edward B. Fiske, *Selective Guide to Colleges* (New York: Times Books, 1982).

28. Earlier in this century alumni sometimes exercised decisive influence at critical points in the development of private institutions. More recently they have been likely, if anything, to exert a rather conservative drag on potential innovations that would affect the character of the school. The fact remains, nevertheless, that they have a vested interest in the betterment of their college.

29. Edward Shils, "The American Private University," *Minerva* 11 (1973): 6–29; Geiger, *Research Universities,* passim.

30. The Carnegie classification (see note 12) identifies ninety-eight Research 1 and 2 universities, including Rockefeller University, an independent medical school not included in this study.

31. Geiger, *Research Universities.*

32. These ten are: the four Ivies of "A1"; the three research-intensive universities of "A3"; Rice, Stanford, and Swarthmore (the most affluent of the LA1+). Bryn Mawr and Haverford have a similar level of selectivity with considerably lower tuition value.

33. David S. Webster, "America's Highest Ranking Graduate Schools, 1925–1982," *Change,* May/June 1983, pp. 14–24.

34. Kenneth D. Roose and Charles J. Anderson, *A Rating of Graduate Programs* (Washington, D.C.: American Council on Education, 1971); Alan M. Cartter, *An Assessment of Quality in Graduate Education* (Washington, D.C.: American Council of Education, 1966).

35. Curti and Nash, *Philanthropy.*

36. Of the "A2" universities only Case Western Reserve received more than $600/student in alumni contributions.

37. W. John Minter and Howard R. Bowen, *Independent Higher Education, 1980* (Washington, D.C.: National Institute of Independent Colleges and Universities, 1980).

38. In arguing the Dartmouth College Case in 1818, Webster is reputed to have brought tears to the judge's eyes by saying, "it is, sir, as I have said, a small college, and yet there are those who love it." Richard Hofstadter and Wilson Smith, eds., *American Higher Education: A Documentary History* (Chicago: University of Chicago Press, 1961), p. 212.

39. Jencks and Riesman, *Academic Revolution,* pp. 20–27.

40. The same conclusion reached by Alexander Astin and Calvin Lee in their comparison of "invisible colleges" with a sample of elite liberal arts colleges. *The Invisible Colleges: a Profile of Small, Private Colleges with Limited Resources* (New York: McGraw-Hill, 1972).

41. Alexander Astin found that "Single-sex colleges show a pattern of effects on *both* sexes that is almost uniformly positive." *Four Critical Years* (San Francisco: Jossey-Bass, 1977), p. 246.

42. Jencks and Riesman, *Academic Revolution,* pp. 312–33; David Riesman, "The Evangelical Colleges: Untouched by the Academic Revolution," *Change,* January/February 1981, pp. 13–20; and C. Robert Pace, *Education and Evangelism* (New York: McGraw-Hill, 1972).

43. Allan O. Pfnister, "Survival and Revival: The Transformation of the American Arts College," University of Denver, Occasional Papers in Higher Education no. 15 (September 1981); and Larry Leslie, Arthur Grant, and Kenneth Brown, "Patterns of Enrollment in Higher Education, 1965–77: Liberal Arts Colleges," University of Arizona Center for the Study of Higher Education, Topical Paper no. 19 (January 1981).

44. Cf. the case of the University of Buffalo. Harold L. Hodgkinson, *Institutions in Transition* (New York: McGraw-Hill, 1971), pp. 160–71.

45. Jencks and Riesmen, *Academic Revolution,* p. 289.

46. E.g., the University of Bridgeport. State systems in recent years have been contemplating contraction rather than expansion, thus precluding the option of private institutions going public.

47. Andrew M. Greeley, *From Backwater to Mainstream: A Profile of Catholic Higher Education* (New York: McGraw-Hill, 1969), pp. 15–17; Jencks and Riesman, *Academic Revolution,* pp. 398–405.

48. Both these universities are located in difficult philanthropic environments; BU inhabits the most congested higher education territory in the country, and the District of Columbia, similarly congested, is a one-industry city—an industry not conducive to voluntary giving.

49. "C3" consists of Boston University, George Washington, Drexell, and Syracuse; "C4" is Boston College, Villanova, Marquette, Fordham, and the Universities of Detroit and San Francisco.

50. In "C5" are Adelphi, American, Bridgeport, Farleigh Dickenson, Hofstra, Long Island, Pace, Seton Hall, Northeastern, and the Catholic Dayton, DePaul, and St. John's.

51. In one of the more resourceful applications of this principle Adelphi has had its professors board commuter trains to teach passengers on their way to and from work.

52. As the case of Adelphi suggests, "responsive" may be too weak a word. At times tuition-hungry universities anticipate or even create consumer demands.

53. Carnegie Council on Policy Studies in Higher Education, *Three Thousand Futures: The Next Twenty Years for Higher Education* (San Francisco: Jossey-Bass, 1980), pp. 32–82; and McPherson, "Demand for Higher Education," pp. 150–59.

54. Humphrey Doermann, *Toward Equal Access* (New York: College Entrance Examination Board, 1978), pp. 33–40.

55. Jencks and Riesman, *Academic Revolution,* pp. 271, 276.

56. See chapter 6 in this volume.

57. Cf. McPherson, "Demand for Higher Education," pp. 168ff.

58. For 1984–85 total federal student financial aid from all programs was about equal to 1980–81 levels in current dollars. This represented a decrease of almost 19 percent in constant dollars. During the same period state programs increased by 27 percent in constant dollars, while institutional financial aid remained flat. Together, however, these two sources comprise only one-quarter of federal aid. Thus, financial aid from all sources declined by more than 14 percent adjusted for inflation. *Chronicle of Higher Education,* January 23, 1985, p. 20.

59. Enrollments at the four largest urban private universities rose by 13 percent from 1974 to 1979—the national average for both the public and private sectors for those years. Perhaps more importantly, their total full-time students rose 16 percent during those years. *Digest of Education Statistics,* 1975 and 1981.

60. On the increased importance that marketing has played see Riesman, *On Higher Education,* pp. 105–61. On the trend toward vocationalism, see Roger L. Geiger, "The College Curriculum and the Marketplace," *Change,* November/December 1980, pp. 17–23, 53–54.

Chapter 6

1. William Bowen, *The Economics of Major Private Universities* (Berkeley: The Carnegie Commission on Higher Education, 1968), pp. 12–16.

2. E.g., Alexander W. Astin, *Four Critical Years* (San Francisco: Jossey-Bass, 1977), pp. 227–31; Roger Geiger, "The Role of the Research Universities in Undergraduate Education," forthcoming.

3. Howard Bowen, *The Costs of Higher Education* (San Francisco: Jossey-Bass, 1980), p. 15.

4. Roger L. Geiger, "The Limits of Mass Higher Education," Yale University Institution for Social and Policy Studies Working Paper, YHERG-41 (February 1980). Cf. Arnold Heidenheimer, "Education and Social Security Entitlements in Europe and America," in *The Development of Welfare States in Europe and America,* ed. P. Flora and A. Heidenheimer (New Brunswick: Transaction Press, 1981), pp. 269–304.

5. "Basic Guidelines for the Reform of Education: Report of the Central Council for Education" (Tokyo: Ministry of Education, 1972).

6. Richard Hofstedter and Wilson Smith, eds., *American Higher Education: A Documentary History,* vol. 2 (Chicago: University of Chicago Press, 1961), pp. 568–69.

7. Richard C. Axt, *The Federal Government and Financing Higher Education* (New York: Columbia University Press, 1952), pp. 85–142.

8. Lawrence E. Gladieux and Thomas R. Wolanin, *Congress and the Colleges* (Lexington, Mass.: Lexington Books, 1976), pp. 8–9.

9. Ibid., p. 11.

10. Ibid., passim.

11. Supplemental Educational Opportunity Grants (SEOGs) were continuations of the federal opportunity grants established in 1965. See Chester E. Finn, Jr., "Federal Patronage of Universities in the United States: A Rose by Many Other Names?" *Minerva* 14 (1976): 496–529.

12. Estimated from Finn, "Federal Patronage," and National Center for Educational Statistics, *Digest of Education Statistics, 1980* (Washington, D.C.: Government Printing Office, 1980), p. 152.

13. SEOGs are awarded by universities on top of BEOGs, thus raising the maximum federal direct student aid to $2,900 under original funding levels, a sum that could only be utilized at a high tuition institution: Finn, "Federal Patronage."

14. This apparently anarchic process is actually highly standardized due to the efforts of two independent organizations. The College Scholarship Service and the American College Testing Student Need Analysis Service both set schedules that are tacitly accepted by both universities and the federal government as the basis for need-based grants. For problems that can arise in this understanding, see, Chester E. Finn, Jr., *Scholars, Dollars and Bureaucrats* (Washington, D.C.: The Brookings Institution, 1978), pp. 162–63.

15. Cf. Chester E. Finn, Jr., "The End of the Liberal Consensus," *Change,* September 1981, pp. 17–21, 60–63.

16. Robbins Committee, *Higher Education: Report of the Committee Appointed by the Prime Minister under the Chairmanship of Lord Robbins,* 1961–63, Cmnd. 2154 (London: HMSO, 1963).

17. Barbara B. Burn, *Higher Education in Nine Countries* (New York: McGraw-Hill, 1971), pp. 76–78. Although the Local Educational Authorities actually award the student maintenance grants, these funds come largely from the national treasury.

18. Need-based student aid exists in some form in all the European countries being considered here (see note 34 below). The United States is unique, however, in the extent to which student aid is an important source of institutional revenue through relatively high tuition charges.

19. The exceptions are the funds still remaining from the Morrill Land Grant Act of 1862, special aid to strengthen "developing institutions," many of which are black colleges, and the direct federal support of Howard University and Gallaudet College. See Finn, *Scholars,* p. 107.

20. Nicole Fontaine, *La liberté d'enseignement, de la loi Debré à la loi Guermeur,* 2d ed. (Paris: UNAPEC, 1978). A private school signing a "simple contract" receives a subsidy based upon teacher salaries with comparatively little government regulation; schools choosing a "contract of association" must accept greater regulation in return for a more lucrative subsidy.

21. I would like to thank Dr. Jose Veiga Simõa for information concerning this policy.

22. E.g., *Times Higher Education Supplement,* November 20, 1981; *Times Higher Education Supplement,* January 8, 1982. With subsequent adjustments the total reduction of the university appropriation was closer to 14 percent over three years.

23. A student of the federal bureaucracy has written, "foundations and institutes have become the preferred form of organization for institutions making grants to local governments, universities, nonprofit organizations and individuals for research in the natural or social sciences, or for artistic endeavors. The unique characteristic of these organizations is an elaborate superstructure of advisory arrangements designed to give representatives of grantee groups maximum influence over the allocation of funds." Harold Seidmon, *Politics, Position, and Power,* 2d ed. (New York: Oxford University Press, 1975), p. 247. The British Science Councils allocate research funds much like NSF and NIH.

24. Carnegie Council on Policy Studies in Higher Education, *The States and Private Higher Education* (San Francisco: Jossey-Bass, 1977). Also, Robert O. Berdahl, "The Politics of State Aid" and Colin C. Blaydon, "State Policy Options," in *Public Policy and Private Higher Education,* ed. David W. Breneman and Chester E. Finn, Jr. (Washington, D.C.: The Brookings Institution, 1978), pp. 321–52 and 353–88.

25. In 1975–76 New York State's general institutional aid for private colleges and universities constituted 60 percent of the total given by all states. Carnegie Council, *States and Private,* pp. 84–85.

26. Susan C. Nelson, "Financial Trends and Issues," in Breneman and Finn, *Public Policy,* pp. 90–94, 134–85.

27. Carnegie Council, *States and Private,* pp. 71, 93.

28. On certain occasions states can exercise qualitative judgments, even though they are not a part of the funding formulae. New York, which is unique in the extent of state authority over private education, has done so by establishing ten endowed distinguished professorships at private universities. Also, at the time it established general institutional aid, the Education Department inaugurated an evaluation of Ph.D. programs in the state, which led to several being terminated.

29. A strong countercurrent of thought has existed in European higher education circles since the late 1960s, often articulated by the Organization for Economic Cooperation and Development, that has advocated integrating university and nonuniversity institutions. Its most notable accomplishments to date have been the Gesamthochschulen in the F.R.G. and the U-68 Reforms in Sweden. Such changes, however, merely manifest the pervasive acceptance of uniform levels of quality in these systems; they have not encouraged hierarchical structures like those of Japan and the United States.

30. Bruce L. R. Smith and Joseph J. Karlesky, *The State of Academic Science* (New York: Change Magazine Press, 1977), pp. 17–18.

31. Finn, *Scholars,* p. 113.

32. Larry L. Leslie, "The Role of Public Student Aid in Financing Private Higher Education," University of Arizona Higher Education Program Topical Paper no. 10 (March 1978).

33. Mark Blaug and Maureen Woodhall, "Patterns of Subsidies to Higher Education in Europe," *Higher Education* 7 (1978): 331–61.

34. Of course, the projected budget cuts constitute a partial repudiation of that aspect of the English university ideal, and may eventually cause the English to cease to be among the leading nations in expenditures per student. This has prompted the observation that Britain appears to be sacrificing one of the world's best university systems in the name of one of the world's worst performing economies.

35. Ignace Hecquet and J. Jadot, *The Impact on University Management of Financing and Control Systems for Higher Education,* The Program on Institutional Management in Higher Education (OECD), 1978.

36. Hans Daalder, "The Dutch Universities between the 'New Democracy' and the 'New Management': Ten Years of Development," in *Universities, Politicians, and Bureaucrats: Europe and America,* ed. Hans Daalder and Edward Shils (Cambridge: Cambridge University Press, 1982), pp. 233–74; and Arend Lijphart, "The Dutch Universities in the Seventies," *International Council on the Future of the University Newsletter* 4, no. 1 (November 1977): 1, 4–7.

37. E.g., Edward Shils, "The Criteria of Academic Appointment in American Universities and Colleges: Some Documents of Affirmative Action at Work," *Minerva* 14 (1976): 97–117.

38. For critical views of affirmative action policies see Nathan Glazer, *Affirmative Discrimination* (New York: Basic Books, 1976); Paul Seabury, ed., *Bureaucrats and Brainpower* (San Francisco: Institute for Contempo-

rary Studies, 1979); the review by Roger Geiger, *American Journal of Education* 89 (1981): 229–33; parts of Walter C. Hobbs, ed., *Government Regulation of Higher Education* (Cambridge: Ballinger, 1978); and Sidney Hook et al., eds., *The University and the State* (Buffalo: Prometheus Books, 1978). For a more benign view of federal regulatory practices, see Finn, *Scholars,* pp. 139–74.

39. Cf. Nathan Glazer, "Regulating Business and Regulating the Universities: One Problem or Two?" *Bureaucrats,* ed. Paul Seabury, pp. 113–40. He attributes this "adversarial regulation" to the combined power of well-organized special interests, partisan regulatory agencies, and the courts.

40. Burton R. Clark, *The Higher Education System: Academic Organization in Cross-National Perspective* (Berkeley and Los Angeles: University of California Press, 1983), esp. chapter 8.

41. Robert Birnbaum, *Maintaining Diversity in Higher Education* (San Francisco: Jossey-Bass, 1983), pp. 1–37.

Chapter 7

1. See Burton R. Clark, *The Higher Education System: Academic Organization in Cross-National Perspective* (Berkeley and Los Angeles: University of California Press, 1983); Robert Birnbaum, *Maintaining Diversity in Higher Education* (San Francisco: Jossey-Bass, 1983).

2. Burton R. Clark, "The Benefits of Disorder," *Change,* October 1978, pp. 31–37.

3. Cf. *Future Educational Policies in the Changing Social and Economic Context* (Paris: OECD, 1979); and the review by Roger Geiger in *American Journal of Education* 88 (1980): 506–10.

4. E.g., see Harold S. Wechsler, *The Qualified Student: A History of Selective College Admissions in America* (New York: Wiley, 1977); Marcia G. Synnott, *The Half-Opened Door: Discrimination and Admissions at Harvard, Yale and Princeton, 1900–1970* (Westport, Conn.: Greenwood, 1979).

Selected Bibliography

Amagi, Isao. *Higher Education in Japan: Problems and Prospects.* Tokyo: Institute for Higher Education, 1977.

Amano, Ikuo. "Stability and Change in Japanese Higher Education." Report to the Second Hiroshima Seminar on Higher Education, Hiroshima University, January 1980.

Ancion, William. "Le système de financement et de contrôle en vigueur en Belgique." Paper presented at OECD Meeting, "The Effects of Present Financing and Control Systems on the Internal Management of Universities." Paris, 1978.

Astin, Alexander. *Four Critical Years.* San Francisco: Jossey-Bass, 1977.

Astin, Alexander, and Calvin Lee. *The Invisible Colleges: A Profile of Small, Private Colleges with Limited Resources.* New York: McGraw-Hill, 1972.

Beloff, Max. "British Universities and the Public Purse." *Minerva* 5 (1967): 520–32.

———. "Starting a Private College: A British Experiment in Higher Education." *American Scholar,* Summer 1979, pp. 395–403.

Berdahl, Robert O. *British Universities and the State.* Berkeley and Los Angeles: University of California Press, 1959.

Birnbaum, Robert. *Maintaining Diversity in Higher Education.* San Francisco: Jossey-Bass, 1983.

Blaug, Mark, and Maureen Woodhall. "Patterns of Subsidies to Higher Education in Europe." *Higher Education* 7 (1978): 331–61.

Blewitt, John E., S. J., ed. and trans. *Higher Education in Post-War Japan. The Ministry of Education's 1964 White Paper.* Tokyo: Sophia University Press, 1965.

Bowen, Howard. *The Costs of Higher Education.* San Francisco: Jossey-Bass, 1980.

Bowen, William. *The Economics of Major Private Universities.* Berkeley: The Carnegie Commission on Higher Education, 1968.

Breneman, David W., and Chester E. Finn, Jr., eds. *Public Policy and Private Higher Education.* Washington, D.C.: The Brookings Institution, 1978.

Burn, Barbara B. *Higher Education in Nine Countries.* New York: McGraw-Hill, 1971.

Caine, Sydney. *British Universities: Purpose and Prospects.* London: The Bodley Head, 1969.

Carnegie Council on Policy Studies in Higher Education. *A Classification of*

Institutions of Higher Education. Rev. ed. Berkeley: Carnegie Foundation for the Advancement of Teaching, 1976.

———. *Three Thousand Futures: The Next Twenty Years for Higher Education.* San Francisco: Jossey-Bass, 1980.

———. *The States and Private Higher Education.* San Francisco: Jossey-Bass, 1977.

Carson, Arthur L. *The Story of Philippine Education.* Quezon City: New Day Publishers, 1978.

Cheit, Earl F., and Theodore E. Lobman. *Foundations and Higher Education: Grant Marking from the Golden Years through Steady State.* Berkeley: Carnegie Council on Policy Studies in Higher Education, 1979.

Clark, Burton R. *The Distinctive College.* Chicago: Aldine, 1970.

———. *The Higher Education System: Academic Organization in Cross-National Perspective.* Berkeley and Los Angeles: University of California Press, 1983.

———. "The Benefits of Disorder." *Change,* October 1978, pp. 31–37.

Council for Financial Aid to Education. *Voluntary Support of Education, 1979–80.* New York: CFAE, 1981.

Counseil nationale de la politique scientifique. *Une nouvelle stratégie universitaire.* Brussels: 1976.

Cummings, William K. *Education and Equality in Japan.* Princeton: Princeton University Press, 1980.

Cummings, William K., Ikuo Amano, and Kazuyuki Kitamura, eds. *Changes in the Japanese University.* New York: Praeger, 1979.

Curti, Merle, and Roderick Nash. *Philanthropy in the Shaping of American Higher Education.* New Brunswick, N.J.: Rutgers University Press, 1965.

Daalder, Hans. "The Dutch Universities between the 'New Democracy' and the 'New Management': Ten Years of Development." In *Universities, Politicians and Bureaucrats,* edited by Hans Daalder and Edward Shils, 173–232. Cambridge: Cambridge University Press.

Dejean, Christian, and Charles-Louis Binneman. *L'Université belge: du pari au défi.* Brussels: Editions de l'Institut de Sociologie de l'Université Libre de Bruxelles, 1971.

DeMoor, R. A. "Diversification in Dutch Tertiary Education." *Paedagogica Europaea* 10 (1975): 73–86.

Doermann, Humphrey. *Toward Equal Access.* New York: College Entrance Examination Board, 1978.

Dore, Ronald P. *Education in Tokugawa Japan.* Berkeley and Los Angeles: University of California Press, 1965.

Douglas, James. "Toward a Rationale for Private Non-Profit Organization: A Review of Current Theory." Yale Institution for Social and Policy Studies Working Paper, PONPO-7 (April 1980).

———. *Why Charity?: The Case for a Third Sector.* Beverly Hills: Sage Publications, 1983.

Finn, Chester, E., Jr. "Federal Patronage of Universities in the United States: A Rose by Many Other Names?" *Minerva* 14 (1976–77): 496–529.
———. *Scholars, Dollars and Bureaucrats.* Washington, D.C.: The Brookings Institution, 1978.
Fontaine, Nicole. *La liberté d'enseignement, de la loi Debré à la loi Guermeur.* 2d ed. Paris: UNAPEC, 1978.
Geiger, Roger L. *To Advance Knowledge: The Growth of American Research Universities in the Twentieth Century, 1900–1940.* New York: Oxford University Press, 1986.
———. "Changing Demand for Higher Education in the Seventies." *Higher Education* 9 (1980): 255–76.
———. "The College Curriculum and the Marketplace." *Change,* November/December 1980, p. 17.
———. "European Universities: The Unfinished Revolution." *Comparative Education Review* 22 (1978): 189–211.
———. "Hierarchy and Diversity in American Research Universities." In *The University Research System,* edited by Bjørn Wittrock. Forthcoming.
———. "Two Paths to Mass Higher Education: Issues and Outcomes in Belgium and France." Yale University Institution for Social and Policy Studies Working Paper, YHERG-24 (April 1979).
———. "Universities and the State in Belgium: Past and Present Dimensions of Higher Education in a Divided Society." Yale University Institution for Social and Policy Studies Working Paper, YHERG-29 (November 1978).
Gladieux, Lawrence E., and Thomas R. Wolanin. *Congress and the Colleges.* Lexington, Mass.: Lexington Books, 1976.
Greeley, Andrew M. *From Backwater to Mainstream: A Profile of Catholic Higher Education.* New York: McGraw-Hill, 1969.
Halsey, A. H., and M. A. Trow. *The British Academics.* Cambridge: Harvard University Press, 1971.
Hansmann, Henry. "The Role of Non-Profit Enterprise." *Yale Law Journal* 89 (1980): 385–901.
Hecquet, Ignace, et al. "Planifier sans planifier: le cas de l'université Catholique de Louvain." Paper for "OECD Programme." Paris, August 14, 1979.
Heidenheimer, Arnold. "Education and Social Security Entitlements in Europe and America." In *The Development of Welfare States in Europe and America,* edited by P. Flora and A. Heidenheimer. New Brunswick, N.J.: Transaction Press, 1981.
Hodgkinson, Harold L. *Institutions in Transition.* New York: McGraw-Hill, 1971.
Isidro, Antonio, and Maximo D. Ramos. *Private Colleges and Universities of the Philippines.* Quezon City: Alemar-Phoenix, 1973.
James, Estelle. "The Public/Private Division of Responsibility for Education: An International Comparison." Mimeo, 1984.
James, Estelle, and Gail Benjamin. "Public versus Private Education: The

Japanese Experiment." Yale University Institution for Social and Policy Studies Working Paper, PONPO-81 (May 1984).

Jencks, Christopher, and David Riesman. *The Academic Revolution.* Chicago: University of Chicago Press, 1977.

Leslie, Larry L. "The Role of Public Student Aid in Financing Private Higher Education." University of Arizona Higher Education Program Topical Paper no. 10 (March 1978).

Leslie, Larry L., Arthur Grant, and Kenneth Brown. "Patterns of Enrollment in Higher Education, 1965–77: Liberal Arts Colleges." University of Arizona Center for the Study of Higher Education Topical Paper no. 19 (January 1981).

Levy, Daniel. *The State and Higher Education in Latin America: Private Challenges to Public Dominance.* Chicago: University of Chicago Press, 1986.

Lijphart, Arend. "Dutch Universities in the Seventies." *International Council on the Future of the University Newsletter* 4, no. 1 (November 1977): 1.

Majone, Giandomenico. "Professionalism and Non-Profit Organizations." Yale University Institution for Social and Policy Studies Working Paper, PONPO-24 (October 1980).

Ménissez, Yvette. *L'Enseignement de la gestion en France.* Paris: La Documentation française, 1979.

Miao, Evelyn Chih-hua. "The Structure and Performance of Proprietary Institutions of Higher Education in the Philippines." Ph.D. diss., University of Wisconsin, 1971.

Ministry of Education and Science. *Contours of a Future Education System in the Netherlands: Discussion Memorandum.* The Hague: Ministry of Education and Sciences, 1975.

Minter, W. John, and Howard R. Bowen. *Independent Higher Education, 1980.* Washington, D.C.: National Institute of Independent Colleges and Universities, 1980.

Moodie, Graeme C. "Academics and University Government: Some Reflections on British Experiences." Mimeo, n.d.

Nagai, Michio. *Higher Education in Japan: Its Take-Off and Crash.* Translated by Jerry Dusenbury. Tokyo: University of Tokyo Press, 1971.

Neave, Guy. "The Nonstate Sector in the Education Provision of Member States of the European Community." Brussels: Report to the Education Services of the Commission of the European Community, 1983.

Nielsen, Waldemar A. *The Endangered Sector.* New York: Columbia University Press, 1979.

Ninomiya, Akira. *Private Universities in Japan.* Tokyo: Private Universities Union of Japan, 1977.

Oncu, Ayse. "Higher Education as a Business: Growth of a Private Sector in Turkey." Ph.D. diss., Yale University, 1971.

Organization for European Cooperation and Development. *Educational Expenditures in France, Japan and the United Kingdom.* Paris: OECD, 1977.

————. *Reviews of National Policies for Education: Japan.* Paris: OECD, 1971: 153–62.

Osborne, Thomas. "The Recruitment of the Administrative Elite in the Third Republic: The System of the Ecole Libre des Sciences Politiques, 1870–1905." Ph.D. diss., University of Connecticut, 1974.

Pace, C. Robert. *Education and Evangelism.* New York: McGraw-Hill, 1972.

Pemberton, Joyce, and John Pemberton. *University College at Buckingham: A First Account of Its Foundation and Early Years.* Buckingham: Buckingham Press, 1979.

Pempel, T. J. "The Politics of Enrollment Expansion in Japanese Universities." *Journal of Asian Studies* 33 (1973): 67–86.

Pfnister, Allan O. "Survival and Revival: The Transformation of the American Arts College." University of Denver, Occasional Papers in Higher Education no. 15 (September 1981).

Philippine-American Educational Foundation. *Profiles of Philippine Universities and Colleges.* Manila: 1975.

Premfors, Rune. *The Politics of Higher Education in a Comparative Perspective: France, Sweden, United Kingdom.* Stockholm Studies in Politics, 15. University of Stockholm, 1980.

Premfors, Rune, and Bertil Ostergren. *Systems of Higher Education: Sweden.* New York: International Council for Education Development, 1978.

Rain, Pierre. *L'Ecole Libre des Sciences Politiques.* Paris: Fondation nationale des sciences politiques, 1963.

Riesman, David. "The Evangelical Colleges: Untouched by the Academic Revolution." *Change,* January/February 1981, pp. 13–20.

————. *On Higher Education.* San Francisco: Jossey-Bass, 1980.

Robbins Committee. *Higher Education: Report of the Committee Appointed by the Prime Minister under the Chairmanship of Lord Robbins, 1961–63.* Cmnd. 2154. London: HMSO, 1963.

Rohlen, Thomas P. *Japan's High Schools.* Berkeley and Los Angeles: University of California Press, 1983.

Shils, Edward. "The American Private University." *Minerva* 11 (1973): 6–29.

Shimbori, Michiya. "The Sociology of a Student Movement—A Japanese Case Study." In *Students in Revolt,* edited by S. M. Lipset and P. Altbach. Boston: Beacon Press, 1970.

Silber, John R. "Paying the Bill for College: The 'Private' Sector and the Public Interest." *Atlantic* 235 (May 1975): 33–40.

Trow, Martin. "The Public and Private Lives of Higher Education," *Daedalus* 104 (1975): 113–27.

Van de Graaff, John H., et al. *Academic Power: Patterns of Authority in Seven National Systems of Higher Education.* New York: Praeger, 1978.

van Kalken, Frans. "L'Université Libre de Bruxelles." In *Histoire des Universités Belges.* Brussels: Collection Lebegue and Nationale, 1954.

Verhoeven, Jef. "The Belgian Universities under Crossfire: Linguistic Communalism, Bureaucratization and Democratization." In *Univer-*

sities, *Politicians and Bureaucrats: Europe and America*, edited by Hans Daalder and Edward Shils, 125–72. Cambridge: Cambridge University Press, 1982.

Webster, David S. "America's Highest Ranking Graduate Schools, 1925–1982." *Change*, May/June 1983, pp. 14–24.

Weisbrod, Burton A. "Toward a Theory of the Voluntary Nonprofit Sector in a Three-Sector Economy." In *The Voluntary Nonprofit Sector*. Lexington, Mass.: Lexington Press, 1977.

Whitehead, John S. *The Separation of Church and State: Columbia, Dartmouth, Harvard and Yale*. New Haven: Yale University Press, 1973.

Williams, Gareth, and Maureen Woodhall. *Independent Further Education*. London: Policy Studies Institute, 1979.

Zwaenepoel, Paul P. *Tertiary Education in the Philippines, 1611–1972: A Systems Analysis*. Quezon City: Alemar-Phoenix, 1975.

Index

Entrance examinations: in Japan, 35–36, 41–42; in the Philippines, 65–67; in France, 118–21, 127, 269n.23

Enrollments in higher education: in Belgium, 82, 86, 100–101; in France, 115–16, 124; in Japan, 21, 24, 27, 30, 46, 48–49, 258n.4; in the Netherlands, 93, 96, 100–101; in the Philippines, 52, 56–57, 66–67; in Sweden, 136, 270n.44; in the United States, 161, 163–64, 189–95, 258n.4, 273n.6, 277n.59

Environmental policies toward higher education, 67–68, 74

Erasmus University, 92

Fabella, Vincente, 55
Falloux Law (1850), 111
Far Eastern University, 55, 58
Feati University, 58
Ferns, Harry, 146–47
Flanders, 77, 83–84, 102
For-profit educational institutions, 3, 9, 14, 53, 60–64, 68–69, 245, 264n.78, 273n.4
Fordham University, 188, 277n.49
Foundations, 152, 172, 179, 279n.23
France, private higher education in: origins, 108–18; Ecole libre des sciences politiques, 118–23; current structure, 123–31; trends, 131–34; mentioned, 208, 233–34
Free University of Brussels (ULB), 77–83, 85, 101, 103, 105
Fukuzawa, Yukichi, 19–20
Functions of private higher education, 165–67, 190
Funds for Assistance to Private Education (FAPE), 69
Fund raising, 148, 152, 155, 158, 173, 178, 184

Gakushuin University, 39
George Washington University, 187–88, 276n.48, 277n.49
Georgetown University, 188
Germany, 2, 8
Ghent, University of, 77, 82, 83
Gothenburg School of Economics, 136, 138
Gothenburg, University of, 135, 137–38, 239
Goucher College, 183
Government regulation of private higher education, 47–48, 64–69, 74, 87–90, 94–100, 118, 223–25, 231, 279n.23, 281n.39
Government support for private higher education: reviewed, 197–98; and rising costs, 198–201; reasons for, 202–7; in Japan, 202–3; in the United States, 203–6; in Britain, 206–7; forms of subsidization, 207–13; consequences, 213–24; conclusions, 224–27; mentioned, 29, 45–47, 67, 74, 81–83, 85–90, 91–92, 93–94, 97, 98–100, 137, 139–40, 262n.50, 263n.60, 266n.10, 279n.23
Graduate service universities, 187–88
Grands corps, 119–22
Grandes écoles, 124–25, 127–31, 133–34, 166, 261n.40
Grinnell College, 182
Groningen, University of, 91

Halsey, A. H., 143
Harvard University, 162, 172, 178, 180
Haverford College, 183, 275n.32
Hierarchy, 15, 23–25, 35–40, 60, 68, 72, 138, 177
Higher Education Facilities Act (1963), 204
Hofstra University, 189, 277n.50
Hosei University, 39